post & Handle
Sales Tax

9.95
85
[40]
_____
11. 20

Received 9-18-78

D1532489

A

MICHIGAN HERITAGE LIBRARY

REPRINT

THE AUTOBIOGRAPHY

OF

THEODORE EDGAR POTTER

PROLOGUE

The Michigan Heritage Library reprint series, commencing with this volume, is designed to bring into general circulation significant out-of-print works. Each volume will illustrate a different aspect of the rich historical experience of Michigan's people.

Too often, important regional histories, atlases, gazateers, journals, and other historical works are available only in a few larger historical libraries or through rare book stores. Our purpose is to make the most interesting and colorful episodes of Michigan's history available to the citizens of the state through reprint editions of these original works.

Our hope is that the Michigan Heritage Library will help the citizens of Michigan to better understand and enjoy their rich heritage.

An important feature of each volume will be an introduction written by a noted historian placing each volume in its historical setting.

Volumes will be selected jointly by the Historical Society of Michigan and Hardscrabble Books with the assistance of an editorial advisory board of distinguished editors, authors, and historians.

Frank C. Wilhelme
Executive Director
Historical Society of Michigan

Editorial Advisory Board

THEODORE EDGAR POTTER

1832-1910

THE AUTOBIOGRAPHY

OF

THEODORE EDGAR POTTER

An American Adventure

Introduction by John Cumming

•

HISTORICAL SOCIETY OF MICHIGAN

Ann Arbor, Michigan

HARDSCRABBLE BOOKS

Berrien Springs, Michigan

This Michigan Heritage Library edition is
an unabridged facsimile reprint of the work
originally published by the family of Theodore Edgar Potter and printed by The Rum-
ford Press, Concord, N.H., in 1913. This
edition contains a new introduction by John
Cumming.

International Standard Book Number 0-915056-08-9

Manufactured in the United States of America

HARDSCRABBLE BOOKS
Berrien Springs, Michigan

To the wife who shared with Theodore
Edgar Potter the perils of frontier life
and whose devotion and companionship
was the source of his greatest joy, this
book is affectionately dedicated.

PREFACE

Theodore Edgar Potter, whose life story fills the succeeding pages of this book, died at his home in Lansing, Michigan, October 25, 1910. The manuscript of this autobiography was found in his library after his death. It is now published in conformity with his last wishes so that his children and grandchildren may appreciate the struggles, privations and dangers that marked the lot of those pioneers, who, like himself, gave their best years to the development of the great western country. The story is told in his own words,—the few changes made have been in the arrangement of matter and in embodying in it incidents which he mentioned in letters and other articles but which he did not chronicle here.

The story is so complete that any addition may seem superfluous. But to the members of Mr. Potter's family, for whom this book is printed, it lacks the incidents of warm personal friendship that in their minds rendered his life so distinctive, and which he in his modesty failed to chronicle. The writer will be pardoned therefore if he calls attention in this preface to a few phases of Mr. Potter's life which are of extreme interest and tender memory to his family.

Theodore Edgar Potter was a fond husband and father. He lavished upon his family the affection that flowed so freely from his deep and generous nature. To him and his wife were born five children, and to them all and their children in turn, he was endeared by his generous affection. The writer can speak for the grandchildren. He was especially interested in their receiving the benefits of the education which poverty denied him in his youth, and never lost an opportunity to urge them forward in their studies. He was extremely anxious that they should learn the value of money and acquire the habit of saving. His plan of encouraging them to save is illustrated by his habit of giving each grandchild a dollar to invest at Christmas and offering prizes for those who could show the best return on their investments at the next Christmas season. Undoubtedly the happiest day in his life was October 5, 1908, when in the midst of a gathering of all their children and all their grand-children save one, he and his devoted wife celebrated their golden wedding. His death in 1910 broke the family circle, for his wife, five children and thirteen grandchildren all survived him.

He was a public-spirited citizen. He answered the call of duty whether it demanded service on the battle field or in public office. He was twice a supervisor of the township of Vermontville. In 1896 he was elected alderman for the third ward in Lansing, Michigan, a position he held for two terms, at the end of which time he refused renomination for a third term. His public service was not rendered entirely through public office. Many a person in Lansing owed food and fuel to his generosity during the winter of 1893–4.

He was a devoted worker in the Grand Army of the Republic and a member of the Military Order of the Loyal Legion of the United States. During the last few years of his life, after retirement from business, he devoted practically all his time to the work of the Grand Army of the Republic. In 1898 he was elected Commander of the Charles T. Foster Post in Lansing, and in 1899 was reëlected. In 1899 the department commander offered a silk flag to the G. A. R. post in Michigan gaining the largest percentage in membership during the year. Commander Potter went after this prize for his post and in the year increased its membership from 191 to 320. A small post in the state having only eleven members won the prize by an increase of 100 per cent but the increase in numbers in the Charles T. Foster Post was so large that the Department Commander had a second flag made and presented it in person to the Post.

Mr. Potter's interest in the G. A. R. was not confined to the local organization. From 1901 to 1909 he was each year a special aide-de-camp of the Commander in Chief, and attended the national encampment during most of these years. In 1903 he was appointed Special Aide in Charge of Military Instruction in the Schools of the State of Michigan. In his work in this field Mr. Potter aimed to inculcate patriotism, and accomplished this by offering a series of prizes for the best essays submitted on Abraham Lincoln. The contest was a spirited one and aroused much favorable comment throughout the state.

The influence of such a life as his cannot be measured. His country has expressed its gratitude for the years of patriotic effort

PREFACE.

on the frontier and in the battle line; his comrades in the G. A. R. have acknowledged the worth of his service in perfecting their organization; young men everywhere have testified to the influence which he had upon their lives; but the true measure of his influence will never be known because it will flow on through the lives of those whom he met and will in turn be transferred by them to others. May this book keep fresh in the minds of his children's children, and in turn their children, the story of the unfaltering steadfastness, the devotion to high ideals of service and the generous spirit that made unique the life of Theodore Edgar Potter.

NEW YORK, October, 1913.   *G. C. S.*

CONTENTS

INTRODUCTION

TO THE

MICHIGAN HERITAGE LIBRARY

EDITION

Winter in 1849 was a period of excitement and anticipation for the young men, and some of the older ones, too, in most Michigan communities, as it was for the men in all the settled parts of the country. It was a time of planning and organizing for the long, arduous journey to the gold fields of California, across the plains and mountains, through the vast expanses of terrain that was inadequately mapped or explored. Little did it matter to these men that such a trail lay before them; they had leveled their sights on California gold and could see nothing in between.

Although January 24, 1848, has been designated as the official date of the discovery of gold in California by James V. Marshall, an employee of John Sutter engaged in the construction of a grist and sawmill on the American River, news of the discovery was slow in reaching the Eastern seaboard. The news was reported in the summer of 1848, but even then it was dismissed by many as rumor. It was not until late fall that the reports began to gain credence. Then, when on December 5 President James K. Polk in his message to Congress reported on the discovery in optimistic terms, the news became official; and the gold fever started to spread until it reached epidemic proportions by the following spring. From every state in the Union, from Europe, South America, far-off Australia, and China, men responded almost spontaneously to the promise of instant wealth.

Throughout Michigan in every village and town preparations were being made for the grand exodus, the great American adventure. President Polk's message was no sooner read before plans were under way in Marshall, Michigan, where the editor of the "Statesman" had called for a meeting of those interested in organizing an expedition to California. Out of this meeting emerged the Wolverine Rangers, the most carefully planned and most skillfully organized company which left Michigan for the gold fields.

In Monroe two companies were being formed, the Pioneers and the California Association of Monroe; from Adrian it was Colonel Avery's Company; and from the Hillsdale-Jonesville area, it was the Fayette Rovers.

Early in the year a notice in the Jackson "Citizen" invited interested parties to contact Hiram C. Hodge of Pulaski to learn about the company being formed there. Each member, the article stated, would be required to be well-armed with pistols, rifles, and ammunition. Each mess would furnish themselves with a team, wagon, tent, other necessities, and provisions sufficient to last throughout the journey. The group would be known as the Central Michigan Emigrant Company. Throughout the state newspapers carried similar appeals.

As early as January 13, 1849, the Niles "Republican" printed a notice that Major Timothy Smith had received a letter from his son in California, informing him that he was making from seven dollars to seven hundred dollars a day. Young Smith urged his brothers to come to California. "It will not take much more to start a crowd from the St. Joseph Valley," commented the editor.

The same newspaper reported that the gold fever was already raging to an alarming extent. Many men were being initiated into the Masonic order so that they might enjoy the benefits of brotherhood should they encounter problems on the trail.

The Niles editor was in a good position to record the excitement of the gold fever. Niles at this time was at the terminus of the Michigan Central Railroad on which parties going west frequently traveled, proceeding from Niles to Chicago or New Buffalo by stage. Niles was also on the Chicago road over which wagons and horses carrying gold-seekers passed.

On February 24, the Niles editor reported, "Teams begin to pass through our town on their way to California. Mr. Nicholson, of Cass County, passed through yesterday." Then on March 3, it was reported, "California teams are plenty. Companies now pass through our village almost daily on their way to the gold region." One week later: "Westward the Star of Empire makes its way. Team after team, party after party, are pushing westward, eager to reach the golden El Dorado."

In towns along the Michigan Central editors recorded the tearful departures of men who bade farewell to parents, wives, and sweethearts. In some towns the departures of companies became a ceremony. In Battle Creek ten young men organized as the Battle Creek Mining Company listened to a speech, "a few appropriate remarks from B.F. Graves, Esq.," and then heard three hearty cheers. They were then escorted by the brass band and quite a number of their friends on horseback for the first half mile of their trip.

Some men sold or mortgaged their farms in order to raise funds for an outfit. Others secured the backing of optimistic investors who hoped to share in the golden wealth of California without sharing the hardships. The Monroe company, officially known as the "California Association from Monroe, Michigan," had the backing of Erastus C. Benedict of New York City and David Noble of Monroe. The men signed an agreement with their backers that they would remain together for two years and that they would share their earnings with the investors. Of all the income above basic expenses Benedict would receive twenty-five per cent and Noble would receive a like amount. The investors supplied twenty-five hundred dollars each. The venture did not prove to be a sound investment for the backers, as the company broken by dissension dissolved before reaching California.

Those who could not afford to make the trip to California, who were unable to find backers, looked with envy upon those who were able to go. Some tried to borrow funds from relatives; others offered their services as teamsters. The urge to join the exodus to the gold fields was hard to resist. In 1849, Theodore Edgar Potter, the author of this book, was seventeen years old, too young to leave home on such an adventure. He felt the excitement and the urge to migrate; but he had to resign himself to the realization that it would be a few years before he could seriously consider such an adventure.

Within a few weeks after the last departures from Michigan, letters began to appear in the newspapers from points along the overland trail. They told of deaths from cholera, accidents, and drownings; they told of stampedes, storms, breakdowns; and they told of the grueling hardships of driving a team and walking day after day. Then after their arrival in California, the gold-seekers began to write letters warning those at home that the finding of gold was not such an easy task as they had been led to believe. It was not easy work and it was not nearly as plentiful as they had permitted their initial optimism to picture in their minds. For every one who struck it rich, there were scores who failed to make enough to live on. Letter after letter expressed the wish that the writers had stayed at home; and they warned their friends back home that they should forget about California.

One would think that such admonitions would have taken some effect; but the opposite proved to be the case. Nearly double the number of gold-seekers crossed the plains to California in 1850. The year 1851 saw some slackening in the pace of emigration; but in 1852 the numbers rose again.

Michigan at this time had a population slightly under four hundred thousand. Although it had been enjoying success in attracting immigrants in great numbers during the 1830's, the pace had slowed considerably during the 1840's. The financial failures of that decade in which the state itself was virtually bankrupt discouraged some prospective settlers. Then, too, the availability of lands in Iowa and Wisconsin exerted an influence, drawing away settlers who might otherwise have selected Michigan. The state still had vast areas of government land to settle; and private speculators had holdings which they were anxious to sell. Newspaper editors bemoaned the fact that so many young men were leaving the state, perhaps never to return again; and to make the matter more serious, they were taking from the state large sums of money. To counteract this influence the state hired promoters to attempt to attract settlers from abroad, particularly from Germany.

By 1852, Theodore Edgar Potter's mother and his older brother, his father having died earlier, gave into his entreaties to make the trip to California. They succeeded in negotiating a loan of one hundred dollars at thirty per cent per annum interest, putting his 120-acres up as security. Thus in 1852 at the age of twenty, young Potter with a friend boarded the Michigan Central at Marshall and headed for St. Joseph, Missouri, where they planned to purchase an outfit. At Peoria, Illinois, they met a woman with five children whose husband had died causing her to decide to return to her home in Toledo, Ohio. Potter and his companion purchased her outfit, consisting of three yokes of oxen, a wagon, and other supplies for two hundred and fifty dollars. They then went on to St. Joseph, Missouri, where they joined a company for the long overland journey. This was the start of a long series of adventures which would extend over the next twenty years and would ultimately become the subject of this autobiography.

Theodore Edgar Potter, the son of Michigan pioneers, was born in Saline, Michigan, in 1832. After several moves, the Potter family settled in Eaton County in 1845, where the father died soon after. The village of Potterville in that county is named after the family.

It was from this home that Potter left for California. According to his account, Potter remained in California until 1856, returning then by way of Nicaragua, where he had enlisted in William Walker's attempt to take over that country. In the same year he returned to Michigan but was not content to remain at home. He related that he was seized with a restlessness which caused him to continue his travels. After some touring he decided to settle in Minnesota. His account includes adventures in the Indian Wars, service in the Civil War, and many other unusual adventures which are all part of this autobiography.

He returned to Michigan with his wife and five children to settle on a farm near Vermontville in 1875. Subsequently he engaged in the lumber business with two brothers in Potterville and had a furniture factory in Lansing, where he died on October 25, 1910.

The "Autobiography of Theodore Edgar Potter was written when the author was seventy-two years old. He was looking back upon events which had occurred over a half-century earlier. From the account of the overland journey to California, it is apparent that he had a diary to which he could refer. George S. Sprague in his introduction to the autobiography which the family published in 1913 noted that incidents which Potter had narrated in letters or articles were inserted into the manuscript by the family.

Writing years after the occurrence of an event, the author is quite likely to have lapses of memory or a tendency to romanticize adventures he experienced. What he has read in other sources sometimes becomes intermingled with his own experiences. One may find such faults in Potter's reminiscences. There are inaccuracies and inconsistencies in the narrative of the overland trail and the events in California which may not have been recorded if the autobiography had been composed at a time closer to the events.

Theodore Potter's reminiscences are, in spite of such faults, an intriguing and exciting reading experience. Few men enjoyed such a variety of adventures over such a long period of time, extending from the pioneer days in Michigan into the twentieth century, as well as the pioneer period in California and Minnesota. The changes which he witnessed would by themselves make an impressive volume; but the fact that Theodore Edgar Potter was an active participant in bringing about many of these changes makes his narrative even more significant.

John Cumming
Central Michigan University
Mt. Pleasant, Michigan
1978

THE AUTOBIOGRAPHY OF
THEODORE EDGAR POTTER.

CHAPTER I.

BOYHOOD DAYS IN THE WOODS OF MICHIGAN.

I was born in Saline, Washtenaw County, Michigan, March 10, 1832. My father and mother with two small children had come to Michigan in the spring of 1830 from Cayuga County, New York, by way of the Erie Canal to Buffalo and thence by steamboat to Detroit, a journey requiring seven days' time. From Detroit they walked to Plymouth, a distance of thirty miles, carrying their two children in their arms. They stopped a few days with relatives at Plymouth and then walked on to Saline, twenty miles further, where they settled. Here my father built one of the first frame houses in that part of the country which he used both as a house and as a tailoring shop, for he had learned the tailor's trade in his youth at Huntington, Pennsylvania, his birthplace. His father had died when he was a mere boy and he had been forced to earn his own livelihood from that time on. At the age of eighteen he had been one of a small party to survey through a line from Cleveland, Ohio, to St. Louis, Missouri, and at nineteen he had joined a larger party that surveyed a broad road through Ohio, Indiana and Illinois to the Mississippi River at Quincy, Illinois. In this way he had picked up the rudiments of surveying and gained some knowledge of the vast wilderness of the Great West. It was doubt-less the glamour of these youthful days as a surveyor that led him to leave the comparatively well-settled community in New York in which he lived for the wilderness of Michigan.

My early life was spent like that of other boys born on the frontier. My earliest recollection is of an occurrence that happened when I was three and a half years old. Our family was then living in a log house on a new farm. My parents had gone to the home of a settler two miles away, to attend a funeral, leaving me with an elder brother and sister. There was a long ladder leading from the main room to

2   1

the loft above where we children slept, and in trying to climb this ladder I fell and catching one leg between the rungs broke the limb above the knee. I suffered great pain from the injury and my brother, who did not know that the leg was broken, carried me from one bed to another, my leg dangling, trying to stop my crying. It was not until four hours later that my father reached home. The nearest doctor was at Saline five miles away, and as father had to make the trip on foot through the woods in the night it was some hours before the physician arrived to find my leg badly swollen and causing me terrible pain. After the doctor had set the leg my father took a two-inch auger and, boring holes in one of the logs which formed the side of the house, drove long pegs into them and built a wide shelf upon these pegs. Mother fixed up a bed for me on this shelf and for six weeks I lay on this firm bed that could neither jar nor spring before I was allowed to get up.

Another painful recollection that comes to mind occurred not long after. The year after my accident father made the trip to Detroit with his ox-team to meet some relatives of ours who were coming on from the East to locate a farm near us. The newcomers, among other possessions, brought a bright new wagon. While my father and my mother's nephew Louis Phillips, the head of the family of newcomers, were away looking at the last piece of government land left in our township I took an axe and chopped off the tongue of the new wagon. This was a serious offence and in those days the vigorous application of a green birch was the common mode of punishment for a four-year-old offender. But for the intervention of one of the newcomers, the wife of the owner of the wagon, I might not have survived the ordeal to tell this story.

Soon after this painful occurrence we moved back to Saline where my father secured work as a surveyor which took him away from home much of the time for the next two years. At that time Saline was the largest village on the old stage route between Detroit and Chicago, and when the six horse stage-coaches came in with a grand flourish, whips cracking, tin horns blowing and horses prancing, nearly every person in town was at the tavern, to see who had come or who was to go, and all business came to a standstill until the horses were changed and the stage had passed on. But even at that time the days of the stage coach were passing. I well remember when the Michigan Central Railroad was finished

as far West as Ypsilanti, and in celebration of this event all were
invited to attend a barbecue there. My father went and took me
with him. When we reached the town, early in the day, we found
the one street decorated with flags and a brass band entertaining the
visitors. We visited the place where the ox was being roasted over
a huge log fire, to make sure with our own eyes that we were not
to be disappointed in the great dinner we had come so far to enjoy.
At the depot we witnessed the arrival of the first passenger train
from Detroit carrying the officers of the road together with General
Cass and other prominent men who were to speak at the exercises.
About two inches of light snow had fallen that morning and when
the train came in view on the slight up-grade near town we saw two
men sitting on opposite ends of a cross-beam in front of the engine
holding large splint brooms with which they swept the light snow
from the track. Such was the railroad snow-plow of sixty-five years
ago. The train consisted of several flat cars loaded with passengers,
and two passenger cars for the officers of the road and speakers
made like the old-fashioned Concord Coaches, with doors on each
side.

For a new country the crowd of people present was very large,
and to a boy of eight years it was a wonderful sight. After the
dinner of roast ox, baked potatoes, pumpkin pie and ginger-bread,
the people formed in line behind the band and marched to the
stage where the railroad officials spoke eloquently of the great
growth and prospects of Michigan. As my father had just returned
from a surveying trip, he was called upon for a short description
of a part of the new country. On reaching home late that night,
my mother asked me what I had seen and heard that day. I told
her that I had seen the roasted ox, a brass band, a railroad train,
two men with brooms sweeping the railroad track, and had heard
General Cass and my father make speeches to the people. Such
were my boyish impressions of an event that typified so much in
the development of a great state.

Another event that appealed to me as of more than ordinary
importance was connected with the presidential campaign of 1840.
My father was a strong Whig politically, and when he learned
that General Harrison, "Old Tippecanoe," was to speak at Fort
Meigs in Ohio, seventy-five miles from Saline, he and a Mr. Parsons
who owned a saw-mill in the village got up a party of sixty men to

go that distance to hear him. The trip was made in style, the party
using their own conveyance. They fitted up a huge wagon by
building a platform with rows of seats upon it which they attached
to a set of large wheels used to cart logs to the saw-mill. There
was a flag-staff near the driver's seat from which waved the Stars
and Stripes and part way up this flag-staff was a platform to which
two live coons were chained. At the rear end of the wagon was a
miniature log cabin in which were two barrels of cider with faucets
and cups to accommodate the oft thirsty passengers. A brass band
of eight pieces and a team of sixteen horses completed the jolly
outfit. As the grand cavalcade passed our log house on the road I
remember that my father, who was in charge as marshal, stopped
it long enough for the band to play one of its favorite airs and for
the men to take another drink of cider and give three cheers for
"Tippecanoe and Tyler too." Then the big train moved on, to
return seven days later from its campaign with no other loss than
the two barrels of cider and the time that had been spent. This was
my introduction to politics.

After the campaign of 1840, my father traded farms and moved
three times within two years; the last time onto a well-improved
farm of eighty acres near Plymouth, Wayne County, purchased
of a relative who had turned Mormon, and gone to Nauvoo, Illinois.
This farm had good buildings on it and was near a district school.
The school was a great advantage to all of us children and we
improved our opportunities during the two and a half years we
remained in the locality. Previous to this we had been pretty constantly on the move (our family moved twelve times during the
first ten years of my life) and when we did settle near a school,
which was not often, there would soon be another moving. Two
exciting events occurred during our stay at Plymouth. One was
a cyclone which came in the night when we were all in bed, and
carried away the roof of our house compelling us to seek shelter
in the barn in the midst of a heavy rain storm. With the help of
neighbors, we had a new roof on our house within two days, though
we had to go to Ypsilanti for the materials. The other event,
nearly a fatal one, occurred on Christmas day, 1844. A boy of
about my age by the name of Clayton came to our house to get
me to go with him to hunt partridges. My father and eldest brother
were away, and unknown to my mother I took the old musket

that my father had carried in the battle of Oswego, with its flint lock and steel ramrod, and went off hunting with Clayton. After shooting several times at squirrels and partridges, but killing none, we went to shooting at a mark. Tiring of this, we varied our sport by loading with powder only, without bullets, and firing at each other at a distance of three or four rods. In my excitement I forgot to take the steel ramrod out of the barrel after loading my gun, and when I fired the rod passed through Clayton's coat sleeve, drawing blood, but doing no serious injury. That ended the mimic warfare. We agreed to go home and keep perfectly quiet about our Christmas celebration. In 1856, I met Clayton at the State Fair in Detroit and he said he had not yet found the ramrod.

Ten days after that Christmas hunt, our family was on the move again going to the then unbroken forests of Eaton County where we were to occupy a new double log house built in advance by my father and eldest brother. To young persons who may never have seen these pioneer shanties, much less have seen one built, a description may be of interest. The only tools used were an axe, a saw and an augur, with sometimes an adz. After clearing a plot of ground sixteen by forty-eight feet, the straightest beech and elm trees, ten to twelve inches in diameter, were cut into logs sixteen and twenty feet long, and hauled to the clearing. The thickest logs were selected for the front, so that when the structure was ready for its roof the front wall would be ten feet in height and the rear wall about seven feet, giving a good pitch to the roof. Basswood trees were cut for the roof, split in half and the centers dug out like a trough. A row of these hollowed logs was laid trough-side up from the front to the rear wall, then another row was laid trough-side down overlapping the upper edges of the first tier and making a waterproof covering, without either rafters or shingles. For floors white ash trees were cut, split, lined, hewed to make straight edges, and laid. Each shanty was twenty feet long and stood eight feet from the other, both being under this one roof which gave a covered alley-way between them. The doorways were cut in the walls so as to open into this alley. The doors were made of hewn split ash, hung on wooden hinges, and closed by a wooden latch, with a piece of rawhide string to pull the latch up to open the door. Not a nail was used in the construction of these two shanties. All the money spent on them went to buy two windows, each containing six 7 x 9 panes of glass. Fireplaces were cut through the logs, and stick chimneys were built upon the outside, laid and plastered with clay.

It took four days to make the trip to the new home and required two neighbors with their ox teams to move the family, furniture, provisions and corn. Though I was not quite thirteen years old, my father sent me ahead one day in advance with a drove of stock, consisting of three cows, two yearlings, five sheep and four hogs. A neighbor's boy of about my age accompanied me and we were guided by a rough map which my father had made of the route, and by the names of the taverns where we were to spend the nights. I was allowed six days to take the stock through and was not overtaken by the teams until we reached Eaton Rapids on the fifth day. We had twelve miles to go the next day, four of them over a new road just cut through the woods which no team had ever travelled. We reached our shanty home before night, and received a warm welcome from my brother who had been left by my father to guard the place. Cheerful fires were blazing to greet the family of seven children.

As we had no fodder for the stock, and our only food was the corn in the ear which we had hauled seventy-five miles, browsing was the only hope of life for the cattle and our principal business for the next three months was in cutting down trees for them to feed on. Within two days after reaching our new home my eldest sister and myself came down with the measles, followed within the month by the rest of the children. My eldest brother had a relapse and came near dying from this disease; all his hair fell out, leaving his head as bald as a bare rock the rest of his life. In spite of our troubles we managed to clear seven acres of land and to get in spring crops, such as corn, potatoes, pumpkins, and squash. After selling his Wayne County farm and paying off the mortgage and settling other debts, my father had $300 left with which to begin life anew and make another home. But necessary expenses until a crop could be raised reduced that amount to $100 which was just enough to buy eighty acres of government land. Father decided to go to the land office at Ionia, fifty miles away, and make the purchase of our land. The evening before going he laid the one hundred silver dollars out on the cherry table, the finest piece of furniture we had, and let us handle and count over the largest amount of money we children had ever seen. After he had gone we were greatly worried for fear he would be robbed, carrying so much money alone and travelling on foot, and talked a great deal among ourselves about it until he returned on the fourth day, safe and sound, to our great relief and joy. The crops on the seven acres of new ground proved very successful and when harvested, three acres were sown at once to wheat.

During the winter my father hauled tamarack logs to the saw-mill at Eaton Rapids to be sawed into lumber for a frame barn, giving half of the lumber for the sawing, and in the spring he built the first frame barn in that part of Benton Township, Eaton County. This was in 1846. The barn was thirty by forty feet in size and in its stable my sister taught the first school in that vicinity, having seven pupils, three of whom were from our own family.

In the following July my father cut our three acres of wheat with a sickle, and I bound it and set it up. The next day he cut one acre for a neighbor, binding and setting it in shock, and taking three bushels of wheat for his pay. I went with him to do the binding. It was very hot that day and the field was surrounded by heavy timber which shut out all movement of the air. He drank frequently and freely of cold water from a nearby spring, until we finished the work. It proved to be his last day's work. He was taken very sick, became unconscious, and on the 26th day of July, 1846, we buried him in the little wheat-field on his new frontier farm at the early age of forty-eight years. He left a widow with seven small children, whose only possession was a farm of eighty acres of which only seven acres had been cleared.

As soon as my mother's two brothers, who owned fine farms near Auburn, New York, heard of my father's death, they came out to see us with the purpose of taking us all back with them to New York and caring for us. But my mother would consent to no offer of theirs. They pleaded that the family could not support themselves in such a wilderness as Michigan then was, and that they could not leave us there to starve. But she replied that all she had to live for was her seven children, the oldest now nearly seventeen and the youngest two years of age, and that as she had moved fifteen times since her marriage she did not intend to move again as long as she could keep the family together. The winter before my father's death my oldest brother and sister had been sent to

Vermontville to school for one term and I was told that I should go the next winter, but my father's death put a stop to our schooling until four years later, when a district school house was built on the corner of our farm and a school opened, which greatly relieved the anxiety of my mother, lest her children should grow up without educational advantages. At the time of his death my father was planning to sell his farm and move on to the prairies of Wisconsin where he thought we could get a living easier, and this he would have done, no doubt, had he lived. But death put an end to the roving habits of eighteen years. My mother firmly decided to stay where she was as long as her children would stay with her.

My father had been elected Justice of the Peace for two townships in 1845, and Supervisor in 1846, and was filling both offices, so that his death was deeply felt by the community. The day after his burial we drew the wheat into the barn, and the day following, threshed ten bushels with flails and shelled five bushels of corn. The next day I was sent with our ox-team and the ten bushels of wheat and five bushels of corn to the Delta Mills to be ground into flour and meal. On the way I met a Mr. Nickerson with a horse and buckboard at a place in the road which was too narrow for the teams to pass each other. Having an axe with me, I went to cutting the road wider, and in doing so, stepped near a large rattlesnake, that warned me by his vicious rattling to keep out of his way. I killed the snake and we finally got the teams past each other. Mr. Nickerson learned who I was and told me that he was a lawyer and that he had tried a case before my father as Justice of the Peace at Dimondale, only four weeks before his death. I reached the mill before dark, but had to stay over night to get my grist. I slept that night in the mill, and got home next day with flour and meal enough to last us for three months. Early in the spring we had chopped three acres of timber near the new barn, and mother wanted us to log and burn it and put it into wheat that fall. In September, we arranged to exchange work with two men to help do the logging. We cleared the ten acres, chopped the previous winter, and sowed it all to wheat in the fall, from which we harvested nearly four hundred bushels.

About two months after my father's death I had my first experience with big game. We had only a small piece of cleared land and this we used for the growing crops, letting our cows run at large in the woods to get their pasturage. In stormy weather they often laid out over night and it was my duty to look them up early the next morning. One morning after a storm I started out with my younger brother to drive home the cows. We could hear the cow bells at a distance of about a mile and so had little trouble in finding them. We had sighted the cows when the dog rushed forward and began to bark at a large buck deer. The deer had great antlers, and used them and his feet upon the dog. He was having a hard time of it and I ran up to help, whereat the deer turned upon me. I ran back, dodging from tree to tree, the deer striking at me with his hoofs and the dog snapping at his heels. My younger brother stood looking on about ten rods off, badly frightened, and screaming at the top of his voice. The dog's biting worried the deer so much that he finally turned upon him and gave me an opportunity to pick up a dry oak stick which lay on the ground and which I used as a club. When the deer had scared away the dog, he renewed his attack upon me and we circled around an oak tree, he striking at me with his feet and antlers and I hitting him on the head with my club whenever I saw an opening. I finally succeeded in knocking him down and pounded him on the head until I thought he was dead. My brother came up and we attempted to drag the deer home, but soon found that he was too heavy for us. We forgot all about the cows in our excitement and started home on the run to carry the news to the family. We found our oldest brother at home with two neighbors who were there helping him with some work. We told them what had happened, but it was difficult to get them to believe our story. They finally concluded to go with us and see for themselves, and they were greatly surprised to really find the largest deer that they had ever seen. They dressed it and our family had plenty of venison for a whole week. The story was published in our only county paper and copied by Detroit papers and it was spoken of as a great adventure for a boy of only fourteen years. The most important result of the occurrence was that my mother told me that from that time on I should have a gun to carry whenever I went after the cows.

There had been handed down in our family a revolutionary musket with a history that could be traced back to 1775. It had been used by my father at the Battle of Oswego in the War of 1812. It was an old smooth bore flint lock, with steel ramrod, cartridge box and belt. This was my first gun and I was very proud of it. Whenever I had occasion to go into the woods I carried it with me, loaded, primed and ready for any large game that might appear. The same month that I killed the deer with a club I shot at no less than five deer and missed every one of them. My mother thereupon said to me, "Ed, if you expect to supply the family with venison, you had better trade off your gun for a dry oak limb."

One evening during that same fall, a messenger brought word that a bear was killing the hogs of a Mrs. Jones, our neighbor, two miles north of us and asking us boys to come at once bringing our guns and lanterns. The man who brought the word said that he would go after Lile Cogswell, who lived two miles farther away, and who owned bear dogs. My oldest brother and I started at once, he taking his rifle and I my old musket. When we reached the farm we found that the bear had injured one of the hogs badly, breaking its back, and had only been kept from killing and carrying it off by Mrs. Jones and her dogs. The night was very dark, but it was evident from the way the dogs were barking and howling that Bruin was not far off. We killed the hog and told Mrs. Jones to take the dogs to the house and shut them up, so as not to scare the bear away. We decided that we would drag the carcass of the hog to a log bridge that spanned a small stream nearby, place it on the bridge, which was about ten feet high, and then secrete ourselves beside a large elm tree near the bed of the stream.

My brother conceived this plan, declaring that as the bear was hungry he would follow the carcass to the place where we had dragged it. We took our position several feet lower than the bridge, so that we could look up toward the sky and see the bear if he came onto it. We had not been waiting more than thirty minutes before Mr. Bruin made his appearance on the bridge. He evidently scented us and was suspicious of danger. As he squared himself broadside to us and looked down, my brother whispered, "Now is our time, give it to him." The bear made a jump at the sound of the guns, struck the bank within six feet of us, and ran into a large beech top a few rods away, groaning as if in great pain and breaking the branches near him. Not knowing what he would do next, we lit our lanterns and took up a position on the bridge, thinking that that was the safest place for us just then. In all new countries the settlers have certain signals for such occasions. In the timber, where settlements are few, the blowing of horns, ringing of cow bells and firing of guns are the usual signals. No sooner had we fired at the bear than we heard three shots from a distance, which meant that Lile Cogswell and his bear dogs were on the way. In a short time we heard the blowing of horns and the ringing of cow bells and within an hour from the time we had fired our first shots twenty men were on the bridge listening to our story and to the groans of the bear. Lile Cogswell and two of his dogs were selected to interview Mr. Bear at once. The dogs were let loose and we followed them with lanterns and guns. We found that the bear was so badly wounded that he could not run, but he made a desperate fight with the dogs. One of them was killed by him, and the other was accidentally killed by one of the men in shooting at the bear. Cogswell, to save the rest of his dogs, rushed forward to within ten feet of the bear and shot him through the head.

We then held a council and decided that two of the men should go with me to get my mother's ox-team and stone boat and draw the bear to our place that night and dress it. It was also voted that the next day should be a holiday, so that all the neighbors of that section could come and receive a share of the largest black bear that had ever been killed in that part of the state. It was a great relief to the settlers for miles around to know that this particular bear was dead. He had been a regular visitor for the past two years and had not slighted any farmer in the township who kept hogs. At least one hundred settlers visited our home the next day and received a portion of the carcass that had cost them so dearly in pork. The bear weighed, before being dressed, a little over four hundred pounds. It was found that both my brother and myself had hit the bear and that either of the shots would have proved fatal as they passed clear through his body. My mother then advised me to do my hunting after dark, as she said it was evident that I could see to shoot better in the dark than in the light.

The year of our bear hunt the State Capital was located at Lansing within twelve miles of us, settlers came in rapidly, new roads were surveyed and opened to the Capital from the surrounding towns and villages, and general improvement and prosperity was manifest. A company of ten men, surveying an air-line road from Battle Creek through Bellevue and Charlotte to Lansing, stopped over night at our house, sleeping on the cabin floors, my mother getting supper and breakfast for them. In the morning, the head surveyor needing another hand, and offering twenty-five cents a day and board until their return, I was selected to take the position. My duties were to carry water, make fires, and do other miscellaneous work as required. The foreman asked me if I was the boy who killed the buck with a club, and said that they had two guns in their party, but that they had killed no game except a few partridges and a woodchuck since starting. He told me jestingly that they would expect me to furnish the party with venison, even if I had to do it with a club, although I might use their guns if I wished and could take time to hunt while they were at work on the way. We started early but made only three miles that day as the route from our place on was almost wholly through an unbroken forest of hard wood timber, the only cleared land in the vicinity being my mother's farm. My first day's hunt netted seven partridges for supper. The next day we made less than a mile, crossing the Old Maid Swamp which was covered with a thick growth of tamarack and willow brush, with mud and water underneath. I cut brush and small trees for a path nearly all day. As soon as we reached solid ground I was ordered ahead to locate a good camping spot which I found near a stream of water. While preparing the camp I saw two deer coming towards me on the trot. I seized my gun, dropped behind a log, and when they were within five rods of me I bleated, and they stopped. I fired and broke the back of one. After cutting his throat I went back and reported to the party that I had located the camping place but said nothing about killing the buck. When the party came up they were all greatly surprised to find a deer, dressed and hung up ready for cooking. We had plenty of venison that night, and in fact during the rest of the journey. This was my first deer killed with a gun. My former failures were from excitement and aiming too high. After this I never had another attack of "Buck Fever."

The fourth night we camped near the present location of Waverly Park, west of Lansing. Next morning we heard cow bells, and the sound of someone chopping. Some of us followed the sound, and on reaching Grand River saw a log house on the other side where a Mr. Cooley lived. He came across in his boat, told us we were within three miles of Lansing, and took one of our party in his boat to town. They returned about noon, accompanied by Charles Bush, a prominent citizen of the new capital. We pushed on and at four o'clock P. M. we were at the corner of Washington Avenue and Main Street, where they were then building the Benton House to accommodate the first Legislature, which was to meet in January, 1848. I had seen brick buildings before, but had no idea how they were put together until I saw them using mortar with the brick on the Benton House. The influx of people was so great, and the houses so few, that we could find no roof to sleep under that night. We followed Washington Avenue, which had just been underbrushed, north to Briggs' store where we bought supplies for our supper and then pitched our tent under a large elm tree just south of the store and camped for the night. Next morning most of the party, after breakfast, walked farther north, past the frame of the first capitol building on to North Lansing where there were two or three small stores, and a saw-mill.

All the settlers around Lansing had been invited to the "Raising" of the capitol that day. Jugs of whiskey, and dinner and supper were provided free for all. The whole proceeding of the erection of the capitol building of the State was after the fashion of an old-style raising of the heavy frame of a barn or house. The most of our party assisted at the raising, and also at the dinner and supper and helped to empty the jugs, but all rallied at our tent under the the elm-tree that night, every man sober.

Next morning we started on our return, following our previous trail for the first four miles, then making a new survey half a mile south of the previous one to avoid a part of the swamp. In after years the Peninsular railroad followed our first survey west of Charlotte most of the way to Lansing. On the tenth day after my leaving, I reached home much elated over my first visit to Lansing, the infant Capital and hub of the State of Michigan.

In the following month of September, I made my second visit to Lansing, under the following circumstances. A man by the name of Corydon P. Sprague, a relative of my father, with his young wife, both school teachers, visited us on his way to Wisconsin. He went to see Lansing and concluded to settle there and open a school instead of going further west. Having no means to build a schoolhouse, five families of his relatives volunteered to go and build one for him and make him a present of it. So on September 10th, 1847, Samuel Preston, John Strange, George P. Carman,

Wm. H. Taylor, and Theodore E. Potter, who represented his
mother's family, with axes and teams met in Lansing near the
junction of Grand and Cedar Rivers, where Bush & Thomas had
given a lot for the purpose and near the spot where the Potter
Manufacturing Company's factory was afterwards built. We cut
timber on the lands of speculators, who were not there either to
consent or object, hauled the logs to the lot with our ox teams and
in ten days had completed a two-story log schoolhouse and residence—the first schoolhouse ever built in Lansing—hauling the
pine lumber for the floors and desks from Flushing, a distance of 40
miles. In this two-story log house Mr. Sprague and his wife lived
and opened the first Select School in Lansing, having a full attend-
ance the first winter, Mrs. Sprague teaching the primary classes,
and he the more advanced. During the summer of 1848, new
schools were opened in other parts of the city, as most of the
people were settling along Washington Avenue on the north side
of the river, which left the Sprague school out of reach and incon-
venient of access. In the fall of that year Mr. Sprague opened
but one department and his wife taught a district school at Delta
Mills. The same year she was taken sick and died, and he became
disheartened and returned to his former home near Auburn, New
York. Afterwards he went to California, located at Sonora, and
in 1850 was elected a member of the California Legislature, serving
two terms. He later moved to Oregon and began the practice of
law, and still later returned to California.

While building the log schoolhouse, old Chief Okemos, then
eighty years old, and a few of his tribe were camped near us. They
had been hunting near our home not long before, and he knew me;
and also about the story of my killing the buck with a club. He
delighted to prove his own bravery and many dangerous encounters
by showing the numerous scars he carried from conflicts with
both Indians and white men, made by the tomahawk, knife and
rifle. History tells of the British commissioning him as Colonel
of an Indian regiment which fought the Americans at the battle of
the Thames, and how he afterwards went to Detroit and agreed
with General Cass to lay down the tomahawk and scalping knife
and to become a good Indian, and how he never broke his agreement. He took great interest in me, calling me his "Pick-a-nin-ne
She-mo-ke-man" (white young man). He watched me intently

while I hauled and skidded logs with the oxen and a log chain. As it was very warm, I was working with bare feet, and he pointed to his own feet, and said—"Squaw make moccasins—you wear moccasin." That night he took me to his wigwam. The squaws looked at my bare feet and at each other and then began to shake with laughter. One of the men said they were making fun of my bare feet. Soon one of them handed Okemos a pair of new, nicely beaded moccasins and he asked me to put them on. I offered to pay him for them but he refused. I walked proudly around displaying the moccasins in all the wigwams, greatly to the delight of Okemos. I did not go barefoot again in Lansing. Since that time I have been acquainted with numerous tribes of Indians but Okemos is the only Indian I ever knew to give a present to a white man.

One day Okemos asked me to take a night hunt with him up the Cedar River. Three of us went in a large canoe, Okemos in the bow, I in the center, and another Indian in the stern to steer. We paddled up the river about two miles where we stopped until it was dark. The weather was warm and sultry, and the mosquitoes very thick and tormenting. As soon as it was dark torches were lighted, and the boat was permitted to drift slowly and silently down the stream. Okemos sat in the bow of the boat armed with a hatchet fastened to a long pole. In a short time we saw the antlers of a large deer protruding out of the water, his body immersed to keep off the mosquitoes, and his eyes shining like two small brilliant stars. Before we reached him we discovered the heads of two more submerged deer, all intently gazing at the bewildering lights and unconscious of danger until Okemos with his hatchet struck the antlered one in the head. With a quick movement he then struck one of the others, which made such a splashing in the water as to frighten the third one away. Before midnight we were back in camp with two fine deer. This was the first time I ever had a hand in this kind of a still hunt, though I had heard about it before, and often practiced it on the lakes and rivers of the West years afterwards. Okemos lived to be over one hundred years of age, and died at one of his camps on the Looking Glass River east of DeWitt. His body was lashed to his favorite pony, and taken to Shim-le-con, an Indian Mission Village on Grand River, south of Portland, where it was buried.

After going home from Lansing and finishing up the fall work, we bought eighty acres more of government land adjoining us on the east. During the winter we chopped twenty acres of the new land, burning a large part of the timber while green and gathering the ashes to make into "Black salts" at a neighbor's ashery. The black salts were sold to merchants in Charlotte, who had them made into potash, then drawn in wagons to Marshall and shipped to Buffalo, where they were made into saleratus, ready to be shipped back to the merchants and sold to the same families who had cut the timber and burned the logs. In those days this was the only paying way of disposing of the now very valuable hard wood timber. As an example of the profit in black salts let me say that my eldest brother George filed a claim on forty acres adjoining us on the north, and before the time for payment expired he had made enough black salts from the timber which he cut to more than pay for the land.

Hunting bee trees for honey was another business the settlers engaged in to their profit in the fall and winter. There were three methods of finding a bee tree. One was to make a box with a sliding glass top, put some honeycomb and honey in it, leave the slide open and set it in the woods in the sun where the bees would find it. The bees would fill up with the honey and fly straight for their home. The hunter would take his ax and mark the trees in line with the flight of the bees, then close the box with some bees still in it, move some distance to the right or left in the sunshine, open the box and line the bees from that point. At the point where the second line crossed the first the bee tree was sure to be found. Another way was to follow the line of flight of bees on a warm day and detect the bee tree by their buzzing. Or again, when there was snow on the ground and there came a warm sunny day when the bees would come out, the settlers would locate the tree by the dead bees that had been chilled by the frosty air and lay on the snow at the foot of the tree trunk.

Our family all enjoyed good health during this period except for the usual attacks of fever and ague. This complaint was very prevalent in Michigan during the early days and hardly a family escaped it. Ague shakes was the fashion, and quinine the remedy, some carrying it loose in the vest pocket so as to be able to take a pinch of it at any moment while at work. My mother said she finally drove it out of her system after a ten years' fight, by the bitter help of that drug and that every fall all the children of our family were sure to have it but me. And, seeing the example of it around me so much, she said that I became an expert in imitating the shakes, although I never had a genuine experience of the bone-rattling, teeth-chattering and flesh-burning, which no amount of resolution, perspiration, quinine and cold water could fully prevent.

Young people of today must not think that we young folks of those days had no fun. Amusements of various kinds were common, such as young people and children play in all ages and countries. Besides in that new country we had our house and barn raisings, huskings, apple-parings, spelling schools, coon hunts and other sports not known now, which have passed away with the pioneer days which were their only proper setting—amusements in which old and young participated. At these gatherings might be found practically all the people of the district in which the gathering was held. Many were the queer characters that were brought together, and many the stories that were told about them. I cannot vouch for the truth of all these stories, but from such incidents originated much of the gossip, story-telling, and amusement of the people in those days of scattered neighborhoods, sparse population and few books and newspapers. One of the characters of our neighborhood was a man by the name of Bailey who lived about two miles north of Charlotte. He was one of the first settlers in the county, noted as a violin player and a very sociable and agreeable fellow. He was called "Rail Bailey" because of an exploit for which he was given credit at the first election held in our precinct. Here were gathered the voters of four townships and after voting they all stayed over to have some fun. Some had come on horseback, and for amusement Bailey offered to run a race of ten rods on foot, with a heavy fence rail on his shoulder, against a man on horseback from near Delta, the stake to be a gallon of whiskey. The Delta man, being a temperance man and Christian, be it said to his honor and consistency, refused to bet with whiskey or make any bet at all, but consented to the race. The conditions of the race were that Bailey, with the rail on his shoulder, which was to be selected by a committee from among the largest ones in a neighboring fence, was to start one rod in the rear of the horse, to get under way, and on getting even with the horse the word "Go" was to be given and both were to start together. Bailey won the race and ever after

3

went by the name of "Rail Bailey." Many other stories were
told about him. Shortly after this, it is said, he went to a store in
Charlotte to get a pair of rubber boots. Finding a pair that fitted
him, he put them on and walked out into the mud and came back
with them covered with mud and told the merchant that they
suited him, and that he would like to keep them, but had no money
to pay for them. The merchant replied that as he had soiled them
so badly that no one else would buy them, he could keep them and
pay when he was able. The old settlers still claim that Bailey
never paid for those boots. The spring of the year when the race
was run a new doctor came with his family to Charlotte and Bailey
employed him. When his corn was ripe the doctor asked Bailey to
take a hog he had received for doctor's fees, that had been fatted in
part on beech-nuts, and to fat it on corn, when he was to kill it and
dress it for half of the meat. Bailey consented, told him to bring
the hog out next day and he would have a place ready. When the
hog came he put it in the pen, fed it corn that night and next
morning, then killed and dressed it and took the doctor his half saying that it was fat enough for his own use and he thought for the
doctor's too. The doctor was angry but could do nothing but make
the best of it, and he said afterwards that the story, circulated all
over the country, gave him such a reputation that he had no lack
of patronage.

In the spring and summer of 1848 the jobs to open the State
road from Battle Creek to Lansing which I had helped to survey,
were let to different parties. Among the successful bidders were
four men by the name of Gilkey, living near Lansing, who took
four miles of the road near our home, making their headquarters
at our house. I took a contract from them to build eighty rods of
the road one mile east of our farm for which I was to have $250.00
in State land script, good for 200 acres of land anywhere in the State.
I was in my seventeenth year and strong and rugged for one of
my age. I first cut the timber four rods wide and then cleared the
center of the road one rod wide by pulling out the stumps. Twenty
rods of the road had to be corduroyed with logs 12 feet long. I
always took my dinner and gun with me, and twice during my
noon hour killed a deer near my lunching place.

While on this job I had another hunting experience, one which
lacked all the enjoyment of my other successes and which resulted

in a loss that was almost irreparable to our family. One noon I had left the ox-team for their rest, and carrying my musket had stepped into the brush when I saw three deer coming towards me and, as I thought, stopping within ten rods of me in the thick willow brush. I fired at the spot where I supposed they were, and the next moment my mother's best cow came rushing out towards me from the willows and fell mortally wounded within two rods of where I stood. I started back to my work broken-hearted, asking myself, "What shall I do? How shall I break the news to my mother?" I knew it would be a great loss to the family, as that cow furnished nearly all the milk and butter for a poor family of seven children. I bethought myself that the cow would at least be good for beef, and went back to where she lay to cut her throat and let the blood from her body. When I got there she was still alive and struggling for breath. She looked up at me with her great soft eyes as much as to say, "You have made a great mistake in shooting me." It took all of the nerve I could muster to end her struggle. I couldn't work any more that day and started for home to break the sad news to my mother and the family. As I neared the two log shanties that constituted our home, I saw my mother and the smaller children standing in the yard, and when mother saw me she called out, "Ed, what is the matter?—What have you come home so early for?" I broke right down and cried, and told her I had killed "old Brinn." As soon as she and my younger brothers and sisters realized that what I said was true, they joined me and we all wept together. My oldest brother who was out at work was called in to hear the sad news and the only thing he said was, "I have always told you that Ed was too young to handle a gun."

We hitched the oxen to a wooden sled made out of small logs, and my older brother going with me, we loaded the cow onto it and drew her home. When we got there I joined the family in another weeping time over our loss. We dressed and prepared the cow for market and started in the middle of the night with the ox-team for Charlotte, eight miles away, arriving there early next morning. As very little money was in circulation at that time we were obliged to trade the beef for groceries, dry goods and other necessaries for the family. The financial loss to my mother was not great, but the loss of milk and butter to the family was felt painfully for the next two years. Since that time I have never killed a deer without its reminding me of my mother's brindle cow.

After finishing my road job I sold $100 worth of my script in Lansing for $20 cash, and with the remainder located eighty acres of land in Kent County, and forty acres in Shiawassee County near Corunna. During the winter of 1848-9, we cut twenty acres of timber, and burned most of it to ashes to make black salts and saleratus.

The California gold excitement at that time was taking many men out of the country, and would have taken nearly all the young men if they had had the means with which to go. I was only seventeen years old, and tried in every possible way to get enough money to go. I had 120 acres of land, but could not raise money with it for nobody had money to loan, and nobody seemed to want to buy land.

In the spring we made three hundred new sap troughs out of split ash logs hewed out with an axe and charred inside to keep them from leaking, tapped four hundred maple trees and made eight hundred pounds of sugar to exchange for goods and family supplies. During the summer we harvested ten acres of wheat with grain cradles, threshed it with a horse power machine, and had a fine crop of over three hundred bushels for use and market.

In October of this year a very distressing occurrence happened that kept the entire half of the county excited for some time. Four miles east of us, in Windsor township, stood a log schoolhouse in the woods. One day in October a boy of six years by the name of Wright, who was attending school, strayed from the path on his way home and got lost in the woods. Nearby settlers looked for him in vain that night. The next day people for miles around were notified, and a searching party of about two hundred men turned out to look for him. They found where he had rested over night, and during the day found his cap two miles southwest of the schoolhouse. Next day fifty men from Eaton Rapids joined in the search. Towards night on the third day, I was on the extreme right flank of the searching party about three miles from the schoolhouse and south of Taylor's Lake near the head of Thornapple River. The willow brush was very thick here and I could make little progress. It was growing dusk and I was about to turn back to the main party when someone at my left fired at a deer. Instantly something that for a moment I supposed to be a wild animal sprang up in a thick clump of willows not more than ten feet from me. A second glance showed me that it was the boy, and I at once shouted to the others that he was found. He was so frightened and exhausted that he could not speak, and his feet were badly frost-bitten. We took him on our backs and carried him to the nearest house where he was treated by a doctor who was in the searching party, and then taken to his home. He never fully recovered from the shock and exposure. Four years later the boy was a pupil in the same school house of Miss Diantha O. DeGraff, whom I married in 1858.

In the spring of 1850, I was still hoping some way would open to enable me to go to the gold fields of California. In the mean time one of love's romances occurred. My oldest brother, George, in attending one of the log house dancing parties met a young lady by the name of Gladden. It was a case of love at first sight and they were married the same month. He at once built a log house for himself on his forty acres which adjoined our farm and was living in it the month after their marriage, though still working and managing our mother's farm. In the following spring while making sugar, some differences occurred between us on the subject of his managing mother's farm, I wanting to work it and he claiming that I was too young. His decision and that of my mother left me nothing to do but obey his orders, with which I was not satisfied as I thought that they were not giving me the privileges to which I was entitled at home.

There was helping me that spring in our sugar-making a young man twenty years old by the name of Verplanck, who was the eldest of eight children, of a very poor family living on a new farm near us. To him I confided my troubles. He in return told me that he and his father did not agree, and that he was planning to leave home and look out for himself. His father would not give his consent to his leaving home but he said that he had decided to go even if he had to run away. We finally agreed to go off together, tramp the forty miles to Jackson, and see if we could not get work on a farm or on the railroad. The next night we filled the large potash kettle full of sap, left it boiling, and taking a change of clothes tied up in a bandanna handkerchief and a fresh loaf of bread, some fried cakes and a cake of sugar as provisions started out. We had about three dollars each in silver. On reaching Jackson the next day at noon we went to a hotel and told the landlord we were looking for work. He said that he had a farm near Jackson and wanted to hire some men to split rails for fifty cents a hundred and board. We told him that we were from the Eaton County woods and accustomed to that sort of work. After an agreement with him, he gave us our dinner, wrote an order to the tenant on his farm and gave us directions to reach the place. We reached the farm about three o'clock, and found an Irish family in possession. The man gave us tools, took us to the woods and marked the trees we were to cut and split. We worked until night cutting logs 11 feet long, and after a good supper slept well. Early next morning we went to split up the logs we had cut, but found the white oak so very tough that after working hard all day we had split less than 200 rails. The next day we worked until noon, and then told the Irishman that we could make no money on such timber and would have to quit unless our wages were raised. He took his horse and went to Jackson to consult the landlord, but came back saying there would be no increase in our pay. We told him he was welcome to the 300 rails we had split, but on leaving he gave us fifty cents each. We walked back along the railroad track to Jackson and thence to Grass Lake where we boarded a freight train for Ann Arbor, working our passage by helping unload freight along the way. At Dexter we heard of a farmer two miles out of town who wanted to hire help. We went to his farm, helped him do his chores that evening, and took supper with him. He told us he could pay us but $5 a month besides board and washing which was less than we cared to stay for. We stayed all night with him and helped him do his morning chores in return for the lodging and our breakfast, and he then offered us $6 a month, which we declined. We walked on to Ann Arbor, where we tried to get work on the railroad but were told we were too young.

We now concluded that we had made a mistake in leaving home and decided to return unless on our way back we could find a good job. We walked to Whitmore Lake and stayed over night with a farmer, then went on west through a good farming country, paying our way with work. On the seventh day after leaving home we reached Eaton Rapids, and found one of our neighbors there who had come to get a grist ground and had to stay over night to get it done. He had two bushels of corn to be ground for my mother. I asked him what she had said about my leaving home. He replied that she had told him that I thought too much of her to stay away long; and then said to me—"Your mother will be glad, but not surprised to see you return." We slept on the mill floor that night, and next day rode home with this neighbor. I was warmly welcomed by all our family and became fully convinced that my troubles were mostly imaginary, and that there was "no place like home." Verplanck was not so well received, his father telling him that he had hoped he would never return.

In August of that year the "bloody flux" or dysentery, raged among the settlers and many died, among them my friend John Verplanck and his three younger sisters. All the people were greatly alarmed and nobody could be had to help care for the sick. Those who died were buried at night by the county coroner, without any funeral ceremonies.

After my return home from my futile journey I diligently made up all lost time and learned to value home as never before, gave up my wild boyish habits and notions and concluded it was time to make more of a man of myself and do the best I could at home. So well did I do that when I was twenty years old my mother and brother obtained means for me to fulfil my long desire of going to California. In closing this story of my boyhood days I will copy an extract of a letter from my mother, written when eighty years of age to a grandson, Pitt R. Potter. After a sketch of Michigan life, she closed by saying: "I kept my family with me until they became men and women, and neither of my five boys, to my knowledge, have ever used liquor or tobacco, and all have good homes and families." Thus she fulfilled her purpose formed at the time of my father's death, and kept the family together until she saw them all married and gone. She lived with her eldest daughter in plain sight of her old home and died at the ripe old age of eighty-three, a remarkable age considering the labors, trials and hardships she had gone through in a new country. Neither my father nor my mother ever united with any church organization, but I believe that they were Christian people, doing to others as they would have others do to them, and that they died as they had lived, in the full belief that all mankind would be ultimately saved.

AT THE AGE OF TWENTY

Reproduced from a daguerreotype taken at Marshall, Michigan, on the day Theodore
Edgar Potter started on the overland trip to California

CHAPTER II.

Across the Plains.

From the day when I first heard of the rich gold discoveries in California I was ambitious to reach the Golden West. But in 1849 I was only seventeen years old, too young, so my mother thought, to make the hard trip into the new country. Moreover I had no money with which to buy the necessary equipment. I had located 120 acres of land but it was not valuable, for everyone had land to sell and few cared to buy. But in 1852 when I reached my twentieth year my mother and elder brother aided me in raising the money for my equipment thus making it possible for me to realize my fondest hope. There was but one man in the county who had ready money which he was willing to loan. He was a retired naval officer who had been wounded at the Battle of Vera Cruz in the Mexican War. He was a good friend of my mother's and she induced him to loan me one hundred dollars on good land security, with interest at 30 per cent per annum.

In 1852 there were but three routes by which one could reach the Pacific Coast and a man's choice of the three depended absolutely upon the amount of money which he had on hand for the journey. If he had $300 he might take the railroad to New York or the boat down the Mississippi to New Orleans, then a steamer to Nicaragua or the Isthmus of Panama, cross to the Pacific and take another steamer up the Coast to California, the entire trip requiring about thirty days. If he had $150 he might ship on a sailing vessel, go down the Atlantic Coast around Cape Horn and reach the Golden Gate in any time from three to six months according to the season. If he had not enough money for either of these routes but sufficient to purchase an ox-team and wagon, rifle and ammunition he could cross the plains, the then so-called American Desert, and after spending anywhere from four to six months on the way would reach the golden valleys of California. My money was barely sufficient for an ox-team outfit and I, perforce, chose the last mentioned route.

Erastus Jacobs and Edwin Spears from the same township left

their new made homes and started with me. The three of us had less than $400 with which to buy our outfit and supplies for the long journey. We decided to defer purchasing this outfit until we reached the border of the frontier. On April 6, 1852, we started from our homes, my brother taking us by ox-team and sleigh to the nearest railroad station which was at Marshall, thirty miles away. At Marshall we bought tickets to New Buffalo, at the foot of Lake Michigan, which was then the Western terminus of the Michigan Central Railroad. We crossed by steamer from New Buffalo to Chicago, a town which was so young and small that it had only one railroad and that running for a distance of only ten miles. We stopped in Chicago one day and then took passage on a canal boat to Peoria at the head of navigation for river boats on the Illinois River. We disembarked at Peoria, for here we planned to buy outfit and supplies and make our start on the long overland journey.

We were very fortunate in getting our outfit but our good fortune was due to the misfortune of another. On the day of our landing at Peoria we found a widow with five children who had started with her husband for the West a few weeks earlier; he had died on the way and she now wished to dispose of her outfit and return home with her children. The outfit consisted of three yoke of oxen, one covered double wagon, one riding pony, one double-barreled shot gun, one rifle, one tent, cooking utensils and a large quantity of provisions for all of which she asked the moderate price of $250 which we paid her without a word. We saw her and her family on board a river boat started back for her old home near Toledo, Ohio, which she had left filled with bright hopes and anticipations four weeks previous, only to be wrecked and stranded among strangers. It was the first of the many sad scenes which we were to observe amongst the many thousands who like us were pushing westward in search of fortune.

We hitched up our teams the same evening and made our first camp five miles west of Peoria. We planned to cross the Mississippi River at Keokuk in southeastern Iowa and to strike the Missouri River at St. Joseph, Missouri, about 400 miles distant from Peoria. We reached Keokuk in six days, and finding the country new and the roads bad, concluded to lay over one day and give our oxen a much needed rest. After crossing the river into Missouri we found the roads much better. The country was mostly prairie and the larger portion of it unsettled. Covered wagons were in sight every day, all pushing forward towards the same destination and the same golden opportunities that we were seeking. What settlers there were living on the route were willing to sell their property at a sacrifice in order to make the same venture that we were making. In fact almost every family seemed afflicted with a severe case of "California Fever." We had plenty of opportunities to trade our outfit for a good prairie farm.

We reached St. Joseph on the first day of May, having made the trip from home in twenty-four days, which was a very good record indeed. We had reached the extreme border of civilization. It was now necessary for us to become part of a larger body of travellers for our mutual self protection as we were to cross a country at least 1,600 miles in extent that was occupied and controlled by roaming tribes of hostile Indians. At St. Joseph we met a man named William Sherman who came from our own county in Michigan and who had driven an ox team hitched to a light two-wheeled rig from his home to St. Joseph. We knew him by reputation as one of the best hunters and trappers in Michigan and succeeded in getting him to purchase a quarter interest in our outfit and to add his yoke of oxen to it. Mr. Sherman was about fifty years of age and a pioneer and frontiersman of the highest type. He proved to be of great help to us in many ways before reaching the gold fields, not only because of his ability as a hunter but also because of his constant good humor and clever wisdom which made him the arbiter of the many differences which arose between the members of our train. He was known to us as "Uncle Billy." He added two good guns and two hunting dogs to our outfit and the addition proved to be valuable to us during the next four months. Four days after reaching St. Joseph we had organized a train of nine wagons with thirty-six yoke of oxen, ten riding horses and six cows. Our party numbered thirty-five men with four ladies and two colored servants. Uncle Billy was the oldest and I was the youngest person in the train. The nine wagons represented nine different states, namely: Louisiana, Tennessee, Kentucky, Missouri, Iowa, Illinois, Indiana, Pennsylvania and Michigan. The four ladies were young and unmarried and came two from New Orleans and two from Memphis. They were members of southern hunting clubs and were taking the land route to California for the purpose of hunting large game such as buffalo, elk and antelope. The two ladies from New Orleans accompanied their uncle who was a polished southern gentleman and a noted hunter. This party had four yoke of oxen hitched to a large and heavy covered wagon which had been used as an express wagon on the streets of New Orleans. I remember that this wagon had a very high top, on the side of which was painted in great gilt letters, "Poydrass Street, New Orleans," and that it attracted more attention than any other one I saw during the journey. This New Orleans party had come up the Mississippi River by boat to Memphis where by previous arrangement they met the party consisting of the other two young ladies of our party and their two brothers who were also provided with a complete outfit. They all boarded the boat at Memphis for St. Joseph, and their combined outfit resembled a travelling arsenal. The ladies were dressed in bloomer costume and each had a well trained mustang riding pony for her own use. There were two stout, healthy looking colored men, supposed to be slaves, with the party who were brought along to do the work, such as cooking, driving teams, pitching tents and everything except guard duty, which it was stipulated, at the time they joined our train, they should not do. This party reached St. Joseph and went into camp near us on the second day after our arrival. Uncle Billy and his two dogs were the first to make their acquaintance and before evening of the day of their arrival the young ladies and he were practicing with their rifles at a target.

The Indiana wagon was in charge of a man named Joseph Smith from St. Joseph County, Michigan, who had crossed the plains in 1850 and had returned over the same route in 1851. Before we left St. Joseph on our long journey over the plains we elected him captain of our train. He was about forty years old, had been raised on the frontier and was a well known pioneer and hunter. He proved to us before the journey was over that we had made no mistake in electing him our captain.

On that first evening together in camp Uncle Billy related to us some of his experiences in the woods and before we went to sleep that night we had a complete history of himself, his wife and his son Paul, whom he had left on a farm in the dense forests of Michigan to make a living as best they could, while he made this journey to California to seek his fortune. Before we parted company with Uncle Billy we became convinced that he never told one of his best stories unless his wife or his son Paul was connected with it.

The number of teams waiting to be ferried across the Missouri was so great that four steam ferry boats were kept busy transporting them. Our train of nine wagons took its place in line on the night of the fifth of May, at least half a mile from the ferry, to await its turn and it was not until the afternoon of the next day that we were landed on the west bank of the raging Missouri. We made our first camp west of the Missouri in a dense grove of cottonwood and elm timber. The next morning it was raining as it had been doing for the last four days, but we nevertheless broke camp and made for the prairie which was only six miles away. We were all day ln making this short distance and I can truly say that it was the most uncomfortable day that I had ever experienced. When we reached the prairie we found that all the emigrants who had crossed the river during the five previous days had gone into camp waiting for the rain to cease. It was a grand sight to look over the prairie as far as the eye could discern and see the new white-covered wagons and tents clustered here and there and the great number of horses and cattle, scattered in every direction, trying to get a bite of the short spring grass that had but just started to grow. It was estimated at the time that at least ten thousand emigrants were camped within a distance of ten miles of this point. These men had cattle and horses enough to haul them, and supplies sufficient to last them during the trip of sixteen hundred miles through a country entirely uninhabited except by Indians. Each train had to guard its own stock to keep them from getting mixed up with others and this was considerable of a job where there were so many separate trains.

This great army of people were all bound for the same goal and each person was ready to hitch up his team and be the first one onward as soon as the clouds cleared away and the sun made its first appearance. The morning of the eighth of May brought us good weather and the entire body of people and animals formed a great procession and started on the way. Previous to this time there had been but one trail over which the wagons could pass. But 10,000 people starting from the same locality on the same day made it necessary for more trails, which were very easily made on the open prairie, excepting when we came to a stream that had to be bridged. During the first day's march there were at least twelve roads for twelve teams abreast. Our roadometer which was fastened to the rear wheel of our wagon registered fifteen miles for this first day's drive.

That night Captain Smith called our party together and said that we ought to adopt some rules to govern us on the march that was before us and that as captain he would see that such rules as we saw fit to make were enforced. He reminded us that when we crossed the Missouri River we had passed beyond the border of civilization and the reign of law and that all our disputes and troubles would have to be settled by arbitration among ourselves as there were no civil courts on the road we were travelling to which cases could be taken. A committee of five, including the captain, was appointed to draft such a code for our government. This committee soon reported a set of rules that the captain had travelled under two years previously while crossing the plains and these were adopted. The rules were few and simple but they covered the main essentials of life on the frontier. One rule provided for the formation of our camp each night so as to give protection against an Indian attack. This was to be done by running the wagons close together in the form of the letter U, pitching all tents inside this enclosure and posting four men as guards during the night, two of them at the camp and two with the stock. Any differences that might arise among us were to be settled by a board of arbitration consisting of three persons selected from the entire number of our party including the ladies. I remember also that one of the by-laws stipulated that we should travel only six days in the week, and that this rule was strictly lived up to during the entire time and distance. The day of rest did not always fall on Sunday as our stops had to be governed largely by the presence of grass, wood and water.

Early in the morning of the ninth our nine wagons were on the march again. Some trains that had horses for their motive power, and grain with which to feed them, were on the move all through the night as they knew that Wolf River was but a few miles ahead and that there was but one bridge on which to cross. During the day large numbers of antelope were seen on the hills, but never less than half a mile away, out of range of rifle shot. This was the first opportunity offered the ladies to show their skill. The four, dressed in bright red suits, mounted their ponies and with Uncle Billy and three other men of the train acting as escorts started on the hunt. The red suits seemed to have the same attraction for the antelope that a torch light has for a deer in the night. They stood still and stamped their feet and gazed at the bright object, allowing the hunters to come within close gunshot range. This first day's hunt was considered a great success for the ladies as they killed four antelope, which the men brought to camp lashed to the ponies. When they arrived in camp they were given three cheers for their success, which meant a feast on antelope for the entire train. That evening "Uncle Billy" related many of his exciting Michigan hunting experiences which I will refer to later on but gave the ladies all the credit for the day's successful antelope hunt.

The only bridge at Wolfe River was owned by a person living at the Pawnee Indian Mission nearby, who charged $5 for each wagon that he allowed to cross. Such was the crowd of people and so exorbitant the price that our party joined with some other trains and built a new bridge over which we passed on the morning of the tenth of May. It was said that there were four such bridges built in two days over that narrow stream which ran through a rocky gorge twenty feet deep and forty feet wide.

On the morning of this tenth of May there occurred one of the many sad incidents that we met with on our way. On account of the exposure through which the emigrants had passed during the storms of the previous week a great deal of sickness was prevalent. We had heard that smallpox and cholera had broken out before we crossed the Missouri River and near Wolf River we passed several fresh made graves. About two miles west of the Pawnee Mission a family of seven persons, consisting of father, mother and five children had camped. The oldest girl came to the Mission that morning and reported that her father, mother and two brothers were dead and that the two others were very sick. The missionary was trying to get somebody to go with him to aid them in their trouble and our captain halted the train while he told us of the sad case. After hearing his story Captain Smith said that he believed it was our duty to help bury the dead and that even if they had died from a contagious disease it would be safer for us to go and bury them than to get excited and run away from what he considered was our duty. When he called for volunteers nearly all in our train offered to go and he chose fifteen of us, and left the rest to look after the outfit and guard the cattle which were let out to graze. The missionary led us to the camp which was about a half mile away and there we found living only the girl who had given the information in the morning. We buried the six persons in one grave. The girl was taken to the Mission where we left her with the promise from the missionary that her wishes to have the outfit sold and that she be returned to her friends in Virginia would be faithfully carried out. This incident detained us about four hours. The afflicted family were Germans who had been travelling with a train of six other wagons. When they were taken sick three days before, their travelling associates had gone on, leaving them to take care of themselves. It was an uncommon thing for a train to lay over on account of sickness even for one day, as it was well understood by all, before starting, that even with the smallest possible amount of detention it would take the entire season to get through to California. The Nevada Mountains, sixteen hundred miles west of us, must be crossed as early as October to avoid the deep snows.

Our train went into camp late that sad day having made only twelve miles. The captain told us that evening that we had four rivers to cross before reaching the Platte River valley near Fort Kearney and instructed us to be ready to start at two o'clock the next morning so as to get ahead of the rush and travel over the old road instead of having to make a road of our own. By noon the next day we had forded the Big Mineha River, twenty miles from our starting point, and there encamped three hours. We made five miles more before camping for the night. That evening the captain told us that if we would consent to start out at ten P. M. each day for ten days we would gain at least five miles each day over the other trains and by doing this we would be able to get ahead of the great body of people and find better roads, camping places and pasture. We adopted this plan and before the ten days had expired we had left the crowd in the rear. We forded the three other rivers in the night, namely, the Little Mineha and the Big and Little Blue. The country we were now in was considered the very best part of the now great state of Kansas. At this time the Pawnee Indians were in possession of all this country as far north as the Platte River, while the Sioux claimed all of the lands north of the Platte to the Canadian line.

It was during our journey along the Big Mineha that we had our second hunt. "Uncle Billy's" experience in hunting big game in company with the ladies had not been quite satisfactory to himself, as the ladies had carried off all the honors. We had heard that elk and deer were plentiful in the timber along the Big Mineha River. So when nearing the timber he suggested to me that I take our riding pony and go to a point of timber some five miles down the river while he would take his two deer hounds and follow down the river on foot, keeping in the timber, and that if he started up any big game he would let the dogs loose and drive it in my direction. Taking two other men with me I started out early in the morning. On our way we saw great numbers of antelope which were very wild, and kept out of range of our guns. At seven o'clock we were at the designated point of timber and in a short time we heard the hounds. It was evident that the game was coming in our direction. We picketed our ponies and took our positions some forty rods apart in the timber. I stationed myself on the river bank near the rapids, where game would be quite sure to cross if they tried to get into the timber on the opposite bank. The barking of the dogs came nearer and nearer, then a shot from a rifle was heard, then another shot and still another. The woods seemed to be full of hunters. At least ten elk and as many deer soon came in sight, headed for the rapids. I fired as they plunged into the river. On the opposite bank several shots were fired and the herd turned on their track back up the river. It was not long before we learned that six elk and four deer were killed that morning. At least ten men from other trains had a hand in the sport, but it was "Uncle Billy" and his dogs from the woods of Michigan who were voted the honors of the day's sport and success. We packed our ponies with only the choicest portions of the meat that was allotted to us for we were at least ten miles from the spot where our train would camp that evening. We crossed the river about noon, built a fire and broiled some of the elk steak, by holding it over the fire on sharpened sticks, and had our dinner after which we started a southwest course to find our train. During the afternoon we saw fresh signs of buffalo, and sighted a small herd about two miles away, making

4

north on the run. Our ponies were already loaded down with the spoils of the day and we could spend no time in following the buffalo. We were well tired when we reached camp about sunset where we found that the ladies had brought in two antelopes during our absence.

During this hunting trip we met several Pawnee Indians armed with bows and arrows and gave them what was left of the elk and deer that we had killed. Little did we think at the time that the slaughter of game we had that day participated in was an illustration of one of the primary causes of all the Indian wars of our country since the first of the English settlements. The Indians had fought for their hunting grounds and after killing unknown numbers of white men had been driven back from the Atlantic Ocean to the Missouri River. The question of the final outcome was discussed by the older members of our train. What would this unnecessary slaughter of game lead to in the future? If all emigrant hunting parties were as successful as we had been, what would be left for the poor Indian to subsist upon? The only answer made to this question was that the Indians would never be driven farther west, as white men could not live in such a poor country as this. When I travelled through this same country ten years later all of the Indians on our western border from the Rio Grande to the British line were in arms against the white man fighting to retain their hunting grounds. Much more could be said in regard to the early day abuse of the Indian, but we pass it for the present.

As we had been travelling nights for the past five days and were well in advance of the great rush we voted to take a rest the next day. It was the first Sunday that we had found a choice camping place since our start from St. Joseph. Our encampment was on the banks of the Little Blue River, with grass, wood and water in plenty and numerous large catfish in the river that were easily caught. Large game was plenty. The lady hunters with their southern escorts had kept the train well supplied with antelope meat every day. Uncle Billy had killed his first buffalo of which the entire train had the benefit. After we had cleaned up, changed our clothes and washed our dirty ones which we spread out on the grass to dry, a minister from one of the nearby camps, accompanied by one hundred or more of his friends and followers, came to our camp and asked the privilege of preaching to us. I remember that he took as his theme the duties that we owed to God on this perilous trip. After his sermon he passed on to the next camp, inviting the members of our party to go with him. The invitation was accepted by many of our men and by the four young ladies who went to assist in the singing. These were undoubtedly the first sermons ever delivered by white men to white audiences on the Little Blue River.

The river was lined with fishermen that day, and hundreds of large fish were caught on which we feasted for the next two days. That evening while we were gathered around our camp fire Uncle Billy entertained us with one of his Michigan bear stories, which I will relate as I now remember it. In the fall of 1840 he was living in a new log house, built near the Thornapple River far from any settlers. He was engaged in trapping for furs, and hunting for large game, such as bear, elk, deer and wolves. While he was away from home one day visiting his traps, a large black bear made a visit to his log house. His wife saw the bear looking in the door, and hastily grabbing her son Paul she hurried up the ladder into the attic and let the bear have his own way in the room below. He helped himself to a loaf of bread, drank up and turned over two pans of milk and then went out into the yard where he turned over a bee hive, ate what honey he needed and departed. If there is anything a bear loves it is milk and honey. It was late that night when Uncle Billy got home to find his wife and six year old boy badly frightened. He concluded to stay at home the next day as he thought the bear would return for more milk and honey as soon as he got hungry. On the second day the bear returned, accompanied by three others—a mother and her two cubs. Uncle Billy had secreted himself and was ready for them with two guns. They first went for the honey. He fired and broke the largest bear's back, and than fired at the old mother wounding her badly but not mortally. He killed the first bear with another ball in his head and then started with his dog after the mother and cubs who had fled to the woods. The mother soon became very weak from the wound she had received and the dogs overtook her. She turned to fight them, and when Uncle Billy arrived on the scene he found that she had killed one of the dogs and badly injured the other. He quickly killed the old bear, and with the help of the injured dog tracked the cubs to a large hollow log about two miles from his home. He was determined to capture the cubs alive, and this he did by cutting a hole in one end of the hollow tree, building a fire at the other end and smoking them out. After capturing them he took them home and kept them until they were full grown, when he sold them to a travelling show man for fifty dollars.

After Uncle Billy had finished his story, an amusing incident occurred that led to disagreeable consequences for me. There was a man with us about thirty years of age, who had seen hard service in the Mexican War, and had been given a government land warrant for his services which he had located in Michigan where he had settled. He caught the gold fever, concluded to go with us to California and mortgaged his land to secure the money for his equipment. When we reached St. Joseph and he learned of the amount of sickness among the emigrants he became discouraged and said that if he could sell out his interest he would return to his family as he felt sure he would never live to reach the gold fields. We made fun of what he said and assured him that he was one of the healthiest and most robust men of the company. He changed his mind at this and instead of going back laid in a large supply of patent medicines, advertised to cure every conceivable kind of disease. He bought a strong hand trunk and filled it with these medicines. Soon after starting on our trip he became known as the "Doctor" of our train. He didn't like the name, but the more he resented it the oftener it was applied to him. It was "Good morning, Doctor," and "Good evening, Doctor," every day. While he was absent attending the meeting at one of the camps this Sunday some person handy with an indelible pencil wrote the following sign on the cover of our wagon:

"Dr. E. S———. All diseases promptly treated."

Many of the larger trains had doctors in their parties who made considerable money on the trip, and it was nothing unusual to see a doctor's sign on a wagon. Our Dr. E. S——— soon had a call for his professional services from the members of another train. I pointed out the "doctor" to the man who inquired for him, and it was not until this man spoke to him that he discovered the sign on the wagon. He was very angry and laid the whole affair to me although I had little to do with it. I was told that he threatened me with a good horse-whipping. That night it rained and we did not break camp until morning. It was my day to drive the team. As we were driving along on the high sandy bank of the river, the doctor came up behind me, struck me with a whip, and accused me of painting the sign on the wagon cover. I denied the charge, but his only answer was to strike me again. He was between me and the river bank and I made for him with all my strength expecting to force him over. He grabbed me and we fell down the steep bank together at least twelve feet onto the soft ground below. It was lucky for me that I fell on top of him. He yelled at the top of his voice, "Oh, Ed, you have killed me; what will my poor wife and children do!" I thought for a moment that he was dying and was badly frightened. At my call for help the train was halted. We carried "the doctor" into the wagon, threw water in his face and gave him brandy, and he soon revived. We called a real doctor from a train nearby who found by examination that his left shoulder was out of place and his right arm fractured at the elbow. We gave him five dollars in gold for his services and instructions and after an hour were on our way again. The injury proved to be a serious one. The doctor called to see his patient again that evening, and said that he would always have a stiff elbow, as it was a compound fracture. He had to carry his arm in a sling for the next four months. After that morning's scrap with our doctor, caused by my not submitting to an undeserved horse-whipping, I was given the name of "Bully Potter," and was known by no other name until we separated in the Nevada Mountains. As he claimed that I was the cause of his getting the nickname *Doctor*, with better reason I claim that he was the cause of my getting the name of *Bully*.

This trouble with "the doctor" was the cause of my having more work to do than I had previously had. Instead of driving the teams one-fourth of the time, I now had to drive them one-half of the time to fill his place. I also had to do his share of guard duty, so that my work was just doubled all around. This experience proved to be a valuable lesson to me in my subsequent life. I have never been in company with miners, lumbermen or soldiers but what some one of them has been picked out as the butt of ridicule and nagged for the amusement of the crowd. Sometimes this so-called fun has consisted in giving a man an uncouth and discreditable name, which is sure to follow him through life. Many a man has been led to commit desperate deeds just because of such nagging. This personal affair on the Little Blue River and its unfortunate results led me to avoid such teasing in the future and to disapprove of it whenever it came within my notice.

The Pawnee Indians were very friendly with the emigrants. When we were in sight of the Platte River at least one thousand warriors passed our train. All were mounted on ponies, armed with bows and arrows, spears and tomahawks, and painted for battle. To our questions they answered that the Sioux had crossed the Platte and were stealing their squaws. They pointed over the hill and said that there would be a great fight that afternoon in the river valley on a battle-ground that had often been fought over before. They invited us to go to the top of a hill that was in plain sight where we could see the battle and watch them whip the Sioux, and drive them back across the Platte to their own lands. Some of us witnessed the Indian fight that afternoon on the old battle-field about thirty miles east of Fort Kearney. Without doubt there were as many white men looking down upon this farce of a battle as there were Indians engaged in it, and the whites were far better armed, for at that time the Indians knew practically nothing about handling fire-arms and none of them were using guns that day. It was quite apparent to the spectators that these Indians did not go to war for the purpose of getting killed. They kept well out of reach of each other's arrows and although I stayed for at least two hours I did not see a single dead Indian. What I did see was an exhibition of very fine bare-back riding by the members of both tribes. We learned a few days later that on the following day the Indians got their fighting temper up to the proper point, so that several Indians on both sides were actually killed. There were two companies of United States troops stationed at Fort Kearney for the purpose of protecting the emigrants from hostile Indians. Fort Laramie, three hundred miles west of Fort Kearney, was the next United States post where we would find troops.

Fifteen miles above Fort Kearney we found many emigrants fording the Platte River, which was at least a mile wide at that point, the water being on an average of not more than one foot in depth though the current was very rapid. Their reason for crossing at this point was to reach a road on the north side of the river on which there was but little travel and along which they expected to find better pasturage for their stock.   Platte River is a dangerous river to cross, as its bed is composed of quicksand which is continually changing.   During one week the channel may be on the south side and the next week on the north.   Many wagons were lost by emigrants crossing at this ford.   The breaking of a king-bolt, tongue, wheel or anything that could not be quickly repaired gave the rapid current its chance to wash the loose sand from under the wheels and in an hour's time the wagon would have settled so rapidly that you could see nothing but the white cover above the surface of the water.   If the wagon was ever recovered it would be at some time in the future when the water was running in some other part of the river bed.

These rapids were a favorite crossing-place for the buffalo on their annual migrations northward in the spring.   Thousands of these monarchs of the plains were in sight as we reached the ford. They were coming from the south, marching in single file, in companies of from one to three hundred, each company led by one of the most powerful bulls of the herd.   All the trains in our section had to stop that day while these herds were crossing the ford, for they would neither stop nor turn out of the way for us or for anything else, but as primitive pioneers claimed the right of way. Some of us would go out and select a nice fat looking one and shoot it down, but that did not check the herd nor turn them in the slightest from their chosen course.   We had to wait until the herd had passed before we could get the one we had shot. Where they passed down the sandy bank into the river their trail was worn so deep that they would disappear from sight entirely to again emerge in sight in the river, each company strictly following its leader in single file and close order with no scattering or straggling.   It was a scene that will never pass from the memory of those who had the privilege of viewing it.   It was a wonderful panorama to look upon.   Thousands of buffalo and hundreds of wagons were fording the rapids of the river, each column in plain sight of the other but far enough apart not to interfere with the other, for the rapids were at least a mile long.

The favorite range of the buffalo runs north and south, about five hundred miles wide, commencing at the Arkansas River on the south and extending north into the British possessions. As all the streams in this region take an easterly course the buffaloes have to cross them in their migrations, yet they are known to have journeyed at least a thousand miles north, returning south the same season. All through this country are still to be found the so-called "Buffalo wallows," sometimes several of them in less than an acre of ground. They are usually about ten feet in diameter and from one to two feet in depth and are made by the bulls in the spring when challenging their rivals to combat for the favor of the opposite sex. The ground is dug up and hollowed by the pawing of the two bulls, the challenge is accepted, and the battle takes place. The one that comes off victorious remains in possession of his bride until dispossessed by a more powerful rival. So desperate are these battles that frequently one of the contestants is left dead on the battlefield, while the victor dies in the wallow from the wounds he has received. These wallows have proved of great benefit to emigrants and have saved many a life. The soil is so compact from the treading that after a wallow becomes filled with water it remains until evaporated. Many an emigrant train has found water for man and beast in a buffalo wallow when all the streams were dried up. It must not be thought that this water is of the quality one is accustomed to get at a popular summer resort, but on the plains a thirsty man or beast with a parched and swollen tongue, far from a living stream of water, does not hesitate long about the quality of water he is willing to drink. Many an emigrant and soldier can also truly say that a buffalo wallow has saved his life when attacked by Indians, as it is a safe and natural rifle pit. I well remember in the several Indian battles in which I participated on the plains of Dakota in the summer of 1863, what good use both soldiers and Indians made of them.

Now, before proceeding with the description of our journey, let me give you the estimate which most of us set upon the character and value of the country through which we were then passing. Fifty years ago any school boy if called upon to give a description of the country west of the Mississippi River, would say that it was "The Great American Desert." At that time it was thought to be of little or no value except for the furs it produced. This was the opinion of our party in 1852. But not long after our journey countless numbers of emigrants crossed the Missouri River seeking homes in this very desert, the valleys and plains of which are now fast becoming the richest and most fertile in the world. American-born emigrants were the first to penetrate and settle there, claiming the best land; following them came the foreign emigrants, flowing in that direction in a mighty tide, narrowing down the limits of the supposed Great American Desert, and making a veritable garden of what we considered worthless land. It did not take long to discover that what we in our party had looked upon as a worthless, barren desert, incapable of sustaining a civilized population, was in fact the richest part of our territorial domain with a climate pure and healthful and a soil surpassing that of most of the eastern and southern states and capable of producing indefinitely. The name *"Great American Desert"* has passed away; instead has come *"The Plains,"* a synonym of great things. Of the many persons who crossed the plains at the time I did, whom I have since met, there are none who have not expressed surprise that their judgment regarding the vast country over which they passed at that time was so far from correct.

After leaving the Missouri River the size and varieties of timber constantly diminished. As we left civilization behind and penetrated the vast plains, forests were nowhere to be seen. The few scattering trees, mostly small cottonwood, which grew close to the banks of the larger rivers, continually became smaller and smaller as we advanced westward and finally disappeared altogether leaving only the small willows to mark the water courses. Nearly all of the plains country can be said to be without timber of any kind. Scientific men disagree as to the reason for this lack of timber. Some of them think that the prevailing high winds that blow unobstructed across the prairies prevent the growth of timber as well as of tall grass. The facts show that grasses grow much taller on the prairies of Iowa and Minnesota, than they do in Utah, Nebraska and Nevada. The lands on the prairies will produce grass high enough to conceal a man on horseback, while the plains are covered with a mass of buffalo grass scarcely three inches high. Another theory is that the plains were once covered with a heavy growth of timber which by various causes was destroyed, and that since this destruction timber had been prevented from growing by the annual fires which the Indians set each fall to burn the dead grass and hasten the fresh growth the following spring. As tending to prove this last theory, many trunks of large trees have been found in a petrified condition on the uplands of Colorado, Utah and Nevada, far from any streams of water.

One of the most remarkable and deceiving phenomena to be met with on the plains is a mirage. It is a wonderful distortion of nature; yet it looks so real that the most experienced eye is often deceived by it. The first mirage noticed by our party was while in camp on the Platte River. We saw what we supposed to be a large party of Indians coming directly towards our camp and as they appeared to be moving rapidly we hastily prepared to defend ourselves. It proved however to be only a small herd of elk. Their number was greatly multiplied by the mirage, and their horns and peculiar motion led us to believe that it was a war party on horseback. It was a common thing for us to look in some direction in the early morning or late afternoon and see what appeared to be a large fleet of vessels under full sail on a great lake, which would turn out to be only a train of white covered wagons. Many an emigrant train while looking for water has gone miles out of its course to reach an inviting body of water which the mirage placed in sight, seemingly only a short distance away, beckoning and alluring them, constantly deceiving them with the belief that they would soon reach the greatly-longed-for goal. Throughout this whole country travellers will occasionally run onto the graves of persons who have been led astray by the delusion until they have perished. In locating a route across the plains, water was one of the most important things to take into consideration. Sometimes it would be necessary for us to make what was called a "dry camp," where there was no water. Then we would carry water in cans for ourselves, while the animals would have to depend upon what moisture they received from the dew while grazing at night.

Uncle Billy had narrated all the hunting stories that had been told on this trip so far. It was evident to us all that he was running short on his hunting reminiscences, as he had repeated some of his best ones. But that night after crossing the Platte River and seeing the countless buffalo he told us a deer story that was new to us all and that I am quite sure was strictly true, as years later I talked with men who shared the venison which he killed on the occasion. His story was as follows. Deep snow had fallen that winter and deer were plenty near his cabin. There came a warm spell that melted the snow slightly, and this was followed by a cold snap which froze the wet snow sufficiently to bear up a man on the crust while a deer would break through. A short distance from his home Uncle Billy struck a herd of thirteen deer one morning. He shot and killed three of them before they got out of sight. He followed the rest of the herd and in less than two hours had killed them all, none of them being over one-half mile from his house. He killed some of them with his hatchet as it was impossible for them to get away, as they broke through the sharp crust of the snow. One of the largest deer came near killing him by striking him with his forefeet and breaking two of his ribs. His son Paul, who was then fourteen years old, heard the firing and took his gun to aid his father. He passed several dead deer before reaching his father whom he found so badly injured that he could not walk. He hurried back home and told his mother and together they brought him home on a large hand-sled after which they went for the neighbors and a doctor. It was a close shave for Uncle Billy for he was under the doctor's care for three months before he could do any hunting.

After leaving the ford on the Platte River where so many had crossed to the north side, we had no trouble finding good grass and water for the next three hundred miles. We continued on the south side, travelling on a level plain near the river, with hardly a tree of any kind or size growing on the banks. The only fuel we had was what we could gather from the driftwood which had floated down from the mountains during the freshets, and the dry buffalo excrements, called "buffalo chips" which we gathered and which made a very fine fire. When about one hundred miles above Fort Kearney we met some fifteen hundred Sioux Indians returning from a bloody fight they had had the day before with the Pawnees. They were all mounted on ponies, finely painted and decorated with feathers, and carried their bows, arrows and shields with fresh scalps hanging from their lances. The Indian who had taken the largest number of scalps had the honor of riding at the head of the column and one would say from his appearance that he was the happiest red man on the plains. These Sioux claimed they had fought a great battle and had whipped the Pawnees, but at the same time they seemed to be in a great hurry to get across the Platte River into their own country.

Before we reached the South Platte River our road became very sandy and the soil so poor that grass grew only near the river. It was very hot and dry. Suddenly, without any warning, we saw an immense cloud of dust bearing down upon us from the west. Our captain promptly took in the situation and ordered us to turn our teams around so that they faced to the east, to run our wagons close together, chain the wheels and set the brakes. Before we had completed these preparations we were in the midst of one of the severest sand-storms I ever witnessed on the plains. The wind blew at least fifty miles an hour, carrying the sharp hot sand with such a velocity that neither man nor beast could face it. The storm did not last over ten minutes and our train suffered little damage from it. But we passed several trains that day which had been badly damaged. Wagons were blown over and great numbers of horses and cattle stampeded, while several men were injured and two were killed. We assisted in helping those who had suffered. It was due to the experience and knowledge of our captain that we were brought safely through that brief but terrible storm, as it was admitted by all that our train was right in its path. This storm delayed us several hours, compelling us to camp that night on the east side of the south fork of the Platte, which heads in the Colorado Mountains near Pike's Peak, and upon the banks of which the city of Denver was later built. At that time no white man knew of the presence of gold or silver in the Colorado Mountains for no one had yet dared to penetrate and prospect them.

We camped on the river bank for the night expecting to cross the ford the next morning. The day had been the warmest we had had since leaving the Missouri. Our roadometer registered five hundred and twenty miles from St. Joseph which distance we had covered in thirty-one days. So far we had met with but few storms to detain us. Our captain had told us of the terrific thunder storms he had been through two years before when passing over the same route, and said that the sand-storm of the morning was a sure sign of the approach of a heavy thunder storm. He was very anxious to cross the South Platte River before this storm came, as a heavy rain would make it unfordable, and gave us orders therefore to be ready to cross at sunrise. Before midnight the predicted storm burst in all its fury. There was neither timber nor bluffs to break the force of the wind which blew with such velocity as to raise the water from the river-bed and drench our camp with the river spray in addition to the driving rain. Imagine the continuous roar of thunder, the livid flashes of lightning gleaming through the mist and spray of water that stood out against the inky darkness of the night and you will have some conception of the dismay that the storm brought to us as we lay in the frail shelter of our covered wagons. When the storm ceased, the guards who had been with the cattle and horses came in and reported that our stock had stampeded. When daylight came our cattle were nowhere to be seen. Three out of our ten horses also had either broken their picket lines or pulled up the iron pins and left with the cattle in wild flight. Captain Smith said that the stock would halt as soon as the storm had passed and accordingly some of us mounted our ponies and set out in search of the lost animals. We had no trouble in following their trail and found them quietly feeding in a valley about ten miles from camp. Our cattle and horses were mingled with hundreds of others and it was evident that it would take time to pick them out. A few of the cattle had been killed and many more injured in the stampede. That afternoon a meeting of the owners was held to consult as to the best way to separate the stock of each train from the herd. The rain of the previous night had already raised the river so that it could not be forded for at least three days and Captain Smith advised leaving the cattle undisturbed for that time, saying that they would probably separate by themselves if left alone. The party took this advice and agreed to leave the stock at the valley ten miles from camp until the river could be forded with safety. True to our captain's prophecy, the oxen, cows and ponies of our train came together before the end of the three days and we brought them into camp in better condition to continue the march than before, as the long rest and good feed had done them much good. Several men were drowned in attempting to ford the river on the third day after the storm, but on the fourth day we took our train over without accident. From this point to Fort Laramie, on Laramie River, we had good roads and good feed for our stock.

We were now approaching the foot-hills of the Rocky Mountains, and had passed out of the range of buffalo and antelope. Deer and elk were still plenty and a few brown mountain bears were seen, our southern party bringing in one young brown bear near this point. They said that they had seen a mountain lion and a herd of mountain sheep during the day. The doctor's arm and shoulder were improving, as it was now three weeks since the accident. I had performed all his duties during this time, driving the team, standing guard at night and washing his clothes, and had left the train only one day of the time to go on a buffalo hunt. He was getting quite good-natured over the affair, and now took all the blame for his injury on himself.

At Fort Laramie we had our oxen shod for the first time on the trip, for we were approaching the Black Hills. In leaving the Fort and ascending the steep bluff the road wound over the solid black rock for a distance of twenty-five miles with no vegetation whatever near it. We passed through Ash Hollow, a narrow ravine leading down from the hills into the valley of the north fork of the Platte River, and in this valley, less than a mile long, we counted over sixty fresh made graves by the roadside. As we approached the river valley we saw numerous wagons halted as far from the road as they could get, each flying a red flag to indicate the presence of smallpox. The new-made graves we had seen were those of the victims of this dread disease. For the next two days of our travel we saw these red flags flying from many wagons unhitched at the side of the road.

From Ash Hollow it was forty miles to the ferry where we expected to cross the river. The day that we left Fort Laramie was the warmest and most trying for man and beast that we had experienced since starting. The thermometer indicated one hundred degrees, the sun shone blisteringly hot on those bare, black rocks and we had no water for stock until we reached the river that night. No game could subsist on the rocky barren waste over which we had travelled during the day but our southern hunting party left the train at Ash Hollow, where there was scattering timber and searched for game through ravines and over bluffs during the balance of the day joining the train just as we were going into camp, with the first mountain sheep that had been killed on the trip and two fine deer. Uncle Billy was with them, and received the credit for shooting the mountain sheep. This success made Uncle Billy's tongue run pretty rapidly for the next forty-eight hours, and led him to tell several new stories of his prowess as a hunter.

At Fort Laramie we had been informed that the ferry on the North Platte was owned by Mormons who were charging exorbitant prices for crossing in their boat which was small and unsafe. That evening the captain suggested that he and Erastus Jacobs ride ahead of the train to the ferry, to find out the true situation there and report to us at our next camping place. Accordingly, when we broke camp at daybreak the next morning the captain with Jacobs and two other mounted men galloped off on their mission. We had gone about twenty miles when the two men who had accompanied the captain and Jacobs in the morning met us and advised us of a fine camping place about five miles further on. We went into camp before dark on the river bank opposite a well-wooded island. It was evident that there had been recent heavy rains in the mountains, for the water was very muddy and rising rapidly. The next morning we found that the river was out of its banks and that we were camped on an island, with water running five feet deep a few rods south of us where the previous evening there had been dry ground and a heavy growth of grass. The river must have risen ten feet during the night and it was still rising. We were somewhat alarmed as a further rise of ten feet would float us and our possessions off with the flood. But the waters soon began to fall, and before night the river was in its old channel.

At noon the captain and Jacobs rode into camp and we all gathered around them to hear what news they had from the ferry. They were both exhausted from their long trip and made us wait until they had eaten their dinner before telling their story. After they had rested and feasted on choice sheep and venison steaks, they related what they had witnessed during the past twenty-four hours. As I now remember it, the captain said that they arrived at the ferry about two o'clock in the afternoon and that the river was then high and rising at the rate of about two feet per hour. The channel was narrow at the ferrying place and as the volume of water increased the current became very rapid. A large number of men and wagons were waiting to be ferried across, at a charge of five dollars each for wagons and one dollar each for men, while the women were carried free. The proprietors allowed only two wagons and ten men on the boat at each crossing because of the high water, while the stock had to swim across just below the ferry. As soon as the cattle of one train were well started for the opposite shore with their owners on horseback closely following them, another train would start its stock into the river. Many people were crossing when the captain rode up. One large drove of stock, which the captain thought consisted of over one hundred head, had nearly reached the opposite shore, being driven by fourteen men on horseback, and another large drove was well started in their rear, when for some reason the first drove suddenly turned around and started back to the other shore. The fourteen men on horseback were caught between the two bodies of cattle, each going in opposite directions, and all were drowned. The wives of two of the men were on the boat at the time and saw their husbands go down to their watery graves. As Captain Smith, who was used to the tragedies of the frontier, related this story the tears streamed down his face and his voice was broken with sobs. Jacobs who was my partner and messmate, told me later that he thought the cattle turned back because dogs barked at them as they neared the shore. He said that after the accident the ferrymen refused to run the boat until the river had gone down, so that there would be no danger in crossing. He had stopped at the ferry all night, and said there were probably five thousand emigrants within five miles waiting to cross, and that it would take several days before our turn to cross would come.

The next morning Captain Smith, Jacobs and I walked up the river to the head of the island and found the water falling very fast. A large amount of flood wood, much of which was dry pine, hemlock and spruce timber which had been brought down by the present freshet was lodged near the head of the island. Jacobs, who had been a raftsman for two years in the pine woods of Michigan, thought we could made a raft out of these dry logs and ferry ourselves across the river at this point, but the captain said that the current was too swift. Jacobs and I argued that there would be but little current as soon as the freshet had passed and the river had gone down to its normal depth, and that if the channel was no wider on the other side of the island than on this side we cou'd easily get our things across on a raft. The captain remarked that as we had no boat he didn't see how we were to get onto the island, to which

Jacobs replied that he could get onto the island all right and that he would look the situation over from that point. The captain agreed to let him try it but advised him to wait until the next day when the river had gone down. When we got back to camp Jacobs suggested that we get Uncle Billy and our axes and go up the river and see if we could not get across to the island. We started out about ten o'clock. Jacobs told us that he was going to cut off a length of a dry pine log, roll it into the river, and paddle it over to the island. About noon he launched his solid canoe and started down the river standing barefooted on the log. The entire crowd was at the bank to see him off, for we had told them of his venture. He kept the log at a proper angle to go diagonally with the current and landed safely on the island. He looked the island over and returned to camp with the news that we could easily cross the river there with a raft. When he was returning the ladies who had travelled in Egypt, said that his log looked like a gondola coming down the Nile. From that time on he went by the name of "Gondola." It is in such ways, and on such occasions, that men obtain amusing names which follow them at least until the party breaks up and often longer. It sometimes became a little embarrassing for us when strangers came from other camps to visit us, and our Michigan crowd was introduced by our nicknames of "Uncle Billy," "The Doctor," "Gondola" and "Bully."

We listened with much interest to "Gondola's" plan of making a raft to take the wagons across the river. He said that the channel on the opposite side of the island was no wider than that on this side and that there was a good landing place there. He was sure that we had plenty of rope in camp to safely handle such a raft, and promised us that if we would all join in and help him he would land us safely on the north bank of the river within three days. The party voted unanimously to build the raft and elected Gondola to boss the job. Taking twenty men with axes he went to a willow grove a little up stream and there built a small raft, ten by sixteen feet in size which he had in the water in less than two hours time. A coil of inch rope was fastened to each end of the raft; Uncle Billy was told to yoke up our brindle ox team, and I to bring our riding pony, and our best block and tackle to the shore. As I was the youngest and lightest man in the train, Gondola asked me to swim my pony across the river and carry the rope which was tied to the

5

horns of the oxen.   A large rope was fastened through the ring of the
ox yoke and this was attached to the raft.   The tails of the oxen
were tied together to prevent them from turning in the river, and
making back for the shore.   Gondola, Uncle Billy and three other
men were to manage the raft, which was hitched about two rods in
the rear of the oxen.   Gondola aimed to strike a cove about twenty
rods farther down the bank than the spot from which we started,
and it was my business to see that we reached this cove.   The
men on shore were instructed how to manage the rear rope.   The
word was given and in less than two minutes we were safely on the
island.   We fastened a pulley to a tree, pulled the large rope
through it, and told the men on shore to pull the raft back,
Gondola and Uncle Billy returning with it.   Four more trips were
made by the raft during the day, carrying over tents, tools and
provisions for those who were to go to work on the large raft
early the following morning.   Grass was good on the island and
the cattle were all driven over that evening without accident.

While the captain and Gondola were at the head of the island se-
lecting timbers from the flood wood for the big raft, Uncle Billy and
I started out with our guns to look for deer, with the understanding
that we were not to shoot at anything except large game.   The
timber became thicker and larger as we went down the island, which
was in some places fully a half mile wide, and we soon separated, he
keeping near the south shore and I near the north.   I soon discovered signs of deer and looking over the top of a knoll saw five
of them, one looking straight at me.   I fired and a deer fell.   I
dropped down out of sight and reloaded, then slowly and carefully
raised myself and saw the other four deer still standing there, one
of them broadside towards me.   I fired at this one, thinking I could
kill him on the spot, but he jumped and ran past me out of sight in
the woods, the other three following him.   I cut the throat of the
first deer and then looked for the spot where the second one stood
when I had fired.   I found a trail of blood on the leaves and followed
this a few rods into the woods where I found the deer dead.   I soon
heard Uncle Billy's gun and started off to reach him.   As I came up
I saw him intently looking at an animal which he had just killed,
and he did not seem to notice my approach until I asked him what
he had shot.   He said that he thought he had killed a mountain
lion, but after looking it over I told him it looked to me more like a

lynx or wild cat than a mountain lion. He told me that when he
first saw the animal it was coming towards him on the run, making
about twenty feet at a jump he thought, but that when it saw him it
went up a tree like a flash. He was terribly frightened when he saw
it coming straight for him, for his first thought was that it was one of
the mountain lions that he had read about. He pointed out the
big limb of the tree less than twenty feet from the ground where
the animal sat when he shot it, and said that he stood and
looked at it for at least ten minutes before he could muster
courage to shoot, for he had completely lost his nerve. The animal
sat on the limb looking straight at him with its eyes glaring and its
tail switching back and forth, and he expected every second that it
would spring at him. He finally mustered up his courage, took
aim at the head, and the one shot finished him. He still insisted
that it was a young mountain lion, and when I asked him if he had
ever heard of a lion climbing a tree his reply was that if it wasn't a
lion he would like to know what it was. We tied the animal's
legs together, hung it on a pole and started for camp, carrying it
over our shoulders. I took the lead and went to the spot where I
had killed the first deer which I showed to Uncle Billy who seemed
quite surprised as he had not heard the sound of my gun, so excited
was he with his "lion." He was doubly surprised when I showed
him the second deer. When we reached camp with Uncle Billy's
animal the captain gave his opinion that it was a large mountain
wild cat. Four of us went after the two deer which we dressed and
divided among the members of our company. The lion was hung
up in plain sight of those on the opposite side of the river. Jacobs
and the captain, in looking up raft timber on the island, found the
body of a dead man which undoubtedly was one of those drowned
at the ferry. That afternoon two ladies from the ferry whose
husbands were among those drowned, came across on our raft to
look at the body we had found, and one of them identified it as that
of her husband. It was getting towards evening, so the ladies from
the ferry stayed that night at our camp as guests of our Southern
party.

The next morning Gondola and twenty men were early at work
on the large raft. They first cut six logs twenty-four feet long and
laid them on four green, peeled stringers close to the river's edge;
then cut eight twelve foot logs about six inches in diameter, bored

them with a two-inch auger, and pinned them crosswise of the six large logs. This gave a good strong base, which we covered with small poles and willow brush. By noon we had two rafts finished, one on each side of the island, and were quite ready for the good dinner of venison and lion meat which awaited us at the camp. After dinner the captain gave orders for everything to be ready to be carried across to the island during the afternoon, saying that we would lay by the next day as it would be Sunday. The raft on the south side was quickly launched and loaded and at nine o'clock that night our nine wagons were safely on the island. A large train of twenty wagons that had camped near us the previous night saw what we were doing and asked to join with us, but we told them that this was only an experiment and that if it was successful we would be glad to sell the outfit to them at a fair price. After our outfit was safely on the island, they offered us $100 for the use of our raft to carry their outfit across at once. We told them that we were going to stay on the island over Sunday, but they could have the raft on the south side Monday forenoon, and that on the north side Monday afternoon, and in that way could get over the river by Monday evening. It was part of the bargain that they were to turn in and help us.

This party had a minister with them, and we arranged to have a joint service Sunday on the island for the burial of the three bodies that we had found for our men had discovered two other bodies in the drift-wood in addition to the one that the captain had found. That evening we heard that two more dead bodies had been found further down the river and were to be brought next morning to the island for burial. Messengers were sent out on horseback to all the emigrant trains in the vicinity, notifying them of the services. Sunday was a beautiful day. The raft ran continuously and nearly one thousand people were present at the services. There were at least fifty ladies present and they gathered wild flowers to strew on the single grave in which these five men were buried. There were three ministers to conduct the services, and that burial service in the wilderness left a deep impression upon us all.

On Monday morning at eight o'clock we began crossing the north channel of the river, and at noon our train was safely over. By nightfall we were twelve miles further on our journey for our four days' stop had given our stock a good rest. Before leaving the island the parties that had purchased our rafts offered us $50 for our ropes and pulleys and we accepted their offer, getting that amount for what had cost us $20 in St. Joseph. The captain thought we should give the island some appropriate name, one by which all of our party would remember it hereafter. One of the ladies suggested calling it "Jacob's Island," in honor of Gondola to whose persistent efforts we owed our success in crossing the river, and to this the party unanimously agreed.

During these four days in camp several amusing incidents occurred, one of which was caused by our having two negro slaves in our train. Up to this time these slaves had attended their masters and had not assisted in the work of the general camp but in building the rafts the help of these two healthy slaves was offered and accepted. One afternoon they went fishing with some of the white men. These two occurrences caused a good deal of discussion among the white men as to the proper place for slaves. When cooking the fish that evening one of the white boys said that he didn't propose to work with a "nigger" on the raft, while another replied that these two negroes were good enough to work with him and were much better helpers than some white men he knew of. The disputants soon came to blows and grabbing their sizzling frying-pans struck each other over the head again and again. Uncle Billy jumped into the fracas and separated them and told them that they could never settle the slavery question in that way. He told them that if he had them in Michigan he would teach them not to fight over trifles in the same way that he had taught his son Paul, that is, by shutting them up in his out-door bake oven when it was good and hot. After Uncle Billy's lecture the white and colored boys worked together in harmony.

Our first camp on the north side of the Platte River was made three miles below the ferry where the fourteen men had lost their lives six days previous. The two ladies whose husbands were buried by us at the island were with us by invitation from the captain and at the ferry we met several members of their train still searching for bodies. Thus far the bodies of only seven of the fourteen men had been found, and our captain told off all of us that could be spared to spread out and look for the remaining bodies. The doctor said he would drive the team with his one arm if I

would go with the searching party, and took the whip in his hand
for the first time in over six hundred miles.   Uncle Billy and I
took our guns, for as there was scattering timber and clumps of
willow on the river-banks, we thought that we might get a shot at
some large game before night.   We saw several wolves in the early
afternoon but we were not wolf hunting and paid no attention to
them.   We kept on along the banks of the river exploring the
flooded places, climbing over drift-wood and wading through the
marshy lowlands looking for the missing bodies.   The train was
making faster time than we were, as it was moving in a straight
course while we were following the winding river.   As we neared a
sharp bend in the river we saw some moving objects that we took
to be deer or elk along the border of a small piece of timber about a
half mile away.   They were coming towards us and evidently had
no idea there was danger for the wind was blowing from their direction so that they did not scent us.   We watched them from a hiding
place in a small bunch of willows and soon made out that they were
elk and that there were ten of them.   When within about eighty
rods of us they stopped and looked back, but finally started on a
trot directly towards us.   We agreed that Uncle Billy should aim
at the leader and that I should try for the next one.   As they trotted
into the marshy bayou we fired, immediately dropping into the
bushes and re-loading our rifles.   When we rose out of the bushes
there stood the rest of the herd, looking to see what had happened
and we got another good shot before they made off.   We found that
we had killed three of the herd and had just started to dress them
when three horsemen rode up who had sighted the herd and had
shot at and wounded the leader.   They were members of the party
who were searching for the missing bodies and as their camp was
nearer than ours we offered them half the elk meat if they would
get a wagon to take it to camp.   It seemed that they had already
sent in for a wagon to take back a body which they had found in
the water near the bayou and when this came up we loaded the fresh
elk meat in on green willow brush with which we filled the bottom.
It was now nearly dark and we were about to make for camp when
we saw a herd of six elk, a short distance away making for the river.
Uncle Billy started along the river bank to head them off but as it
was so late and as we already had a considerable load I did not go
with him.   However the temptation of getting another shot was

too much for my good resolution to kill no more game that day, for when we neared a bend in the river where I saw I could get a chance of a good shot I dropped into the bushes and waited. A moment later I heard Uncle Billy's rifle ring out and a few minutes after that took a close shot at the rest of the herd, killing one of the largest ones. This made us five elk for our afternoon's hunt, as Uncle Billy's last shot had killed one. It was long after dark when we arrived at camp with our five dead elk and the body we had found in the river.

Our train camped that night within a short distance of the party that had met with such a sad loss of men and we learned that nearly all of the men drowned were Mormons who were on their way to Salt Lake. The survivors told us that they had decided to stay in their present camping place for several days in the hope of finding the remaining bodies. The next morning we bade the Mormon train good-bye, after they had thanked us for the help we had given them.

CHAPTER III.

In the Rockies.

Our route lay up the North Platte, until we struck the road leading to the Sweet Water River. The country had become barren, with little vegetation except an occasional patch of burnt grass and sage brush, but the roads were excellent and we made good progress. I remember that one day we passed through a valley that looked as though it were covered with snow. This valley was called Soda Lake. In the early spring the basin of the valley was covered with water but like many other lakes in the region it had no outlet, and evaporation during the hot summer months caused the water to disappear leaving upon the earth a crust of alkali or soda several inches in thickness. We used this soda for our bread, biscuit and pancakes, and it seemed to answer the purpose as well as the store soda that we had purchased in St. Joseph and had carried with us for eight hundred miles. We passed a large number of these soda lakes in the southern part of Wyoming and speculated upon the probable value of the product when the region should become more accessible.

We reached the Sweet Water River the day after crossing Soda Lake and found it a narrow, rapid stream, flowing through a valley hardly a mile wide, which was covered with the finest grass we had seen for the last three hundred miles. We were now about one hundred miles east of the South Pass where we were to cross the divide of the Rocky Mountains. As we had been driving our teams for at least eight hundred miles on a gradual up-grade, we looked forward with anticipation to reaching the summit, for then we would have the advantage of a down-grade. Near the head of the valley was Independence Rock, its walls rising almost perpendicular, for three hundred feet from the surrounding plain. It was the only great rock in the vicinity, and as it covered an area of several acres it was a landmark. It had been given its name by General Fremont who, on his first expedition to the western border of the continent, raised the Stars and Stripes from its summit on July 4, 1848, the first flag-raising in the Rocky Mountains. We camped near this rock, and examined it with curiosity, finding thousands of names chiseled upon its face with the dates when the parties passed it. A party of Mormons with stone-cutting tools were located on the spot and did a profitable business in cutting names in the rock at a charge of from one to five dollars, according to the location. We were fortunate in having a man with us who could do the work with a hammer and cold chisel and as the rock was of sandstone and very easily cut we soon had the satisfaction of having our names on that great roster. Men who passed there a year later said that the names previously cut in the rock had nearly all been erased and new ones cut in their places. So transient is our fame! We learned that the scheming Mormons made a nice fortune from the emigrants in a few years by cutting their names in the rock for a fancy price, and when they had passed on erasing these names and cutting others in their places.

Less than five miles from this rock the Sweet Water valley came abruptly to an end. As we toiled up the valley it seemed as if it were entirely enclosed by solid rock walls three hundred to five hundred feet in height, and our eyes were strained to see the spot the river entered where the trail would lead us out of this enclosure. As we drew nearer to the bold bluff of solid rock we caught sight of two openings, one a narrow gorge called the Devil's Gate— just wide enough to let the tumbling, swirling river through, the other, to the left and wider than the first, the opening through which our trail ran. This opening soon broadened into a narrow valley with a steep up-grade for the first two miles, which led to a level plateau with a good road and plenty of grass for our stock. We could see the mountains now only a short distance away, the lower ranges covered with a thick growth of timber while Pike's and Long's Peaks towered above the timber line with their summits covered with snow.

We made our camp in this beautiful plain near a snow-bank the melting water from which ran into a small creek flowing east into the Sweet Water River. As we toiled up the valley from the Sweet Water River more than half of our party went hunting in the timber that lined the valley, for we had secured no game since leaving the North Platte River. The Southern members of our party with Uncle Billy and his dogs and Gondola hunted along the timber to the left of the train and brought in two mountain sheep and a brown bear. The other and larger party that I was with skirted the timber on the right of the trail and killed a black-tailed deer. Uncle Billy's dogs had been a detriment to our hunting parties on several previous occasions, but on this trip they were given the credit of finding the bear. For the past five days we had been eating bacon that had been smoked and cured in Cincinnati and had been carried fifteen hundred miles and the fresh meat was a great treat. As I think of our supper that night and our breakfast next morning, consisting mainly of fresh mountain sheep, bear and deer, eaten in that beautiful spot near the summit of the Rocky Mountains, I think that if the voices of the forty persons in our party could be heard with mine we would declare unanimously that those two meals were the most enjoyable that we had eaten since crossing the Missouri River. The beauty of the scenery, the rarity of the atmosphere due to the elevation, the encouraging prospect before us all combined to give a relish for the fresh and tender wild meat that nothing before had done.

We had still about twenty miles before reaching the highest point in the South Pass with a gentle grade most of the distance. Because of the altitude the atmosphere was light and rarified, affecting the efforts of both man and beast; the teams were easily tired and would lie down while hitched to the wagons, as soon as we stopped. For this reason the captain gave orders to make only ten miles the next day and to camp at a spot where he had camped two years before.

That evening many stories were told about our camp fire. The captain told us of some of his hunting experiences in this same region which were so thrilling that a hunting party was gotten up at once under his leadership to put in the full day hunting. Early next morning, as we were ready to start, the captain asked me if I would take charge of the train while he went on the hunt. This I agreed to do on condition that they make a day of sport out of their hunting, dividing the party into two squads, one taking one side of the trail and the other the other side, with the penalty upon the squad that secured the least amount of game of cooking supper and breakfast for the company at the summit of the Rocky Mountains. The suggestion met with a cheer and arrangements were quickly made, Captain Smith and Gondola being selected as leaders and choosing up sides. The captain instructed me to push on at once and to make the agreed camping place by noon if possible, and at three o'clock to send out two empty wagons to get the game. Both parties were to kill any game they could find and the result of the contest was to be decided by a majority vote of all the persons that stayed with the wagons.

At noon, after an up-hill drive of ten miles, we made camp on the west side of a snow-bank several feet in height which had been left from the previous winter. While I had been attending to the various interests of our train during the forenoon the Doctor, with his arm still in a sling from the injury received at the Little Blue River, drove our team of four yoke of oxen handling the whip with his well arm. At three o'clock in the afternoon, as we had previously agreed, two of our wagons were unloaded and started out in opposite directions, one north and the other south, towards the timber and foot-hills of the mountain ranges, to bring in the game which the twenty hunters had secured during the day. The teams returned nearly at the same time, each wagon well loaded with game, dressed and ready for use. The parties of hunters marched alongside the wagon with their rifles over their shoulders and made an imposing and martial procession. Nearly all the varieties of animals to be found near the summit of the Rocky Mountains from a rattlesnake to a mountain lion were killed that day. Captain Smith's party, hunting near one of the branches of the Sweet Water River, brought in four mountain sheep, one black-tailed deer, twenty-five rabbits, one bald-headed eagle, and two large rattlesnakes. Gondola's party, hunting on the south, secured a mountain lion, a deer, and twenty rabbits. The bodies of all the game except the mountain lion were brought to camp while the lion's skin was presented to the Southern party who were saving all the furs and valuable hides that were obtained on the journey. The vote taken on the relative success of the hunting parties resulted in Captain Smith's party coming out victorious, and Gondola's party had the task of preparing the next two meals, which they did with much merriment and to the satisfaction of all. Supper was announced in good time and we all gathered in a circle around the fire and were served in genuine Southern style by the two colored men.

That supper was a memorable occasion for us. We were all in good spirits over our success thus far, delighted with our fine game supper and enthusiastic over the novel and romantic location we occupied. The stars shone brilliantly above us in the rarified atmosphere, our eyes took in a depth and outstretch of landscape which they could not fathom, our memories spanned with interest the incidents and distances of the route already covered, and our anticipations sought to grasp the future of our way. This induced thoughtfulness and reflection, as well as exuberance of spirit and hopefulness. Our hardships and exposures seemed forgotten or discounted, and our future prospects rose above par in the market of our anticipations and hopes. The hour following supper was an interesting and enjoyable one, each member of the party being called upon for a five minute speech. I think that there were some very witty and even brilliant things said that night, but, as no secretary had been appointed for the occasion, no record of these speeches was made and they were soon lost in the echoes of the nearby mountains. But the hour and the speeches served their best purpose, for they brought us into closer touch and sympathy with each other than we had been before.

After supper and oratory we came down to plain business again. Captain Smith told us that we would find very little game for the next seventy miles of our way. The hunting parties had that day secured about a thousand pounds of fresh meat that we could easily preserve for use during the next ten days, as meat would keep for weeks in that pure air and altitude if it were merely cut into narrow strips and hung to the loops of our wagon covers. The captain also told us that our next camping place would be near the junction of two roads, one through Salt Lake City, crossing the Green River at Fort Bridges, and passing through Emigration Canyon; the other taking the most direct route which the country would permit for the northern end of the Great Salt Lake. The latter route would take us over a very rough country that had been travelled only two years, but through beautiful scenery as the road passed the hot springs on the Bear River and went through the valley of the White Pyramid Rocks. The captain himself preferred the latter route both because he had been over it and knew all the camping places and also because it would save us one hundred miles of travel, but left to the members of the party by a majority vote the decision as to which route should be taken. By common consent the determination of this question was left until the next day.

When the sun rose the next morning not a cloud was to be seen. Peaks one hundred miles away were as distinct in that pure mountain air as if but a few miles off. As we started on everyone remained with the train and all were deeply interested in watching for the spot where the waters would be found running westward to the Pacific Ocean. The road was good and we could no longer discern with our eyes that we were any longer on an up-grade, but the water from melting snow in the ravines still ran in an easterly direction. Before noon we came to a small mound of rocks piled around the base of an iron post to mark the exact dividing line, and soon afterward discovered the water from melting snow-banks running westward. Five miles further on we came to Pacific Springs, where we found an abundance of the purest mountain spring water. Here we turned the stock out to feed on the short grass and to rest while we took our lunch. We concluded to go ten miles further before camping for the night. The vote was then taken on the choice of route, resulting in a decision to follow the shorter, but rougher and newer, road by way of the Bear River and White Pyramid Rocks. The only ones who wanted to go by way of Salt Lake City were our Southern people, and their reason was that they were curious to see Brigham Young and his multitude of wives.

During the next five miles that afternoon we passed the point where the road to Salt Lake City branched off. In beginning the descent of the mountain, a marked change came over our animals. Since leaving the North Platte River we had been obliged to use a great deal of persuasion, expressed in the forms of oxgads, to keep our oxen on the move. Now they kept their drivers on a sprint to keep up with them. Two men were sent ahead of the train on horseback to look up a good camping place for the night. It was getting late in the afternoon when they returned and met us, with the news that we could find one of the best of camping places by going off from the road about a mile to the north. We followed their advice and found it indeed an excellent place. As we had made a thirty-mile drive that day the captain said that we would only attempt to make fifteen miles the next day, and would camp on the Big Sandy River the next night. We all rolled in early that night with the exception of the four guards, for we were very tired. It happened that I was one of the relief guard that went on duty at two o'clock, and I do not remember ever having a harder time getting awake than I did that night. The only thing that helped me keep awake on guard was the howling of a pack of wolves not far off. The next morning while driving the stock into camp a deer followed by a dozen wolves ran past us within easy gunshot but it all happened so quickly that none of us had a chance to get a shot at him. The deer's bold strategy probably saved his life, for the wolves turned back as soon as they saw us. Wolves were so plenty in this belt of country that elk, deer and sheep were very scarce.

At nine o'clock we were on the move, and before nightfall had crossed the Big Sandy River, after a hard drive over pulverized sandstone rock three or four inches deep. We were now penetrating a country where nearly all the streams disappeared in the loose sand or emptied into some lake that had no outlet. In fact we crossed but one river that finally reached the ocean in the seven hundred miles after we left the summit. The Big Sandy was a sample of such rivers. It had a broad channel, which was evidently all used during the spring freshets, but on this day there was not a drop of water to be seen. A few miles above us there was water fresh from the melting of perpetual snows running in its channel; ten miles below us, where the river entered the mountains again, the water came once more to the surface and formed a considerable stream which finally emptied into the Green River.

After crossing the dry channel of the river we went up the west bank a few miles until we found water in the channel and good grass on the banks. Captain Smith told us that the next two days would be hard ones for our oxen and horses, as the road was rough, and as there would be practically no grass for them to pick. At his suggestion we employed the early evening in cutting the luxuriant grass on the river-bank with our scythes and packing it into sacks and blankets to be carried along for the use of our stock. We packed this grass in every empty place in the wagons and even tied bundles of it on the sides and on top of the covers, until some of the wagons looked almost like travelling hay-mows. We made an early start the next morning and as the weather proved cool and favorable, covered thirty miles before we made camp that night. Twenty miles of this distance was through country covered with sandstone rocks, which protruded above the ground in every conceivable shape, and which made the roads very difficult to travel. In places our heaviest wagons would sink six inches into the sand rock. The sides of the roads were so lined with boulders that there was no possibility of turning out to make a new track so our wagons had to follow in the deep ruts already cut into the sandstone rock.

We all wondered that a road had ever been made through such a country and soon learned that the only reason for it was that the emigration passing through the country in 1849 was so great as to demand another and shorter route to the coast than the one via Salt Lake City. In the year just mentioned several large transportation companies were organized which made a business of carrying passengers to California for a certain price per person, including board and lodging. They carried first, second and third class passengers. The first class travelled with horse teams hitched to light spring wagons paying two hundred dollars apiece and covering the journey from the Missouri River in sixty days; the second class passengers travelled in wagons drawn by mule teams, at a cost of one hundred fifty dollars, it taking them eighty days to make the trip; the third class travelled with ox teams, paying one hundred dollars for the trip, which took them one hundred days. The first year's experience of these companies proved that grain-fed American horses were a failure for this purpose and route, and that mule teams were little better; only the ox teams could live and successfully endure the trip, for with proper care they would thrive on the native grasses along the way, while the horses and mules could not do so. It was these transportation companies that cut this road through the rough sandstone country for the purpose of saving one hundred miles in the trip to California.

Our camp was made right on the trail that night for we were hemmed in by rocks. We threw down the grass which we had cut the previous day and our stock spent the night beside the wagons doing away with the necessity for a double guard. We had no water for the stock and only that which we had carried during the previous day for ourselves, so we made an early start the next morning in order to reach water and grass on the Green River which was ten miles away. The sun rose bright and clear on this, our Uncle Sam's Birthday, July 4, 1852, and we celebrated right merrily by starting down the steep descent into the valley of the Green River. It was a beautiful and inspiring view from our elevation. The delightful valley, broad, green and picturesque in the glow of the early morning sun, looked as if it might well have been selected as a quiet and happy Eden for the home of a primitive race. It spread out for ten miles in front of us to the river itself and then ten miles beyond the river to another range of mountains which we must pass in order to reach the Bear River valley beyond. The most dangerous part of the descent came soon after our start. There had originally been a bluff fifty feet in height here and when the road was first put through all wagons were let down over it by ropes and tackles. When the Mormons got possession of the road and the ferry on Green River, they charged ten dollars a wagon for lowering them over the cliff and taking them across the river on the ferry. This was little less than robbery and the emigrants, in 1851, decided to cut a road down the soft sandstone bluff and save the charge. This was done and the Mormons lost a large source of income; they still kept the road in good repair, and published and sent a guide-book through the country explaining the advantages of this route in order to get good returns from their investment at the ferry. At this steep road down the bluff we found two men connected with the ferry, who gave us instructions and aid in making the dangerous descent. The captain told me to go ahead and take my wagon down first, giving me directions as to how to do it. Three of the four span were unhitched and driven down the road to the foot of the bluff; the remaining and best span was left attached to the wagon to take it down while the speed was regulated by a heavy two-inch rope attached to the rear axle and running over the drum of a windlass. With this arrangement the descent which had looked so hard was made with ease and safety.

After leaving the bluff the road wound through a deep sandstone ravine for about seven miles and then emerged in the valley which was one of the finest and most beautiful I have ever looked upon. We found water for the animals in the ravine through which we passed, and while we were watering them the captain and Uncle Billy rode ahead to the ferry to see if there was any chance of our getting across that day. I was left in charge of the train and was told that if I did not hear from them to move right on until we reached the ferry. We arrived at the ferry-house at noon and found that one of the owners also owned the ferry on the North Platte. He had been at the North Platte at the time of the drowning and recognized Captain Smith as the leader of the train that had helped to search for the bodies of the unfortunates after the accident. He told us that we might cross at once and that there would be no charge for us because of the help we had given to his people in their trouble. We drove onto the ferry, all the stock except the ponies swimming the river, and in less than an hour our outfit was across. The ferrymen and their helpers lived in log-houses on the west bank of the river and were very insistent upon our coming to see their homes, seeming anxious to have us see how Mormon families lived in a country two hundred and fifty miles from their nearest white neighbors. Of the women whom we met living here, four were said to be wives of the two owners of the ferry. These ferrymen were also stockmen, owning a large number of cattle which they kept at the south end of the valley, well out of reach of the passing emigrants. The beginning of their herd had consisted of the sick, lame and stray cattle which had been left behind by passing emigrants and had been supplemented by others that had been run off in the night by thieving men in the Mormon settlements and secreted in mountain valleys until the trains from which they were stolen had ceased their searching for them.

The man who had taken us over on his ferry free of charge went with us to show us a good camping place which we found within a half mile of a spot where about a thousand Snake Indians from the upper waters of Green River were camped. They were on their annual visit to the Utah Indians, who were to meet them in the valley. The ferryman informed us that the Utahs would probably be in the valley before night, and advised us to stay over the next day as by so doing we would see the greatest exhibition of bareback riding we had probably ever witnessed. He said that he and his partner were well known to the chiefs of both tribes and that he would be glad to take a crowd of us over and introduce us to them if we wished to go. All of us, including the ladies, welcomed the idea and a party of ten was soon ready, of which I was one. When we got to the Indian camp the ferryman spoke to them in their own language. The chiefs gathered around him, while he told them that we were on our way to the setting sun, having come from where the sun rises, and that we had called upon them as friends in passing through their country. The eyes of every buck and squaw were fastened on the four ladies who were dressed in their brilliant red suits and mounted on fine ponies, and our guide told us that these Indians had never witnessed such a sight before. He told them that the ladies were great hunters, and had many furs with them which they had taken in the past two moons. Our captain asked him to invite them to come to our camp and see the furs which the ladies had taken and tanned on the trip. The Indians said they would wait until later as they expected the Utahs before the sun went down, and as every Indian who had a pony wanted to be on hand to meet them. We bade them good-bye and rode back to our camp after arranging with the ferryman to bring some of the Snake and Utah chiefs with him to our camp at five o'clock that afternoon. The ladies busied themselves during the rest of the afternoon in getting their furs in shape for exhibition, not omitting the bald eagle which they had mounted, nor the two rattlesnake skins which they had dried and stuffed. They had stuffed and mounted many other small animals, such as prairie dogs, rabbits, four or five different kinds of owls, and a large cat-fish. Much of this exhibition was new to even the members of our train, as the work had been done by the ladies in their own tent.

Promptly at five o'clock the two ferrymen, with two of their helpers, their ladies and about twenty Indians from the Utah and Snake tribes rode into camp. The Mormon ferrymen interpreted for both sides. Our ladies were the center of attraction. They were dressed in their bright red suits, and appeared to be exceedingly attractive to the Indians, so much so indeed that they paid but very little attention to the exhibition of furs and stuffed animals. They were told how well the white man's squaw could shoot with a rifle, but, as they were still using bows and arrows this statement made little impression upon them until the ladies offered to show them how well they could shoot. The target was set up about ten rods away and the Mormon explained it to the Indians. Every time the ladies hit the bull's-eye and rang the bell attached to the target, the Indians were so pleased that they gave their savage grunt with such vehemence as to make it a howl sufficient to raise the hair on a white man's head. They were very much interested in the target and asked permission to shoot at it with their bows and arrows, but had very little success. When the shooting was over Uncle Billy showed the Indians the skin of the strange animal he had killed on the Island of the North Platte, but they and the ferrymen all said they had never seen anything like it before, and were not sure what it was.

When we separated that afternoon the Indians invited us to come to their camp that evening to attend their reception to the Utahs which would conclude with the Snake Indian dance. They also invited us to watch their horse races the next day, which the Mormons said would be the finest thing of its kind in the country. In view of their invitation our party voted to lay over the next day. Our ladies were quite pleased with the impression they made on the "Big Indians" of two prominent tribes, and the chieftains no doubt felt that if they could capture and retain them, it would be the highest possible honor and glory they could attain to.

Every one in our train was anxious to witness the Snake tribe dance that night. Our captain who was cautious and not to be put off his guard by Indian strategy told us that it would be very necessary to keep a strong guard out that night, for there were bad white men as well as Indians in the neighborhood who were on the watch to take advantage of just such opportunities as this to steal the stock belonging to emigrants. It was arranged therefore that one-half of our party should go to the Indian camp and see the dance for a period of two hours, while the other half stayed on guard, and should then return and stand guard while the other half visited the encampment. All the emigrants in the valley had been invited by the ferrymen to go and see the dance and those who were still camped on the east side of the river were given free passes across the ferry so that they could attend. Some twenty ladies in all were present to see this Snake Dance. The first dance was performed by eight Indians, four Snakes and four Utahs. The bodies of the Snakes were nearly naked and were painted in bright colors to represent the different kind of snakes which are found in that part of the country. As they came into the large dancing ring each one of the four Snake Indians held a live snake in his hands. At the same moment four Utahs entered the ring decorated with all kinds of different colored feathers, and reciting a form of Indian chant. A number of other Indians were seated just outside the ring, and made their kind of music—which was not extremely melodious—on different kinds of rude instruments, the dancers keeping time to the music by the movement of their feet and the motions of their bodies. In the movements of the dance the four Snake Indians exchanged snakes with each other, and at different times had them coiled around their necks and their arms. When the dance was over the snakes were liberated and left to go free. They were believed by the Indians to be sacred and so close to their deity and so high in his favor, that they were sought as mediators to bring the wants of the tribe before the Great Spirit. The Snake Indians also believe that the original mother of these serpents was the common ancestor of both snakes and Indians.

This opening dance which lasted a few minutes seemed a solemn affair, but its mildness soon changed to scenes of amusement and finally almost fearful excitement. As many as a hundred Snake squaws came into the ring followed by the same number of Utah braves; all were painted in brilliant colors in every conceivable style, each one to suit his own taste and fancy, and their heads were covered with fanciful decorations of feathers of all shades of color. Each Indian selected his partner for the dance, and at a signal given on a rawhide drum all started in at once, and the public test commenced. At the signal the Indians outside the circle struck up a peculiar guttural chant, difficult to describe or imitate, and the dancers tried to keep step with this jumble of so-called music. This dance continued until the participants became exhausted and left the ring. When only one couple remained on the floor the crowd gave what was intended as a cheer, in the deep guttural grunt of Indian approval which assured the last dancer that in their view he had fairly won his prize. The winner received as his reward the squaw who had finished the dance with him and was entitled to take her home with him as his own. Through the Mormon ferrymen, who understood the language of both tribes, the Indians invited the white people to dance. As we had two good violin players, and a clarionet player in our party, their invitation was accepted. Twelve ladies volunteered to take part in three sets of a cotillion, a man was selected to call the changes, the dance commenced and we had our evening Fourth of July celebration which seemed to please the Indians for they gave us a grand grunt of approval. After entertaining them with three styles of white men's dances, we returned to our camp and relieved our guards, who went over to the Indian camp and remained until the performance closed for the night.

The next morning we attended the great horse races. Before noon about five hundred members of each of the two tribes, mounted painted and feathered in their gayest styles, gathered at the course. The first race was on a straightaway about half a mile long. Each tribe took its position, mounted. on opposite sides of the race track about six rods apart and at a given signal three Indians from each tribe at the head of the column swung into line on the race track and at another signal the race between these six began. At the end of the course the horses were jumped over two poles fastened horizontally about three feet from the ground, turned, and raced back to the starting point. The Indians who won took as their prizes the horses of the three beaten men. Several such races took place that day, some of them quite exciting, but we soon tired of the sport although it was a fine exhibition of skill in riding. Among the redskins' feats was to get a white man to lay a nickel or dime on the ground, when one of them would mount his pony, start him on a run and leaning over his side, pick up the coin and recover his seat. As long as the white boys would advance the money there were plenty of Indians ready to make the running dash and pick up the coin with rarely a failure.

During the day reports came to us that large numbers of stock had been missed from the camps on the east side of the river, and that no trace of them could be found. There was little doubt in our minds that they were stolen on the previous evening when the emigrants were enjoying the festivities of the Indians, and that they had now been driven into hiding places in the mountains where it would be both difficult and dangerous for the emigrants to follow the trail of the robbers. Our captain knew very well at the time that both the Mormons and the chieftains of the Indian tribes knew where the stolen cattle were. No doubt all were in the plot, expecting to share in the plunder, and would have fought to retain their booty if the emigrants had united in a determined effort to regain it. But the emigrants were helpless. They had readily fallen into the trap, and now must bear the penalty. From our camp we could see no opening in the high rocky wall that surrounded us; we seemed to have been caught in a complete cul-de-sac—bagged, as more nearly expressed it—where a few hundred Indians could have held and captured a strong force. Our captain alone of our train knew where the trail out of the canon was.

There was nothing for the pillaged emigrants to do but to take their medicine.

Many of the Indians came over to our camp on the evening of the fifth and we tried to entertain them by having our colored men sing plantation songs with banjo accompaniment and give plantation dances, but our attempt was a failure. The Indians gave no manifestation whatever of the least interest in the efforts of the negroes. The ferrymen told us that very few of the Indians had ever seen a negro, and that they all looked upon them as an inferior race and beneath their notice. When they bade us good-bye that evening they neither spoke to nor took any notice whatever of the colored men. I learned later from association with other Indians that all American Indian tribes in their primitive condition possess this same prejudice, and that the negroes rarely overcome it and gain their friendship.

Our two days experience in the Green River Valley made a deep impression upon me. I saw here the clashing extremes of civilization. There were two tribes of savage Indians still bound by their primitive habits and instincts; and there was the group of men and women of the white race called Mormons, who claimed to be civilized, educated and highly religious, professing to have received a new revelation for the guidance of their lives and conduct in an age when civilization demanded more from the individual than ever before. I saw these two extremes, the savage Indian and the civilized white man meeting and indulging in the same practise of polygamy, the Indian determining the number of his wives by the number of horses he owned, and the Mormon determining his by the size of his bank account. Then there were the members of our own train consisting of the refined, college educated and world travelled ladies and gentlemen from the south, and the rest of us plain, rough and hardy pioneers with little education, yet honest and true men, loyal, each one of us to the standards of American civilization. Here we were, this human conglomeration of college bred and savage, of honest pioneersmen and hypocritical Mormons walled up in a natural garden, surrounded by cliffs towering hundreds of feet high that seemed to shut us off from the rest of the world. I could not but wonder what type would have predominated, had we at that time been the only representatives of the human race. Surely not the Mormon for by his standard, the lowest, most primitive and savage, was also the highest, noblest and best. There is no possibility of evading this logic. The Indian did not degrade a higher civilization by becoming what he was, for his faults and habits were the product of his place in civilization and not the fruit of retrogression from a higher stage; while the Mormon owed his low condition to his voluntary betrayal of all that was best in the civilization to which he once belonged, for he had prostituted his training, education and morality, and thereby placed himself on a plane beneath the savage. For honesty, purity, truthfulness, trustworthiness and honor, as between the two, Indian and Mormon, give us the Indian by all odds. While he acts out his nature, he acts it for himself alone knowing no better; but the Mormon know-ingly descends to his degeneration, and without excuse or reason adds to his crime by deceiving, dragging down and degrading others to his own low level.

The time had now come to leave this interesting valley, with its beautiful stream of pure fresh mountain water, the only one we were to cross from the Rocky Mountains to the Nevadas, a dis-tance of eight hundred miles, all the other rivers and streams sink-ing and disappearing in the salt lakes and deserts of Nevada. The Green River heads two hundred miles north of the valley we were camping in, flows through eastern Utah, then into the Colorado River and Gulf of Mexico, and is one of the most picturesque rivers of the continent. We started on our way early on the morning of July 6. After rounding a rocky bluff we began to climb the hills again by a road similar in character to that by which we entered the valley. The up grade was very steep and we made slow prog-ress winding through crooked and rough ravines for six or seven miles until we reached a spot where we could look down over the entire valley, and with our field glasses see the Indians repeating their sports of the previous day. The view was so beautiful that we halted to give our teams an hour's rest and a light feed, while we feasted our eyes on the loveliness of the scene. Seeing it now from the West, as we had earlier from the East, added to and enhanced its charm and we felt that the dullest intellect could not but be aroused to the deep consciousness that this was none less than the creative handiwork of God, a material and permanent expression of his supreme beneficence and goodness.

We were soon on the move again, reluctant to take the last

backward look. The roads were heavy but as our oxen had been well fed and rested for the past two days they made good progress and at sunset we had passed the summit between the two rivers and were over twenty miles from our camp on the Green River. We made a dry camp that night and fed our stock on the grass which we had cut in the valley before we left. No hunting parties were out that day, and no game larger than a rabbit had been seen. Our fresh meat had been used up, and we were again living on our Cincinnati smoked bacon. As the stock were all kept in camp that night, we had out only half the usual guard. We fed out all our grass in the morning and made an early start for it was fifteen miles to the nearest grass and water. We made this distance before noon and after a two hours' rest started on a down grade over a good level road to the valley of Bear River. We camped on the banks of a small mountain stream with the best of grass near the camp. Wolves were plenty and very bold, a large pack of them attacking our stock that night and injuring a cow so badly that we had to kill her in the morning. They were so hungry and ferocious that they did not leave until the guards had killed two of their number.

Trouble that we were not looking for developed that night. The two days' drive over the sandstone rocks had made several of our ox-teams foot-sore and in the morning we found one of the best oxen we had on our Michigan team hobbling around on three legs, with the other one badly swollen. At first we thought that he might have been bitten by a rattlesnake, but on examination we found that a large sized gravel stone had worked in between his hoofs. Another wagon had two oxen in a similar condition. We could not go on with the oxen in this shape and we had to choose between delaying and doctoring them up, turning them out and leaving them to the wolves, or killing them and taking their flesh with us for food. The captain advised us to lay over where we were for two days and doctor the lame cattle, while the rest of our train drove on twenty miles further to Thomas' Fork on Bear River and a better camping place, where they could wait for us. We took his advice and stayed at our camp, faithfully applying all the remedies we had to our sick oxen. We could not save the one on our team so on the second day we killed and dressed it. The two oxen belonging to the other wagon recovered from their lameness by the second day.

During this stop Uncle Billy and I put in our time hunting in the mountains, while the doctor and Gondola were trying to heal the ox's foot. The first day we killed an elk and several rabbits and saw a number of wolves and bears. While we were returning to camp that night we came across an ox and a cow that had no doubt been left behind by some train or had strayed away and could not be found. Our ponies were loaded with our game and we were five miles from camp; but Uncle Billy thought we had better drive the ox and cow along with us for if no one claimed them we might use them to fill the places left by our own cripples. The second day we hunted along the banks of Bear River. We saw several elk but could not get near them and so returned to camp early concluding to hitch up our teams and drive ten miles that night. We hitched up the ox we had found and driven in the day before, and he made our team as good as ever. We expected however, to be called upon to give him up at any time, for during the trip we had found stock several times but the owner had always appeared to claim it. Once on the Platte River a fine pony, saddled and bridled came into our camp early one morning and we rode him over two hundred miles before his owner appeared to claim him. Up to this time we had lost no stock, our good fortune being due to the fact that our captain was continually on his guard and would allow no carelessness on the part of the men.

The next morning at eight o'clock our train was all together again. As Captain Smith had not expected us until evening he with fifteen others had gone on a hunt up the Thomas River. Our party of southern people had been out the day before and had brought back an elk and two deer. This day they had gone out for bear. When they left they had said they wished that Uncle Billy and his two dogs were with them, and when Uncle Billy heard this he started out at once to have a hand in the bear hunt. Gondola, the Doctor, and I divided the beef we had killed the day before and spent the rest of the day fishing near the camp with good success. From our encampment we would see clouds of steam from what was called Steamboat Springs which were nearly twenty miles away. When the party of bear hunters came in towards night, they had to their credit four mountain bear. They had seen several elk and deer during the day but they did not try to shoot them as they had agreed to shoot nothing but bear. Uncle Billy and his dogs were responsible for the day's success. The result was a great surprise to the captain as he had found no game in the valley two years previous. The bear meat was taken care of, and we judged there was enough to last us until we reached the Great Salt Lake, if it kept well.

We had a good night's rest and were on the road for Steamboat Springs at sunrise. As we neared the springs we could easily distinguish one large cone shaped mound that every few moments would send large volumes of steam spouting up from its center, the vapor drifting away like a transparent cloud on the clear blue sky. On approaching still nearer we saw a great white mound surrounded by hundreds of smaller ones, all composed of the alkali or soda which occurs so abundantly in this vicinity. At times the entire underground system would seem to be put in operation, and the whole group of mounds that looked like old fashioned beehives would set to gaping, spouting and belching out steam and hot water in a fierce bubbling competition. Our road passed so near them that we could feel the spray from the hot water falling on us. The largest mound covered several acres and could not be approached on account of the extreme heat of the ground around it and the hot water and spray which spouted forth and fell to the ground from the cone. The center of the mound seemed like an immense boiling caldron sending forth tremendous blasts of hot water and steam as often as every thirty minutes. We were in sight of these interesting springs for two days.

We went into camp that night near the great North bend of the Bear River and here the river was deep and wide enough to be navigated by a large sized steamboat. In looking down the river, a clear stretch of a few miles to the southwest, the valley seemed to be walled in by an unbroken cliff of white rocks. Some of our party, including the ladies, rode the next morning to the point where the river entered the rocky gorge, and said that it was a great sight to look down on the rushing, foaming torrent which struggled as if enraged at the sudden opposition and limitation forced upon it by the rocks, presenting a great contrast to the quiet calm of the waters just opposite our camp. About noon on July 13th we left the valley of the Bear River and made for a small valley about ten miles distant. Shortly after leaving Bear River valley we came to a series of unique and beautiful natural wonders called the "White Pyramids." These were sandstone rocks as white as the purest snow rising in the shape of regular cones and varying in height from one foot to one hundred feet. We passed through this singular and beautiful formation for a distance of about three miles. That evening we reached an excellent camping ground in a narrow valley where there was an abundance of good grass for the cattle and pure mountain water, for both man and beast.

Our camp was visited that evening by a number of Flathead Indians who, with their families, were on their way to the camp of another tribe in the Bear River valley. They were all well mounted on fine mountain ponies. This tribe is not numerically strong, and its members are very friendly with other tribes and with emigrants who pass through their country. They were the first Indians we had met who were not prepared for a fight on short notice. They were not decorated in the hideous war paints of the usual Indian tribe, nor did they dangle any display of scalps to prove their valor. Instead they claimed to be a tribe of peacemakers, visiting neighboring tribes in the interests of peace by the special direction of the Great Spirit. We found that some of them could speak English sufficiently to understand us, and they took much pleasure in showing us their squaws, pappooses, and ponies. The Flatheads cremate their dead, and some of us witnessed that evening the burning of the remains of a small child. After the burning of the body the ashes were gathered up mixed with pitch and plastered on the face and body of the child's mother as a token of remembrance and a sign of mourning.

The ladies of our train who had been at first anxious to go by way of Salt Lake City, were now delighted to think that they had come by this route, and two of them who had travelled abroad declared that in all their travels they had never witnessed such beautiful and splendid scenery as they had seen on this day. We were now about one hundred miles from the north end of Great Salt Lake, which we were anxious to reach as soon as possible. Our captain informed us that the first fifty miles would be over a rough country with but little pasture for our stock. We were three full days in making that fifty miles. Our southern hunters and Uncle Billy were out in the hills and small side valleys all this time looking for large game. In the three days they brought in five black-tail or mule deer and a large number of jack-rabbits. Our captain told us that there would be no large game after we left the Bear River Mountains until we reached the Nevada Mountains, a distance of six hundred miles or more, and that it would be well to get what fresh meat we could.

CHAPTER IV.

ACROSS THE DESERT.

When we reached a point where we could see the Great Salt Lake and its surrounding valley we were greatly cheered, not only because we were near one of the great landmarks of our journey, but also because we were sure of having good roads for the next four hundred miles. During the next three days we crossed several small streams of pure mountain water, along which the grass was good, but a short distance away from them there would be no vegetation except sage brush and no animal life but an occasional rabbit and a species of sage hen about the size of a prairie chicken. These sage hens would fly up out of the brush along our path, and such of our hunters as had shotguns were kept busy trying to shoot them. This was good sport, for they were the same color as the sage brush and could not be seen on the ground so they had to be taken on the wing. The main road led several miles north of the lake in order to keep on firm ground, but as our party was determined to strike the lake at some point and go into camp for one day in order to see the sights, we took a road that branched off from the main road and camped on a stream of fresh water two miles from where it emptied into the Salt Lake. Some of our party who were out riding visited the lake that afternoon and found a good bathing place with hard banks and bottom. Uncle Billy was the first one of our party to take a swim, and told us that evening that the only trouble he had was to keep out of the way of the large flakes of salt which were floating on the surface of the water. He said that he felt as if he had enough salt sticking to him to supply our train for the balance of the way to California, and that he must have a fresh water bath before he went to bed or else he feared he would experience the fate of Lot's wife before morning. Uncle Billy's experience so interested the rest of us that we all determined to go to the lake early the next morning and try the bathing. The captain said that at least two men must remain to guard the train while the rest went to the lake, and Uncle Billy and I were the two who were chosen. We put in our time washing our clothing. I had done the doctor's washing ever since his arm was injured, and as he was still conveniently carrying it in a sling it became my duty to do it again. There had been no general regular wash day since we left Green River and orders had been given for all to clean up before starting next day. The water we used was quite soft, and with the free use of soap our washing looked very respectable when hung out on the lines which were stretched from one wagon to another. The party returned from the lake before noon and while they cleaned up, Uncle Billy and I took our turn at bathing. As there was no wind the sensation was a pleasant one although we had to wade some distance before reaching water of any depth. As soon as we reached a depth of four or five feet our bodies would begin to float, in fact we could not avoid floating, for it was impossible to keep the whole of the body under water at one time. If you got your head under water you could not keep your legs from coming up above the surface.

After our day's rest at the Great Salt Lake we felt very refreshed, and quite ready to start on the next stage of our journey, the objective of which was the Humboldt River Valley, a distance of one hundred miles on our way towards the setting sun. On July 23rd we made twenty miles through a sage brush country, and camped in the foot hills of the Humboldt Mountains. During this day not a living thing of any kind in the way of game was seen, if we except an occasional gaunt looking rabbit which jumped from one bunch of sage brush to another to keep out of our way. We found fresh water, but very little pasture for our stock. On the morning of the 24th we were on the move before sunrise, and after driving ten miles found good grazing and went into camp for the remainder of the day. On the 25th we had to make twenty-five miles before we found a good camping place, which was near the beginning of the descent into the upper valley of the Humboldt River. The country was the poorest we had travelled over and we did not see an animal or bird of any kind during the day's drive of twenty-five miles. The grass was very short and burned by the scorching rays of the sun. That night we had to double our guards as the stock was restless and constantly roaming about in search of better feed. On the morning of the 26th the captain and three others started in advance of the train to look for a camping place where our stock could find sufficient grass, even if we had to drive off from the main road to reach it. We were now on a down grade. The day was one of the hottest we had experienced and not a breath of wind was moving. After driving fifteen miles we met the captain who told us that by driving down a small valley about three miles distant we could find good grass and water. But our stock were now exhausted and could go no further, so we halted until sunset and then hitched up and made the three miles to the place which had been selected. The next morning the sun shone so bright and hot that it was decided best, on account of the extreme heat, to remain in camp for the day. Many of our men became uneasy and dissatisfied at this delay and for the first time on the journey fault was found with the captain and he was criticized for holding the train over for a whole day when we had so short a time left us for reaching our destination. Three of the wagons were so disaffected as to hitch up and leave us but when they finally got out on the trail and the sun became hotter and hotter they saw their folly, and turned back to camp. This rest proved the best thing that we could have done for we learned afterwards that trains which moved on those two extremely hot days lost considerable stock by the excessive heat.

By the 29th the hot wave had passed on and as our road was now on a down grade we made good progress. Our two days' rest, combined with the cool breezes that came from the mountains to the north put new life, vigor and cheer into man and beast. In these narrow valleys through which we were now passing we often came upon both hot and cold water springs at the same place. At one camping place we found at least twenty deep natural wells of pure cold water walled in by rocks of volcanic origin. In Thousand Springs Valley which we crossed we found numberless springs of hot and cold water which were so near each other in some places that if a person would lie at full length on the ground he might bathe his feet in a spring of hot water and at the same time bathe his hands and face in another spring of cold water. The pasturage was good in all these small valleys, and camping places were easily found but most of the streams disappeared in the sand after reaching the end of the valley. There was no timber of any size in the region. Our party agreed that this section of country was absolutely worthless and the history of the fifty years since that day has confirmed our judgment in this respect.

A description of the features and character of this section of the

7

country and the incidents and details connected with one day's travel through it with an ox team is sufficient for the four hundred miles of travel from the upper waters of the Humboldt River down its valley to Humboldt Lake, for the scenery showed little variety. The river was important owing to the fact that its valley furnished the only east and west route by which emigrants could reach California. It was the largest river in Nevada, its valley extending three hundred miles although it was only about two miles in width. The Little Humboldt and the Reese River were its main tributaries bringing down a huge volume of water during the spring but in the summer drying up in the sands of the desert before reaching the Humboldt River channel.

After making about twenty miles on this day—the 29th—we went into camp at a spot offering plenty of good feed and water. No large game had been seen during the day although Uncle Billy said that he had found deer tracks along the bank of the little brook on which we were camped. This statement was sufficient assurance that he intended to hunt deer the next day. A few Digger Indians came to our camp that evening armed with very inferior bows and arrows. They were the most degraded lot of Indians we had met with on our travels. Hunting parties started out on both flanks of our train early the next morning, eager for the chase after several days abstinence from its excitement. Uncle Billy and his party on the south side of the road saw no large game, but the party on the north side got two small deer which were a great addition to our store of fresh food. The following day was the last day of July, the date which we had set for reaching the Humboldt Valley, but in spite of the long drive that was before us in order to keep up to schedule Uncle Billy started out with his dogs in the morning determined to make up for his poor luck of the previous day. Soon after leaving camp his dogs started a deer which crossed the road just ahead of the train. Two of the ladies had mounted their ponies and as the deer crossed the road they galloped after him and brought him down with their rifles much to Uncle Billy's dismay. This was all the game that was killed that day, so Uncle Billy's hunt brought little credit to him.

That evening we went into camp on the bank of the Humboldt River. At this point it was only about four rods wide but quite deep though with little current. The next morning (August first) we started down the valley for Humboldt Lake, three hundred and fifty miles away. At the first camp on the Humboldt the captain explained to us fully his plan of trying to reach Humboldt Lake the latter part of August and of resting there a few days to get the stock into good condition for the sixty mile trip across the desert that lay west of the lake. We took an inventory of our supplies and found that we would have to live on short rations, if we did not find game along the way. This scarcity of provisions led us to plan to send out large hunting parties every day to bring in any game that could be found, whether large or small. Our trip thus far had taught us a valuable sanitary lesson, namely that those who lived on fresh meat were seldom troubled with sickness. Captain Smith thought that our party had killed more game than any emigrant train that had crossed the plains that year, and as he was experienced in the life of the plains we believed him. Certain it was that we had had less sickness than any train of the size we knew of, and we attributed our good fortune to nothing except the active mode of living and our almost daily fare of fresh wild meat.

We made only fourteen miles the first day in the valley and camped at night near the river, but the mosquitoes and sand flies were very numerous and rendered our camp anything but enjoyable. A party of fifty California miners returning to the States, all mounted on mustang ponies, came into our camp that evening. They presented a very picturesque appearance, as they were dressed in Spanish costume, with bright colored leggings and sashes, and broad brimmed Mexican hats, and well armed with heavy Colt revolvers. They had started from Sacramento, seven hundred miles west of us, on the 15th of July. Some of them had been over this same route one or two years before when on their way to California. The evening passed very pleasantly in listening to the experiences of these miners fresh from the wonderful gold fields. They were making their trip homeward at the rate of fifty miles a day on their tough little horses, the best in the world for such a purpose and such a country.

The party planned to go by way of Salt Lake City to obtain supplies and said that they expected to reach the Missouri River in less than fifty days. They told us that they had buried that morning one of their number who had been accidentally shot; but we learned a few days later that the so-called accident had been a fight with pistols in a dispute over a trifling matter. Three days later we passed the grave of this man who had been so foolishly sacrificed. It was marked by a large willow stake driven into the ground to which his Mexican hat was fastened. On the hat was written his name, the date of his death, and the statement, "Killed by accident." During this period many such "accidents" occurred.

The next morning Uncle Billy asked me to be one of the day's hunting party. We crossed the river and made our way to the foot hills on the other side where we found deer tracks leading down to the river bank. We decided that deer came to the river in the night to get water and also to rid themselves of the mosquitoes and flies, and that at daybreak they had gone back into the brush or timber, and so we rode towards the mountains about five miles to the northwest. The foothills were covered with groves of man-soneto or small apple trees, the fruit of which is mixed with acorns from the scrub oaks of the lower ranges and used by the Indians as their staple food during the winter. We followed along the base of this range of mountains, crossing two small streams of water that disappeared from sight before they reached the river and although we saw several deer, one of which was within rifle range and was wounded by us, we were unable to secure any of them as they plunged into a thick growth of mansoneto brush where we could not trace them. After a long hard ride of thirty miles we rode into camp without any game. The other hunting party which included the ladies brought in two deer and several rabbits, so we had fresh meat for breakfast the next morning.

I took up the ox-gad instead of the rifle the next day, giving Gondola and Billy a chance to go with the hunting party. On account of the intense heat we made only ten miles that day. The hunting party returned to camp early, having obtained no game worth mentioning. What game there was kept to the patches of timber and brush on the mountain side where there was shelter from the rays of the sun. Our hunting parties met with little success in this section, and for ten days we lived on short rations of Cincinnati bacon that we had brought with us a distance of twelve hundred miles.

On the thirteenth of August we camped at the mouth of the Reese River, a large stream coming out of the Reese Mountains, and heading over two hundred miles south of us. The spot where we camped was called the mouth of the river although there was no water on the surface of the ground; ten miles south of us it became a fine mountain stream. Our hunting party that day went several miles south and secured two deer and upon returning home reported splendid feed and water in a small valley only five or six miles away. The prospect of good feed for our oxen was so alluring that we voted to break camp that evening and move at once to this valley and to remain there until our stock was rested. It was the first time since starting that we had made camp and broken it the same evening. As there was a full moon we experienced no difficulty in the night march and our new camp which we reached about midnight proved to be one the of best we had found during our trip. We delayed at this spot for two days, resting our cattle for the hard drive which lay before them and taking advantage of the good hunting to lay in all the fresh meat we could carry, thus giving us a change from the bacon diet which had become rather monotonous.

On the morning of the fifteenth we broke camp bright and early and with both men and oxen well fed and rested retraced our steps past our old camping ground, and made twenty-five miles before going into camp for the night. Our course was now almost due north around the great bend of the river, which we passed the next day and arrived at the point at which the Little Humboldt River, after flowing two hundred miles from the Humboldt Mountains, disappeared in the sand. As the roads were good and the weather cool, we made another twenty-five miles the next day and on the three succeeding days totalled sixty-five miles. Our fresh meat was keeping well, owing to the cool weather, and so we sent out no hunting parties but pushed on as rapidly as possible, taking full advantage of the cool weather and the excellent food which we found for our stock. When we went into camp on the evening of the twenty-fourth, eight days after leaving our camp on the Reese River, no one had been on a hunt during the time nor had a gun been fired by anyone of our company. We were now about one hundred miles from the Humboldt Meadows, which the captain said we could reach by the evening of the twenty-ninth provided the weather continued cool. At the meadows we planned to take another two days' rest in preparation for the trip across the sixty mile desert which lay to the westward.

On the morning of the twenty-fifth Uncle Billy headed a hunting party to the neighboring mountains, and this party was very successful, killing two deer and a young mountain bear, which furnished us with fresh meat for the next two days. This success so aroused Uncle Billy's story telling spirit that that evening he entertained us all with Michigan hunting yarns, one of which I still remember. This was the story of a neighbor who lived about three miles from him and who invited him to come to his place one evening in September and shoot the deer that were eating his new sown wheat. He accepted the invitation and told his wife and son Paul that he would come home in the morning with fresh venison. He shouldered his gun after dark that night and started for his neighbor's house by a short cut through the woods. As he neared the house he heard a rustling in the leaves and saw a large black animal moving slowly through the brush with its head down, evidently eating acorns and beechnuts. He heard the animal grunt and concluded it was a bear and as it was five or six rods off and coming towards him he slipped behind a tree and waited for it to come nearer. It was too dark for him to see the sights on his gun, but he felt perfectly cool and putting three buckshot on top of the ball he leveled his gun at the animal and fired. The bear gave a grunt and was out of sight in an instant. He reloaded his gun and went forward to where the bear had been but as he could find no signs of it, went on to the neighbor's house and told his story. They went back together taking two dogs with them, and found the bear, which proved to be his neighbor's only hog which had been feeding on beechnuts in the woods. Two of the buckshot had proved fatal so he was bled and dressed on the spot. The next morning Uncle Billy surprised his wife and boy with fresh pork instead of the venison which he had promised them. This story was greeted with shouts of laughter and led me to repeat a similar incident in my own experience when I had killed my mother's only cow, leaving our family of seven children without milk and butter for a period of two years.

We were on the road early the morning of the twenty-fifth with the determination to reach the great Meadows at the sink 'of the river as soon as possible. The roads were good, the weather delightful, and as no hunting party went out that day we made a twenty-five mile drive before camping. A large number of Digger Indians visited us that evening. They were engaged at this season in gathering their winter supply of food. This consisted of mansoneto berries and acorns, gathered from the nearby mountains, ground in stone mortars by the squaws, and the meal obtained from them mixed with the flesh of frogs and large white grubs which they secured in the loose black soil along the river. Their way of getting these oily grubs was to take a sharp pointed stick about three feet in length which they pressed into the loose soil and whirled around until the hole became larger than the stick. The worms and grubs came out of the soil and clung to the stick, and the squaws carrying woven willow baskets carefully drew out these sticks, scraped the grubs off into the basket with their hands and replaced the sticks for another catch. When grasshoppers were plenty, they used them instead of the grubs, as they could get them very quickly by driving them into the water, and scooping them out in long pointed baskets made for the purpose. These grubs or grasshoppers were mixed with acorns and mansoneto berries and then ground together and baked into bread, which was stored away in mounds along the river bank. During the winter months the tribe moved from one storehouse to another as the supply of food dwindled. The Digger Indians never use ponies or horses for any purpose.

The doctor offered to drive the team on the morning of the twenty-seventh, and, as the roads were good and his arm nearly well we thought that it would be safe for him to do so, so Captain Smith, Uncle Billy and his dogs, Gondola and myself arranged to make up a hunting party that day, keeping along in the scattering timber of the foothills. We borrowed two of the ladies' horses and taking our noon lunch and canteens filled with cold coffee made for the hills. We rode all day through brush and timber, over hills and through deep ravines and travelled nearly forty miles before reaching camp that night, but failed to find any game worth shooting. We had trouble finding water for our horses, but finally discovered a little lake of brackish water which was hardly fit for use even by animals. Ten miles farther back in the mountains we could have found plenty of game and pure water, but all of the streams that formed in the mountains soon disappeared after reaching the dry sandy plains below. Other trains that camped here for a few days and sent parties into the mountains found plenty of game, as we heard later. That night we decided to send out no more hunting parties until we had crossed the desert and reached the timber in the Nevada Mountains.

We were now about forty miles from the Meadows, the objective point of this stage of our journey. The next morning we were on the road before sunrise, but by ten o'clock were forced by the extreme heat to go into camp. At five o'clock that afternoon we broke camp and after a ten miles' drive went into camp about ten that night, it being understood that we would start out again at daybreak and after making ten miles would lay by during the middle of the day. This plan was followed out to the letter and we arrived at the Meadows late in the evening of the twenty-ninth of August.

On the thirtieth we held a council and decided to abandon four of our heaviest wagons and load their contents into the other five wagons. This arrangement would give us seven yoke of oxen to each wagon on the trip across the desert instead of five yoke as we had had previously. We had planned to delay at the Meadows for two days but the weather becoming cooler we decided to start on the evening of the first day, and to make the first twenty miles to the boiling springs that night. A ton of hay was cut and loaded on one of our five wagons for we knew we would not find any feed for our stock for the next two days. We bade a final farewell to the four wagons that had served us so well for the past four months, and started on our night drive for the Hot Springs, our next camping place, twenty miles nearer our final destination. We passed many booths that night, built of cedar and spruce boughs, where whisky and water were sold at the same price for a drink. Our Michigan contingent invested four dollars in a gallon of water, agreeing to leave the wooden cask encased in the cloth that held it at the Truckee River. During the night we passed hundreds of wagons abandoned by the roadside, and thousands of dead oxen whose lives had been sacrificed on the desert for greed of gold. Some of these animals had died three years before, but such was the influence of the dry atmosphere that their carcasses remained in form, instead of decaying. We saw some of these carcasses propped up with gun barrels or with gun barrels thrust in their bodies and looking like small arsenals or forts, for years before guns and everything else that could possibly be dispensed with by the emigrants were thrown away to lighten their burdens and save their lives. Hundreds of human lives were lost on this desert in the year 1849.

The night was cool and a gentle breeze was blowing from the Nevada Mountains to the westward and had it not been for the deep sand, and the entire absence of every green and growing thing, we could hardly have imagined that we were in the middle of a great desert. At twelve o'clock we halted for thirty minutes to feed our stock from the bundles of grass tied to the wagons and at five o'clock on the morning of August thirty-first we went into camp at the boiling springs. Not a living thing was in sight except emigrants and their stock. All was dry, bare, dreary desolation. The springs consisted of clear hot water boiling out from between deep and wide openings of solid rock, the water running over the rocky basins and disappearing in the sand. Wagon boxes had been sunk in the sand, corked tight and the hot water turned into them to cool for the cattle to drink, but the rays of the sun were so hot that it never really became cool. During the day we lay in the shade of our wagons, feeding our stock twice from the wagon load of hay. Not a spear of hay was left when we were ready to start at evening, so we used our hayrack for fuel to cook by and left the empty wagon to keep company with thousands of others abandoned near the Hot Springs of Nevada.

At sunset we were on our way again. Our captain told us that the sand would now be much deeper than during the past twenty miles and said that we should be very thankful if we reached the Truckee River by noon of September first. Before starting we invested in another supply of mountain water, paying two dollars a gallon for it. Two booth saloons were selling whisky at twenty-five cents a drink and pure Truckee River water for one bit a glass, a drop in the price of water of 50 per cent, from prices of the day before. As we neared the mountains that night the air became fresher and cooler, but the sand grew deeper and deeper. When daylight came we had passed the highest point of the desert and could see the timber which skirted the banks of the Truckee River ten miles away. Our wagon wheels rolled in sand from six to eight inches deep, but our oxen now took on new life for they seemed instinctively to know that they would soon reach good food and water. The head of each ox and horse was lifted high as it sniffed the cool and moist mountain air, laden with the scent of fresh water and grass so that although the sand grew deeper around our wheels our teams only travelled the faster, and at ten o'clock we were on the banks of the Truckee River, a gift of pure water without price. We struck the river within five miles of Pyramid Lake, where it loses itself in the sands of the desert and after watering our stock drove on down near the lake, where we found good feed and made camp. Some of our party visited the lake that evening and caught a nice string of fish besides killing two deer.

This locality was very interesting for the two great lakes, one at each end of the river, are indeed most beautiful. Lake Tahoe, six thousand feet above the level of the sea, is without doubt the most beautiful body of water to be found in the Nevada Mountains. Walled in by high mountains on the south and west it opens to let out the Truckee River, a large stream of pure mountain water, which rushes through deep canons and gorges with a fall of nearly two thousand feet in the first twenty miles; it soon widens into a narrow valley where it slumbers until it reaches Pryamid Lake, a body of water more than thirty miles long and fourteen wide, walled in on all sides by solid rock, leaving no outlet. The two lakes are about sixty miles apart. The mother lake, which is the smaller of the two, is located on the eastern line of California and sends its pure cold waters down into the greater lake to keep it alive; there the massive rocky barriers rise up before it and seem to say imperatively, "Thus far shalt thou go and no farther," thereby constituting for this arid country one of the most splendid reservoirs of water ever created.

The morning of September second dawned beautifully with a clear sky radiant with soft golden hues, and soon the rising sun cast brilliant glories over the rocky walls of the lake, giving us a sight so entrancing and magnificent that I believe the members of our train could not forget it as long as they live. From this point we had before us more than one hundred miles of up grade travel to reach the summit of the Nevada Mountains, and of this distance about forty miles lay up the narrow valley of the Truckee River towards Lake Tahoe. We started from camp about nine o'clock that morning making a good ten miles' drive and then camping for the night on the river bank. The mountain slopes on each side of the river were covered with a fine growth of fir and pine. We planned to make fifteen miles up the valley the next day and as we now had only four wagons, more of us were able to join the hunting parties although the large teams of oxen required two drivers to each wagon. I was one of the hunters on that first day and as deer were plentiful we brought in four that night. The following morning the captain ordered every man to stay with the teams all day, as the river had to be forded many times in going the fifteen miles and this was not now an easy matter since the water was high on account of recent rains in the mountains. We were up early that morning and started in advance of all the trains camped near us. We forded the river soon after starting and repeated the experience seventeen times during the day.

That evening we came to a creek and valley entering the Truckee Valley from the northwest, which we were to follow until we reached Beckwith Valley, which in turn would lead us to the summit of the Nevadas. We camped for the night at the mouth of this creek, and here met parties from California who offered to buy all our stock and wagons and to allow those of us who wished to do so to keep on with the train until it reached Sacramento. The opportunity being a good one, we sold out to them. Some of these men were miners and had plenty of gold dust with them. One of them told us of rich mines at Poor Man's Creek and said that we would pass within five miles of the diggings. I made up my mind then and there that I would stop at Poor Man's Creek. It was nearly one hundred and fifty miles to that point and would take at least fifteen days to reach it, for travelling over the mountains was very slow. One of the stock buyers kept with the train in order to pick out camping places with good grass and to see that we did not drive more than ten miles per day, this being one of the conditions of the purchase, for the buyers intended to keep the stock in good condition so that they could readily dispose of them in California.

We made only eight miles on the fifth and camped that night at the foot of Beckwith Valley, which was hemmed in with a heavy growth of timber. In this eight miles journey we had increased our altitude by fifteen hundred feet. On the sixth the road was rough and stony, and we went into camp in the same valley after a ten mile drive. We were now entering a country where large game was plentiful. Uncle Billy had seen a grizzly bear and the sight had worked upon his nerves until he talked of little else. On the seventh all the good hunters in our train were scouring the mountains on each side of the road for grizzlies, but not a bear was seen by us, although we found fresh signs of them and killed two deer. The next day twenty of our number renewed the quest, but again failed to find any grizzlies; because of the thick timber and steep mountain sides the hunting all had to be done on foot.

That night we camped near the first and at that time the only settler in Nevada. With his family of wife and nine children this pioneer had emigrated from Missouri and settled in the valley in 1849. Since then he had accumulated a fair fortune by picking up worn out stock from the passing emigrants, caring for them until they were in good condition and then driving them over the mountains to the California markets. We met this interesting character that night and when he heard that we were anxious to hunt grizzlies he invited us to camp for a day and promised that he would take us on a grizzly hunt where we could both see and shoot them. The captain let us decide the question and we voted unanimously to take a day off and try real big game hunting. Our pioneer friend informed us that it was nearly five miles to the place where bear could be found and that this distance could be traversed only on foot. Ours was the first party having lady hunters, he said, that had ever camped in that valley and he was sure that his twenty year old daughter who was the best shot in the family, would welcome the chance to go hunting grizzlies with some of her own sex. He told us that it would be necessary to start by sunrise and since this would require very early rising suggested that the ladies spend the night with his wife and daughters at their home and take breakfast with them. The ladies were glad to accept the invitation and were seemingly happy of the chance to get a breakfast that had been cooked within doors. We were up early the next morning and just as the sun was rising thirty-four persons from our train, together with the pioneer, his daughter and four of his sons started to the hunting place. Our guide was made our captain for the day and it was understood that everyone should implicitly obey his orders. We found the way rough and difficult, but the thought of the sport ahead made us disregard all obstacles. The valley where we were to begin our hunt was finally reached and our guide and captain after noting the direction of the wind and the bear signs stationed us in certain positions which we were to maintain while he and his sons beat up the game in a cross valley and drove them past our stations. The hunter and his boys had horns which they were to blow in case they started a bear. Orders were given that no one was to leave the spot where he was stationed, and that no shots were to be fired except at bear or mountain lions.

Perfect quiet was necessary since the grizz'y bear is always very suspicious and on the lookout for danger and trouble, ready to run and hide at any unusual sight or sound. Contrary to general opinion the grizzly is extremely timid a characteristic which is due, doubtless, to the fact that it is the most hunted of any of our mountain animals. Every hunter of any ambition wants to kill a grizzly sometime in his life. That was really the matter with us. What else but this ambition could have induced men who had killed almost all other kinds of game on the continent to stop a train of forty men a whole day, while thirty-five of them went out into the roughest kind of mountain country over five miles of rock and cliffs.

For two hours we lay quiet, scarcely speaking a word, our ears keyed to catch the first sound that should tell us of the approaching game. The wait seemed never-ending to us, but at last we heard the sound of a horn, seemingly not more than a half mile away, followed quickly by a rifle shot. A herd of five deer passed us on the trot, but not a shot was fired at them for we were after bigger game. A few moments later we heard a half dozen shots from the point where the ladies were stationed and in another instant a bear and two cubs dashed up the ravine directly towards us only to turn a short distance away and make off down the mountain. Several of us saw them and fired as they turned, while Uncle Billy and the captain of our train started down after them, forgetting the orders of the guide in the excitement of the chase. A few moments later shots rang out again, and the two cubs came into sight once more again making towards us. We fired as they came into range and one of them fell dead, but the other escaped down the mountain. There was no more firing and soon we heard three blasts on our guide's horn which was a signal for all of us to come to them. As we passed down the mountain we cut the throat of the cub which we had killed and found Captain Smith and Uncle Billy standing proudly over the body of a big grizzly which they claimed that they had killed. The guide and his boys had a large mountain lion which they had shot and when we reached the ladies we found that they had killed one large grizzly and wounded another, which had escaped into the woods. Several of us started in pursuit of the wounded bear whose trail was easily followed by the drops of blood. We were convinced that he was mortally wounded and soon came to him and found him in his death agony. The five shots fired by the

women had all found their mark.   Two struck the wounded bear
and three struck the one which was killed on the spot.   The wounded
one was said by our leader to be the largest bear that had been killed
in that vicinity, and the five ladies received the honors of the day.
The large bear killed by Captain Smith and Uncle Billy had been
badly wounded by our leader and his sons earlier in the chase.   No
one knew which of us killed the cub.   We dressed the game in short
order, and soon had it ready to pack.   The captain and I, with two
of the boys, went to camp to get teams and wagons to bring back
the game.   We made the trip easily, met the party with the game
at a previously designated point and by four o'clock in the afternoon were all on our way back to camp.   While we had been gone
for the teams the hunters had found the other cub which had been
wounded, and had killed it as well as two deer, so that our bag for
the day's hunt consisted of five grizzly bears, one mountain lion
and two deer.   The skins of the five bears were given to the ladies,
making a splendid addition to the collection of trophies which they
had secured on the trip.

We were royally entertained that evening by our Missouri host
and his family, who related to us some of their experiences during
the past three years in this wild mountain country.   They described
vividly the terrible winter storms and told us how two years before
they had been snow bound for nearly half the year, when snow fell
three feet deep in the middle of September and did not go off until
April of the next year.   Only a short distance from this spot a
Missouri wagon train of fifty-two persons was caught in a snow
storm only a month after our visit, so we learned later, and all perished.   Evidence was discovered to indicate that in their sad and
desperate sufferings they cast lots to decide which one should
be sacrificed for food, in the hope that one or more might live to
tell of their sufferings and fate to the world.   This party had been
detained on the road by sickness and death, and only two days before
the storm had camped near the house of our host who warned
them of their danger in attempting to proceed further.   In the
blinding storm they wandered ten miles off from the main road, and
consequently were not found until the snow had disappeared the next
spring.   Their camp was only thirty miles from the Missourian
who had warned them of their danger and who had plenty of provisions to have kept them all during the winter.   He and his boys,

during the early part of the winter, spent many days searching for them but never found their out of the way camp where all had perished until the early part of April, 1852, when they discovered evidence that two of the party were still alive as late as the twentieth of March.

The stories of early snows made us all mindful that it was now the eighth of September, and that it would be extremely well for us to be on the move and over the mountains just as soon as we could, if we wished to escape the serious consequences of a possibly early winter. We were now camped about thirty miles east of the California line, which was the summit of the Nevadas, and at the rate we were tavelling it would take us three more days to pass into California, the golden state to reach which we had been on the long weary road over five months. That night we resolved to spend no more time hunting but to push rapidly on to our goal. We agreed that the day's hunt with its excitement and success would never be forgotten by any of us but that it would be remembered by all as a grand wind up of a two thousand mile trip with ox teams and the best of all the many hunts that we had had. The morning of the ninth we were on the road early and made fifteen miles to the head of the valley, where we entered a dense forest of pine, spruce and hemlock. The next one hundred miles of our way was to be over the roughest country we had covered on our whole route.

On the tenth of September we made another ten miles over this very heavy road and camped that night five miles from the California border. Our camp was now six thousand feet above the sea, and after another five miles of up grade, our trail would be downward for the remainder of our journey. All our talk that evening centered on the cheering fact that we would pass the summit of the Nevadas the next day. The night was cool and we secured a good rest. The grass was thin and scattering and as we let our stock feed until late in the morning we were slow in starting, but about noon we could see that we were on the down grade, and felt very happy at the prospect of soon ending our long journey. We camped that night on the head waters of a small creek that emptied into Feather River. All about us stood the heavily wooded mountains. The sole subject of conversation that evening was the question of where best to locate for mining. Some had decided to go on down into the California valleys. The ladies of our party were going to San

Francisco, but most of the men were anxious to try their hand at mining for the first thing. They had come for gold and gold they intended to get.

Nothing of special interest occured during the next four days. The roads were very rough, running through unbroken forests of pine and spruce timber, the trees towering from one hundred to two hundred feet high. On the seventeenth we came to a place called Eureka where there was a small saw-mill run by water power. Gold has been found in quartz rock here and a company had been formed to put in a crusher with which to pulverize the rock and extract the gold, but the plant was abandoned the following year as the ore was too poor to pay for working. We camped on this branch of the Feather River and most of the one hundred young men located at the mine visited our camp, each one eager to give advice as to the best place for us to go, which advice was offered free to all and without asking. But, while they were so free with advice as to what it would be best for us to do in California to make money, it struck me from their appearance that it was doubtful if a single one of them in the whole crowd had made enough since coming to pay his way back to his former home in the states. The one little saloon in the place seemed to be the great attraction for them all, and was probably the depository of most of their earnings.

The next settlement on our route was Onion Valley, thirty miles away, and five miles from Onion Valley was Poor Man's Creek, the place I had selected fifteen days before as the spot where I would try my fortune at gold mining. The road for the first two miles out of Eureka lay through one of the worst mountain gorges we had anywhere found. The grade was steep and very sidling, so that in some places we had to hold our wagons with ropes to keep them from turning over. We were a full half day in making the distance of two miles. We could distinctly see Pilot Peak its top clad in perpetual snow; and above the timber line toward the foot of the mountain lay the little village of Onion Valley, the supply station for the mining camps in that vicinity. We made eight miles more that day, and camped for the night in a small open space where our cattle could find a little grass. They were so hungry after the day's hard trip that they trimmed and ate all the green brush around as high up as they could reach, and we cut down the willow bushes bordering the brook near us to feed to them. That evening our talk was largely upon the probability of our meeting again after the separation that was soon to come. We had learned to esteem and care deeply for each other during the varied and trying experiences of the long journey, and the thought of parting was painful. As I had talked of Poor Man's Creek for the last fifteen days, all had come to look upon me as the first one who would leave the train. One of them said, possibly to discourage me from stopping there, "Now, Bully, if you settle down there, you will always be poor." I replied that as I had been brought up in poverty it wouldn't make any difference anyway but that I construed the name of the locality just the other way, and that it was so named because it was the only place for a poor man to get rich. Most of the party discouraged me saying that if I stopped up there in the high mountains, I would soon be snowed in and could do no mining for six months, for we had been told the night before that the snow had been thirty feet deep during the past winter. But I held to my purpose and said that unless something unforeseen happened before reaching Onion Valley I would leave them there. On the night of September twentieth we camped within five miles of the village and several miners from Nelsons and Poor Man's Creek visited our camp to induce us to locate at the mining camp. They showed us their buckskin sacks well filled with gold nuggets. Some of them were willing to sell their claims to us as they were now ready to return to their homes in "The States." I was the only one of our party who told them that I was going to do my first mining on Poor Man's Creek.

The man who had bought our Michigan teams and wagons had agreed to pay us in full at Onion Valley. The next morning I packed what few clothes I had in my carpet sack, rolled up my two blankets and was prepared to leave the train as soon as we reached Onion Valley and received our pay for our teams. We made an early start and reached the village by ten o'clock. I sold my gun to a man in Onion Valley for five dollars and after receiving my share from the sale of our teams, pony and cow, found that I was about sixty dollars richer than when I left home one hundred and sixty seven days before without counting the knowledge, experience and pleasure I had gained on the journey. It was the largest sum of money I had ever possessed. The train halted long enough for our financial transactions and then all the members pressed up to give

8

me a shake of the hand and wish me luck.   The four young ladies insisted that, as I was the youngest of the crowd and had been considered by all as the boy of the train, they could not part with me with a mere shake of the hand, but must give me a farewell kiss, and this I received to the great merriment of the other members of the train although I have no doubt each one wished he might have filled my boots that day.   It is now fifty-one years since I stood and watched that little train leaving Onion Valley and slowly disappearing from my sight, and I have never since met but two of its members. These were Ed Spears (the Doctor) and William Sherman (Uncle Billy), both of whom did well in California, returned to their families in Michigan and lived and died among their old friends, respected and esteemed.

CHAPTER V.

GOLDEN CALIFORNIA.

Onion Valley was located in a small valley at the base of Pilot Peak seventy-five miles east of Marysville, the head of steamboat navigation on the Feather River. It was then the supply station for the mines on the head waters of Feather River, as at that time teams could not cover the rough trail to the mines and all supplies had to be packed in from Onion Valley on small Mexican mules or on the backs of men. From Marysville to Onion Valley supplies were brought by wagons carrying four to six tons. These were drawn by from eight to sixteen mules which were driven with a single line by one man who rode the near hind mule. Four and six horse Concord Stage Coaches ran daily between Marysville and Onion Valley for the accommodation of passengers who paid twenty dollars each for the distance of seventy-five miles. All mining towns on the branches of Feather River for forty miles north and east depended on Onion Valley for supplies, making it an important point. The nearest mines were on Poor Man's Creek, of which it was said that more poor men were here made rich than in any other surface digging in California.

At noon on September 21, 1852, I shouldered my satchel, blankets, frying pan, coffee pot, a week's provisions, pick and shovel, a total weight of about fifty pounds, and started for Poor Man's Creek five miles away. With me were three other young men who had just come in by boat, each of them carrying a similar pack. The first mile of travel was over a good trail, with no timber, although the grade was steep. The next four miles was through a dense forest, with deep ravines and gorges, and alongside rocky canyons, where the path was so narrow that I had to use my long-handled shovel to steady myself over dangerous places. I have often heard it said that the Mexicans could take their pack teams of loaded mules and broncos over any trail that a man could take a pack over, but certain it is that up to this time they had been unable to get a pack train within three miles of Hopkinsville, the mining village at the mouth of Poor Man's Creek. We passed several men on our way who were constructing a trail for pack trains, which, however, was not completed until the following spring on account of deep snow falling early so that all supplies for the mines had to be brought in on the miners' own backs. We soon reached a commanding spot on the trail from which we could look down the narrow valley and see the white tents of the mining village of Hopkinsville. We reached the village before dark and sheltered ourselves that night in an abandoned miner's shanty of spruce boughs. That evening we looked for the first time upon the night scenes and excitements of a real mining camp.

The little village had been hastily built during the past six months and the buildings were necessarily rude and cheap. The hotels, stores, gambling houses and saloons were all built of canvas with the exception of the floors, which were made of spruce lumber, sawed by hand and costing from five hundred dollars to eight hundred dollars per thousand feet. There were at least one thousand miners in the village that night, and not a boy, nor a woman nor a gray haired man did we see among them all. Board at the best hotel was twenty-four dollars a week in advance, including a sleeping bunk made out of rough boards and built along the side walls of the dining room. In the saloons all kinds of games of chance were being played. Two bars, one on each side of the room, dispensed cheap whiskey, the signs reading,—"Plain drinks 25 cents, Fancy drinks 50 cents." My three new companions were from the state of Maine, strong, healthy young men who had been brought up in the woods of that State, and who had only just arrived in California via the Isthmus of Panama. The scenes and excitement of that evening were so new and interesting to us, that we did not think of going to our shanty for sleep until after twelve o'clock.

In the morning we prepared a good breakfast from the supplies we had packed in the preceding day and leaving one man to look after our camp and agreeing to keep together for the day started out in search of gold. We were full of hope, and took our picks and shovels with us, expecting to return at night with nuggets of gold in our pockets. We went up the creek as far as gold had been found, but every claim had been taken and everywhere men were at work on them. At least half of the claims were for sale, but of course, those were the ones that were not paying well. We passed one claim where four men had taken out forty thousand dollars worth of gold the day before, and others where the color of gold could not be found. These latter claims belonged to men who were willing to sell out and go somewhere where they could pick up gold out of the water or sand without having to labor hard with pick and shovel to find it.

About noon we came to a store, at the back of which was a slaughter yard. Here about one hundred miners were gathered, serving as a combined jury, judge and executioner. The prisoner was accused of stealing his neighbor's frying-pan, and had been found guilty of the crime at this rude trial. He was tied to one of the posts used for hanging up beef, while a man chosen by lot gave him twenty-five lashes with a heavy whip. After this whipping he was compelled to give up his interest in a good mining claim, and to leave that section of the country. This was the heavy penalty for stealing small things like a frying-pan; it was death by shooting or hanging for anyone caught stealing articles over the value of fifty dollars. Civil courts were not instituted in these remote mining places until two years after I arrived in California. Few men were punished for stealing under the summary methods and severe penalties of the miners' laws for the criminal element soon learned to be honest if they had not been before. If guilty of crime, they did not find it so easy to escape punishment here as in other jurisdictions where courts were established and justice was not so swift. Many of the miners in the early days in California would leave the gold in their sluice boxes or long toms, from Monday until Saturday night and nothing would be touched. But conditions changed when civil courts took the place of miner's laws in 1854, and then every miner had to take good care of his gold every day or he would find that it had been stolen.

On our way back to camp after getting this first glimpse of western justice one of my companions came across a man whom he had formerly known in Maine. This man and his three partners offered to sell their claim to us as they wished to return to their homes in Maine before the winter set in. They told us that they had made good wages during the summer with two rockers, that is, boxes eighteen by thirty-six inches with a wire screen or sieve bottom, placed on rockers, into which one man would shovel the sand and gravel, while the other rocked it with one hand and dipped water into it to wash it with the other hand.   The gold being heavier than the sand settled to the bottom while the water washed the sand and gravel away, and left the shining gold in the rocker.   In those early days there were three ways in which to separate the coarse gold from the gravel on these small mountain streams. These were a rocker, as just described, a twelve quart sheet iron pan, and the long tom.   Where the soil was very rich with gold, a man could wash out a good fortune in one summer with a pan; two men with a rocker could wash twenty times as much dirt as one man with a pan; while with a long tom with four sluices attached and sufficient water running through them two men could wash out a hundred times more dirt than with a rocker.   We got the lowest price at which these men would sell their claim, which was two hundred dollars, and then set out for our shack to talk the matter over.   The man who stayed in camp had a good supper ready for us and we did full justice to it as we were very hungry, not having had any food since breakfast.   We discussed fully the matter of buying the claim and finally decided to test it the next morning.   We went to the village again that evening and the excitement of the previous night was again experienced.

In the morning, we packed our things and carried them to the claim we were to test.   The owners showed us how to use the rockers and we went to work with the understanding that we were to have the gold we took out that forenoon in case we bought the claim.   We worked like beavers for four hours, then cleaned up and found we had taken out something over one ounce of gold, worth about twenty dollars.   We felt satisfied with the result and after taking dinner with the owners, paid them for the claim, including the two rockers, their tools and the log shanty in which they lived.   That afternoon we worked busily again and by evening had about twenty dollars more in gold dust.   Several of our mining neighbors called on us that evening and advised us to put in a long tom, which they said would enable us to secure much greater results.   We had no timber with which to make such a long tom and the sluices that were necessary.   Graham, one of my partners, said he was good at running a whip saw and suggested that we saw our own timber and one of the neighbors who gave us the advice offered to rent us a whip saw for two dollars

a day, and to sell us a long tom for twenty-five dollars. We concluded to work with our rockers another day, and to defer our
decision until then. The next day brought us less than twenty
dollars for our work and that evening we decided to put in a long
tom. Next morning while two of the men worked the rocker,
James Graham and I went up on the side of the mountain in sight
of our claim, where there was a pit and platform already made
for whip-sawing lumber, and having borrowed a broadax and
handax, chopped down a fine spruce tree eighteen inches in diameter
and cut a log twelve feet long. We scored and hewed this log to
two inches in thickness, rolled it onto the platform, lined it on
both sides for one inch lumber and then began our work as sawyers.
Graham took his position on top of the timber as head sawyer,
while I went down into the pit under the timber, as second best
man, where I had the benefit of all the sawdust in my face and eyes
while under orders to look up and see that the saw followed the
line on the under side of the log. By night we had six boards cut,
each ten inches wide and twelve feet long, and by noon the next
day we had twelve boards, sufficient lumber to make four sluice
boxes, with three boards to each box. At the village we bought
ten pounds of twopenny nails, costing fifty cents a pound, and by
night had our sluices ready to attach to the long tom which we
bought next morning at a cost of twenty dollars. We made a
wing dam in the creek to turn the water into the sluices and that
night had over one hundred dollars in gold dust to pay us for a half
day's work with our own long tom and sluices, which greatly en-
couraged us.

The old miners who had spent a winter in the mountains were
anxious to leave before the heavy snow came, which was expected
very soon after the first of October. When we first reached Onion
Valley we had been told that the snow was sometimes thirty feet
deep in the mountains, and I remember that when we were coming
over the mountains we had seen trees on the eastern slopes partly
burned off fifty feet from the ground by fires kindled by emigrants
who, being delayed in crossing the plains and getting caught in
the heavy snows, had left their teams and attempted to save their
lives by crossing the great snow belt on snowshoes. Hundreds
of emigrants lost their lives in trying to cross the mountains during
the fall and winter of 1849, 50, 51. But we gave little heed to

the weather and kept on working our claim for twelve days, each day being more successful, so that on the third day of October we washed out over six hundred dollars worth of gold. That night the snow came. On the morning of the fourth it was nearly two feet deep, and falling so thick and fast that we could not see a man ten feet from us. It snowed constantly for six days, then suddenly turned warm and rained until the snow all disappeared. The miners along the banks of the creek became alarmed at the situation and many of them left their shanties and fled to the higher ground. At Hopkinsville the whole town was torn up bodily and moved up on higher ground out of reach of the surging flood. The water in the creek rose twenty feet that day and the flood swept every movable thing before it,—shanties, tents, sluices, boxes and tools, everything that had been snowed under and left was carried down the valley in the mad rush of the surging waters. How much gold was carried away in the flood no one could estimate.

This flood was the cause of the dissolution of our partnership. During the few days that we had been able to work our claim we had succeeded in obtaining about three thousand dollars. But such was the danger from these terrible floods that two of our party packed up and went with many other miners forty miles to the westward where mining was not so surrounded by difficulties. Graham and I decided to stick by our claim and to start up our bone-and-muscle saw-mill early in the spring so as to replace the sluices and boxes carried off by the flood.

We had a chance to buy five whip saws at a very low price from miners who were leaving the vicinity, and soon we were at work sawing lumber, the demand for which we could not meet, even though we charged eighty cents a foot. We hired men to cut logs and hew them ready to be sawed, while we did only the sawing. In less than a week we were running two saws, Graham as head sawyer for one gang and I now promoted from the pit and receptacle of fresh sawdust for eyes, nose and mouth, as head sawyer of the other, while each of us educated a new hand in the pit below to become a head sawyer at a future day, provided he liked the business. By this process of education we soon had all of our five saws running busily from morning until night, six days in the week. We made money very rapidly at the prevailing prices for we had nearly all the trade. "The Graham & Potter Saw-mill" was soon known the length of Poor Man's Creek. Graham was in the early prime of life, twenty-six years of age, six feet and two inches tall, weighing over two hundred pounds, while I, though only twenty years of age, weighed one hundred and sixty pounds, and was over six feet tall so that we were conspicuous even in that region and day of strong men. We kept our five saws running steadily for two months, moving up or down the stream, wherever the miners wanted the lumber. The best of spruce timber lined the stream on either side, costing us only what it took to cut it, and as our saw-mill was very portable, we could go where the lumber was and there was little expense in hauling. The only real difficulty in our work lay in the steepness of the sides of the mountains rendering it difficult to find a place which was level enough to set up the saw-mill.

In December the snow had become so deep that it was impossible for men to do any kind of work out of doors and we were compelled to give up our sawing. Nearly all of the miners within three or four miles came into Hopkinsville and there was a winter colony there of about three hundred young men, with not a woman in all the town or district around. Provisions in town became scarce before February was over and it looked as if we would soon either have to be put on short rations, or else must leave our camp and attempt to get down to the settlements in the valley. Eighteen of us volunteered to go to Onion Valley and bring in supplies of food on our backs through the snow which was eight feet deep. The first two miles of our journey lay up the creek valley and was made quite easily, but when we left the creek and began to go up the side of the mountain we found the going very hard. It was difficult to make a track through the deep snow, which was so light that one would sink into it up to his armpits. The only way we could make any progress through the snow was for the man in the lead to fall forward his full length, get up, walk forward his length, and fall again into the snow, continuing the operation until he was exhausted, then stepping aside and letting the next man take his place while he dropped into the beaten path in the rear. Most of the men could make from four to six plunges in the loose snow before becoming too tired to advance, but James Graham, who was our leader that day, would make twelve plunges every time he was in the lead before giving up his place to another.

The snow was falling so thick that we could not clearly see one-half the length of our line of eighteen men. We had made about two miles up the mountain at a grade of about thirty degrees and were close to the top, from which we would have a comparatively easy down hill trail to Onion Valley, when, without warning, the deep body of light snow which evidently rested on a harder crust of older snow, started *en masse* down the mountain side towards Poor Man's Creek, from whence we had just so laboriously come, and carried with it our entire party of eighteen men. Such a "sliding down hill" none of us had ever experienced before. The snow was very light and the whole body of it moved at the same time so we were kept from being buried in it, and no one of us was injured except Graham who fell and struck his back and side against a rock, hurting himself quite badly. By the time we had collected our scattered party from the snow it was getting late in the day and as Graham was suffering from his injury we decided to return to Hopkinsville for the night, and start anew in the morning.

It took us an hour to find the trail we had come over, but when we had located it we had little trouble in following it. Graham proved to be badly injured and suffered so much pain that we had to carry him, and if it had not been for the brandy which several of the men had with them, he would never have lived to reach the camp. It was a difficult task, this carrying a badly injured man along the narrow snow trail. One man would go along on the side of the trail tramping the snow down to make the trail wider so that two men could take Graham by his arms and drag him along between them. We kept this up until we reached an abandoned miners' camp about a mile from town. There we made him as comfortable as possible with four men to care for him while the rest of us went on to Hopkinsville, reaching there about midnight. We aroused the only doctor in the village and started him with two fresh men on the way to the shanty where Graham lay injured. One hundred men volunteered to start early the next morning for Onion Valley, over the same route we had taken; but only a few of the men who were in our party were willing to try again. I had very little sleep that night, but felt sure that the trip could be easily made by one hundred men, and determined to go on. When the new party reached the cabin where Graham had been left we found him apparently better and determined to go with us in spite of the advice of the doctor and of all of us. It was snowing so heavily that we could not see a person twenty feet away. At Graham's request I was chosen leader of the party for the day, and before starting I released them all from their promise to make the trip and advised all who were not willing to do their share in breaking the way to go back to camp. Twenty of the party turned back at this and after leaving four men at the log shanty to keep up a good fire and have some food on hand to care for any of our party who should give out and be obliged to return before reaching the top of the mountain, the rest of us, including Graham and the doctor, about eighty in all, started up the difficult trail. A few of the party tired and turned back before the top was reached for it took some time and much effort to break a trail through the avalanche of the previous day. As soon as we reached the hard snow which had been left bare by the slide we made rapid progress and reached the top of the mountain about one o'clock. From this point we were only about one mile distant from Onion Valley and we found it far easier breaking a road down the mountain than it had been going up. When we were within half a mile of town it ceased snowing, and we could see the roofs of the two hotels, but the rest of the village was buried under the snow. We were discovered by the villagers soon afterwards and they started out and broke a path to meet us. Graham had become exhausted in going down the mountain, and when the people met us they hauled him into town on a large hand sled. We reached the hotels before dark, but to enter them by their doors we had to go down snow stairs nearly twenty feet, as the snow was over that depth in the main street of the town. During a period of six weeks that winter the only way of getting from one hotel to the other or to any other place in town, was by tunnels cut through the drifts of snow for that purpose. The houses were kept lighted night and day with oil lamps or candles.

In a couple of days the weather had become settled again and many of our party returned to Poor Man's Creek, carrying supplies on their backs, although a few of them were determined to go farther down into valleys where they would be out of the snow belt. The doctor and I stayed with Graham who was too ill to travel and ten days after his injury in the snow slide the poor fellow died. He knew that death was coming and very calmly told us what he would like to have us do. His personal effects and gold dust he handed over to me to be sent back to his young wife in Maine. He asked the doctor and me to make a coffin out of the timber he and I had sawed together in Onion Valley and to bury him in the snow until spring came when we could dig his grave. We promised faithfully to mark his grave plainly with his name and former home so that his relatives might find his body when they came for it, as he was sure they would do. After he died I hastened over the trail to Hopkinsville, cut the lumber for his coffin into proper lengths and with the doctor's help packed it on my back across the trail to Onion Valley and laid all that remained of my good old partner Graham away to rest. Long before the snow disappeared we made his grave on the mountainside and marked it as he had requested.

Graham's death left me badly broken up. I felt that I could not stay in the place where he and I had worked together so long, especially now that there was little to do. I returned to Hopkinsville, and having sold our whipsaws and what lumber we had on hand, started out for Marysville for the purpose of taking the steamer down the river to San Francisco. I reached Marysville the fifteenth of March, and sent Graham's gold dust and belongings to his wife by express, writing her a letter telling her the sad tidings. A year later I heard from her, and two years afterwards I learned that Graham's body had been taken up and shipped to his old home in Maine.

I paid twenty-five dollars for a first class steamer ticket down the river to the Golden Gate. Sacramento, the capital of the State was our first stop, and here we found the streets flooded with water, on which boats plied as though the streets had been canals, while most of the residents were living on the second floors of their houses. This flood was caused by the melting of the heavy snows in the mountains. A run of twenty-four hours landed us in San Francisco. The beautiful bay was crowded with vessels carrying the flags of all the nations of the world. It was said, and I think truly, that by stopping in the new city a single week one could hear spoken every language of the world. It was a novel and interesting sight to look out over the bay and see the many colored flags floating in the soft spring breezes, as if painted on the distant blue sky. I have often recalled and can never forget the beautiful picture. But one did not spend much time in looking at the scenery here. When he turned from viewing the bay his eyes fell upon the crowded streets of the city, thronged with busy crowds of young men. There were few women, gray-haired men or boys; nearly all were young men, vigorous, stirring and energetic, each preparing to search for the elusive gold. Many of the vessels in the harbor had agents in the city trying to hire sailors, for their regular crews had deserted and gone to the gold mines. In some cases even the officers had deserted their ships, so that the commanders of the vessels in order to keep their crews had been forced to forbid their men to go ashore.

The most exciting happening in the new city was the arrival of mail. There were many thousands of strangers in the city, each anxious to hear from home and friends in the far east. All the mail then brought to the Pacific Coast came by ocean steamer which arrived only once in two weeks. No wharves had yet been built and passengers, freight and mail had to be transferred from the steamers at anchor half a mile from shore, into smaller vessels or "lighters" and then taken to shore, which made a long tedious job. The mails, like everything else, were late in reaching the city distributing office, which always became a center of excitement, clamor, and sometimes violence, before the mail was distributed. The post office would be besieged by a dense crowd extending for blocks and its windows had to be barred to keep men out while the clerks were distributing what sometimes amounted to tons of letters, taking as long as two full days to sort. While the mail was being distributed a great crowd would be clamoring for it, sometimes becoming so impatient as to rush against the building, causing it to shake and tremble as if there had been an earthquake. At the time of this, my first trip to San Francisco the post office had ten delivery windows, each window marked with initials, showing what letters might be obtained there. Ten lines of people were formed in the streets, each person as he came taking his place at the foot of the line before the window bearing the initial of his name, where he awaited his turn as the line moved slowly on. No one could call for mail for more than one name and as soon as he received that he had to step out of the line; even under this rule which kept the crowd moving those at the rear end of the line had sometimes to stand five or six hours before they reached the delivery window. The business men of the city could not afford to lose so much time and often offered from five to twenty-five dollars for one's position near the window, and this practice led men who did not expect mail to go early and get a good position which they would sell to someone who was in a hurry and willing to pay well for it. Some men who could stand the strain of standing still would keep this up, getting pay for their places three or four times in twenty-four hours, as for several days after a mail steamer arrived and the mail was ready to deliver, the long ranks kept formed day and night. Men with supplies of hot coffee, cakes and other eatables passed up and down the line supplying refreshments, and saloon keepers had their runners along the line selling drinks at exorbitant prices.

I stayed in this city of crowds and excitement nearly ten days and then bought a ticket back to Marysville which cost me forty dollars, fifteen dollars more than on my trip to the city, due to the fact that it took a day longer to go up the river than to come down. I had decided to go back to Poor Man's Creek and work the claim in which I had a share, for it would be forfeited unless some one of its owners was back at work by the fifteenth of April. To hold a claim it was necessary to have it registered in all the mountain districts, that giving you the right to leave it during the winter for a period of six months. The Register of Claims was the only paid officer in the district and his position was a remunerative one, as he received a fee of five dollars from everyone registering a claim. The San Francisco papers had been full of glowing accounts of very rich diggings recently discovered in the northeastern part of the state, one of which was called Gold Lake, where it was said one could pick up nuggets of gold on the shore of the lake without any digging. Another great digging that was loudly advertised was Rush Creek, about one hundred miles north and east of Marysville. I was so smitten with the fever that when I reached Marysville I decided to give up my interest at Poor Man's Creek and was caught and carried away in the new "rush" for Rush Creek. The last fifty miles of the journey to the new camp could not be traversed by teams and all supplies had to be taken in on the backs of mules and men. I purchased sixty-five pounds of prospector's supplies and joined in the exciting rush with many others who like myself were eager to be the first there.

Hundreds of men who carried only their blankets and provisions, relying on being able to get extra supplies when they reached the camp, passed others who were more heavily laden. Some of them got there in three days, while others required six days. On the way four of us agreed to stake out our claim together, and stay by each other.

We reached the new mining village called Rushtown at dark on the sixth day and found that there was still a great deal of snow on the mountains and that the water in the creek was very high. Miners were at work along the banks washing the dirt and claiming that they were making money very fast. Our party of four got bunks in a log hotel, and next morning started out to locate a claim, but for a considerable distance found the claims all taken and staked, and someone in possession. We located on the first vacant ground we came to, which was about five miles down the stream, and by night had built a temporary shelter of fir and cedar brush. On the following day we built a comfortable house of small fir trees, and it occurred to me that if Graham with his whipsaw had been with us, we could have made quick money by sawing the pine, spruce and fir trees which lined the banks, and selling the lumber for which there was a good sale at one dollar per foot. I went to the village next morning to get a whipsaw, but learned there was but one on the creek, and that that one was now in use. Through one of the merchants of Rushville I placed an order for two whipsaws, to be delivered as soon as possible by Mule Express. Soon after giving my order I met a company of miners from Poor Man's Creek, among whom was a good sawyer who had worked for Graham and me the preceding year. This man volunteered to go back to Poor Man's Creek and get three saws and two other men who had also formerly worked for us. The trip would take at least five days but I agreed to his proposal and told him that if he would start at once I would have the logs cut and hewn and ready to saw when he got back. I countermanded my order for saws through the merchant, and went back to camp where I told my three partners that I had a good job for them until the water went down enough to allow us to work in the creek. For the next five days we busied ourselves cutting sawlogs at different places along the creek, and before the saws came I had taken orders for five thousand feet of lumber at one dollar a foot. The sawyers with the three saws came in good time and by the seventh day all three saws were running, cutting timber at the rate of one hundred feet per day for each saw. For the next thirty days we did nothing but saw lumber for miners along the creek, and there was such a demand for it that the miners would themselves get the logs ready for us and we had only to saw them up into boards for which we received the regular price of one dollar a foot.

Rush Creek was about twenty miles long, heading near the western summit of the Nevada Mountains, and flowing through a continuous gorge until it emptied into the Feather River. Rushville was located about three miles from its head. Every claim on the entire length of the creek was taken and recorded before the water subsided and the miners could get to work. We soon discovered that the paying claims were confined to about two miles of the creek near the village of Rushtown, which proved to be very rich. The rest of the claims were valueless so that most of the miners who had hurried to this new district the first of April, carrying some gold dust in their pockets, left the country the first of June "dead broke." The only thing that saved me from going out in the same condition was our forty days' work with the whipsaws and the great demand for lumber.

The failure of the mines ruined the lumber business and the only thing left to do was to find some other place to try mining operations again. When I left Marysville for Rush Creek in April, I told my associates that I believed I was making a mistake in not going to Poor Man's Creek and working the claim I had bought an interest in the fall before; I even offered them an interest in my claim there if they would go with me, but the influence of the rush to Rush Creek was too strong and they declined my offer and we went on to our failure. A similar disappointment came to those who went to Gold Lake, for this development proved to be a complete fraud gotten up by some merchants in Sacramento who shipped a large stock of miners' supplies there and then got out advertisements of the finding of gold which were published in most of the California papers. When the crowds of excited miners learned of the fraud they organized a vigilance committee, took possession of the goods of the guilty merchants which they distributed among themselves, arrested the merchants, tried them under the miners' code, and upon a verdict of guilty executed them on the spot. Their act was upheld by the miners throughout the state and put a stop to subsequent speculations and frauds of this nature.

Before leaving Rush Creek I had decided to go to Poor Man's Creek to find out what had become of my claim there. I found that two of the men from whom my partners and I had bought the claim had returned and retaken it, as it had become forfeited because of our not remaining in possession and they told me that I had made a great mistake in leaving it, as they were making money rapidly. I explained to them that I had left because two of my partners had gone away and the other one had died. They invited me to stay over night with them, and in the morning offered to sell me a quarter interest with them for five thousand dollars but as I did not have the cash I could not buy. They showed me twelve hundred dollars in gold which they had washed out that day, and said that the pay had averaged one thousand dollars a day for fifty days. It needed nothing more than this to show me what a great mistake I had made in abandoning the claim through the wild rumors of a place of which I knew nothing. But such was the fortune of miners who followed surface digging in California. In haste to get rich they were not satisfied at doing well, but made hazardous changes in the hopes of finding diggings rich enough to obtain a fortune in a day. My loss was gain to others. Before I left these men made me flattering offers if I would stay with them, but I told them I did not care to run in debt, and could make forty to fifty dollars a day running three whipsaws on Nelson's Creek during the rest of the season. On leaving they gave me a sack of gold weighing six pounds, saying that as I had once bought the claim of them, and no doubt would now be in possession of it but for the death of my partner, they would make me a present of their previous day's earnings worth twelve hundred dollars as part remuneration for my loss. I hesitated to take the gold but they insisted upon it, and said that if at any time I returned they would take me into partnership with them and give me a good chance. I thanked them many times for their kindness and said I might return in two weeks, as I was going to work my saws on Nelson's Creek which was only twelve miles away. As I walked towards Nelson's Creek carrying the six pounds of gold so kindly

9

given me, I asked myself if I would have given away twelve hundred dollars under similar circumstances. How few would have done it. For fifty years the gift and the spirit which prompted it has enriched my memory.

On arriving at Nelson's Creek I found that my lumber partners were all ready to start our three bone-and-muscle saw-mills. The next morning we took a contract to saw ten thousand feet of inch lumber, to be delivered on or before the first of August (it was now the fifteenth of June) for which we were to receive fifty cents a foot, making five thousand dollars for the job. Our camp was about a half mile from Nelsonville, located at the spot where Nelson Creek emptied into Feather River. Good paying gold claims were located the entire length of Nelson Creek which was formed by the union of Poor Man's Creek and Hopkins Creek, at Hopkinsville, fifteen miles above us. The lumber we were under contract to saw was to be used in the construction of a flume to divert the waters of Nelson Creek from the channel and carry them to the Feather River, and the work had to be done in August while the streams were low. If we could obtain help enough to prepare the timber as fast as we could saw it we could easily finish our contract in twenty days and have time to open a claim for ourselves and extend the flume to it. We finally concluded to do this and staked out a claim, paying five hundred dollars for right of way over other claims to build a flume of three hundred feet to carry water to it. Our lumber contract and the opening of our new mine gave us plenty of work for six months. On the tenth of July we finished our contract and received our pay, clearing three thousand seven hundred dollars in twenty-five days. We then moved our camp up the creek to our claim, where our workmen had prepared three new sawpits and had cut timber, and by the nineteenth of July we had three thousand feet of boards ready for our own flume. The dam was soon finished to turn the water into the flumes and on the last day of the month the five-mile flume was completed.

On the first of August mining operations commenced on every claim in the bed of the stream. It was necessary to carry on this work day and night, without intermission, until the claim was exhausted, or the men driven out by high water. More than one million dollars was invested in the claims along these six miles of river bed by young men who had carried in most of their provisions and supplies over rough and steep roads while the work of preparation went on. It was an interesting and impressive sight, one not soon to be forgotten, to stand on Nelson's point, the location of the little village of five hundred people, its members gathered from nearly every state in the Union and to look down the stretch of the Feather River watching the six-mile flume of shimmering water running at a speed of twenty miles per hour, turning great paddle wheels in its progress to pump the seepage water from the claims back into the flume, while down in the bed of the stream hundreds of men could be seen busily washing out gold in rockers or long toms. Then one might turn and look southward up Nelson's Creek for a mile and the same scene would present itself, hundreds of young men literally slaving day and night for gold, as if no other interest existed.

Little gold was taken out during the first few days, but as soon as the claims were well opened large finds were made in both streams. Some claims failed to pay expenses, while others enriched their owners. Our claim failed to pay expenses the first two weeks, but on the fifteenth day we struck a pocket in the bed rock from which we took out over two thousand two hundred dollars worth of nuggets in less than one hour. On the same day the fourth claim below us yielded sixty thousand dollars, which was said to be the largest amount taken on one day from any claim within a radius of six miles. That claim paid its four owners more than five hundred thousand dollars in two months. My partners and I worked our claim day and night whenever we could get sufficient help. We would work for days and obtain very little and then perhaps the next day we would find enough to pay for a whole week's work. The claims on Nelson's Creek paid well, while half of those on Feather River were a failure. Many parties became discouraged and left after a year's hard work with nothing to show for their toil and heavy expense, while often the purchaser of their claims did well.

I had sent word to my kind friends at Poor Man's Creek, who had given me the six pounds of gold, asking them to come and spend some Sunday with us. Two of them came over and I spent the day in showing them the sights on Feather River, and in taking them to dinner at the best hotel in Nelsonville. They told me that their claim was paying better than when I had been there, and that they had been offered $50,000 for it, but had refused to sell for less than $75,000 and had given an option on it at that price for one week. On the way back from the hotel we stopped and examined the claim where gold worth $60,000 had been taken out of a pocket in a rock in a single day, and the owners showed us the gold which they had washed out that forenoon which was worth $12,000, and said that there was as much more in the long tom to show for their afternoon's work. We remained and saw the gold as it was taken out of the box. In the course of our conversation the owners of this claim discovered that my friends from Poor Man's Creek were from the same state as they and on this basis they soon became warm friends. On reaching our claim towards evening we found that this had been a successful day for us for our men were cleaning up the day's findings that amounted to over $1,800. The owners of the rich claim we had visited insisted that we should all go with them to the hotel for supper. There were nine of us in the party, eight from Maine, and I alone from Michigan. We had a splendid visit that night without any aid from the saloon-keeper for we were all temperance men. When our party broke up I persuaded my friends from Poor Man's Creek to stay over night with the promise that if they would do so I would arrange to have them home at seven o'clock the next morning by supplying them with saddled mules. They accepted my invitation and started out early the next morning accompanied by one of my partners and one of their new made friends from the rich claim, both of whom stayed with them during the day and were witnesses of the sale for $75,000 cash of the claim that eleven months previous I and three others had bought for $200, and then forfeited by our neglect.

The day our friends left us we got over $1,200 from our claim and then for five days it failed to pay expenses and seemed to be worked out and worthless. But we kept on working hoping to find a rich crevice or pocket in the bed of the rock where gold had washed in years before and had not been moved by the current. For two weeks longer we labored on without success, but we resolved to keep at it until our claim was entirely dug over or we were driven out by high water. By the 10th of September half our claim had been worked over and been found barren and as the rains and snows would soon be upon us, we decided to work a narrow strip near one bank of the creek where there appeared to be loose seamy rock, in the breaks and fissures of which we might find gold. After working a distance of eighty feet we reached a seam in the rock from which we obtained three hundred dollars in one afternoon. To clear the bed of water we had to change the location of the water wheel and pump which took us a day and then we found gold in paying quantities, obtaining over $600 in a space only two by eight feet. Our hopes arose, and we hired extra men to remove the top gravel that was six feet deep over the crevice, hoping that if this crevice extended clear across the creek bottom we would obtain six or seven thousand dollars for it. By noon of another day we had cleared about twenty feet of rock, and in the afternoon began to take out and wash the gravel in the crevice as far down as gold could be found, running it through sluice boxes and the long tom, and keeping extra men at work all night paying them six dollars for each twelve hours' work. When the crevice was cleaned up we had six thousand seven hundred dollars for our four days work, which caused us to forget the many days of hard work when we had obtained nothing. Two old miners who visited us that day said they were sure this was the same pocket from which four New York men had taken $75,000 the year before, and I told them that I would like to meet those New Yorkers to thank them for the goodly amount of gold they had left behind. The strangers asked permission to look into the riffle box, that held the gold under the long tom and after examining it one of them said that it looked to him as if this second crop were better than the first. We were much surprised the next day to be visited by hundreds of miners from the vicinity who had heard that we had made a find of $100,000 in one day and who came down to congratulate us and to take a look at the crevice in the rock of the creek bottom, now already filled with six feet of water, that had given its owners such a treasure. Even the owners of the rich claim below us came to congratulate us "on the greatest strike ever made on Nelson's Creek." The story was widely published all over the state of the $100,000 gold find in one crevice in Nelson's Creek, the rumor having its whole foundation in the statement of a miner who looked into a box of gold that had less than $7,000 in it. We only wished the story could have been true. Visitors did not ask questions, but seeing the "pocket" for themselves

concluded that the story was true, inasmuch as two of the oldest
miners in the section had seen gold nuggets covering the bottom
of a box three feet wide and six feet long, and were ready to swear
there was a bushel of them. With such exaggerated stories published and believed, no wonder the life of a miner was an exciting
and wandering one.

On September twenty-sixth rain began to fall at the head waters
of the Feather River, raising the water enough to carry off the five
miles of flume on that stream, although the one mile of flume on
Nelson's Creek remained undisturbed. We were able to keep
at work until our claim was gone over, but did little more than
pay expenses after working the pocket. On the twenty-first of
October we sold our flume, long tom, pump, tools and everything
connected with the claim for five hundred dollars to parties who
owned the claims above us which they intended to flume and work
the next season.

It was now eighteen months since I had left home and I had
not heard a word from any of my people during the whole period.
No post offices existed in the mountain mining districts. The
nearest post office was Marysville, one hundred miles away, and
to get mail one had to give an order on the nearest post office to
an official mail man and pay him one dollar for each letter which
he brought. I had often made out these orders but had received
no mail. When leaving home I had promised my mother to write
her every month after reaching California, and this I had done.
I was sure that my mother and oldest sister had written me, and
that there must be letters for me somewhere in California. A
miner told me that he had been in the state two years before he
received a letter from his wife and that then he had advised his
wife to address her letters to him in her name and that thereafter
he had received them regularly and without expense, as no extra
charge was made in California for delivering letters addressed to
ladies. By his advice I at once wrote home, asking them to address
all letters to Miss Louisa Potter, Marysville, California. As a
result of this scheme I received three letters on the tenth of February, twenty-two months after leaving home.

My two partners decided to return to their homes after finishing our job on Nelson's Creek as they felt satisfied with the result
of their six months' work, amounting to five thousand dollars

each, two thousand from their whip-sawing and three thousand from mining. I had done equally well and in addition had the twelve hundred dollars which had been given me, and I also made up my mind to return home, and with my money buy the best farm in our home county. On the first day of November we shouldered our blankets and started for Marysville, going by way of Hopkinsville and Poor Man's Creek to Onion Valley where we could take the stage. We stopped for dinner at Hopkinsville, and I was surprised to find only two men remaining who had wintered there the year before. We examined my old claim that had been recently sold for seventy-five thousand dollars and I made myself known to the present owners, who had heard of me in connection with the death of my partner James Graham. I asked them if the claim was for sale but they declined to name a price for it, having bought it for mining purposes. We learned from them that the men from whom they purchased had bought a claim at Forbestown, which was fifty miles away, out of the region of heavy snows where they could work during the winter. At their invitation we stayed over night with them and saw them clean up over three thousand dollars worth of gold for their day's work.

Starting out at daybreak we took the three mile up grade trail to Onion Valley on which Graham had been injured in the snow-slide of the previous year. At Onion Valley we boarded the six horse Concord stage. I stopped at Forbestown and bade farewell to my three partners who were bound back East and whom I never saw again. One mile north of Forbestown, on a creek running into Feather River, I found the two men who formerly owned the Poor Man's Creek mine. They seemed glad to see me again and I told them that I had spent the previous night at their old claim where I had been informed of their present location and had stopped on purpose to see them again. The sides of the creek on which these two men were located had been worked over but the middle of the stream which was about one hundred feet wide, had not been worked, although it was reported rich. They owned three hundred feet of the creek bed and were planning to build sluices to divert the water around their claim, so that they could work the bed of the stream. The gold here was in the shape of dust, not nuggets as in the mountains, and they were planning on separating it from the other gravel by means of quicksilver. There had been three

partners originally but one of them had gone home and his share
of the claim was for sale, and after examining the claim for two days
the gold fever once more mastered me and I decided to try my
luck again and to buy out this one-third interest. The purchase
took all I had made during the past six months and left me with
nothing but my share of the claim. It was an expensive claim to
open and one that could be worked only during the rainy season
when there was plenty of water for washing. By great effort
we were ready to begin operations in December, the usual time
when the rainy season began, but this year it was late and for
long weeks we waited. About the first of January the rains came
and we set to work with a large force of men on both sides of the
creek, washing out the gravel. We were greatly disappointed
for the daily clean-up for that month was only six hundred dollars
and our daily expenses were over two hundred dollars. We could
work only during the rainy season, three months of the year, and
so we hired help enough to work day and night from January first
to the 18th of March, when the claim was all worked out. In
November I had put six thousand dollars into the claim and in
April after five months' work, I went away with only two thousand
dollars in my pocket.

CHAPTER VI.

WITH THE SONORA GRAYS.

My disheartening loss at Forbestown made it practically impossible for me to go back to Michigan so I decided to keep at mining and to try my luck in Tuolumne County, one hundred miles southeast of Sacramento. My partners, to whom the loss had not meant so much as to me, decided to return home and spend the rest of life among their friends. As soon as our business matters were settled we took passage by stage for Marysville and at evening were on board a boat, my partners bound for San Francisco and I for Sacramento. The next morning I bade my partners a final good-bye and left the boat to take the stage to Sonora, the county seat of Tuolumne County and the largest mining town in Southern California. Our coach was a large six-horse one, with room for twelve persons inside. The first twenty miles was over a good level road, one of the interesting spots which we passed being old Fort Sutter. The second twenty miles was through the foot-hills of the Nevada Mountains, still over good roads, and the end of this stage was Jackson, the county seat of Amadore County and the first mining town on our road. The first forty miles was made in four hours, with a change of horses and drivers every ten miles and with a load of twenty-two, consisting of twelve passengers inside and ten Chinamen on top.

When we arrived at Jackson we found it a center of great excitement. A vigilance committee had the evening before executed a noted Mexican bandit and outlaw, and his body was still dangling at the end of a rope from a limb of a live-oak tree in the center of the town, the committee having given orders that it should hang there all day as a lesson to the robbers and bandits who were numerous in that mountain district. Amadore County is today one of the principal agricultural and fruit-growing sections of the State; Jackson still remains its county seat, and I am informed that strangers who visit the town are shown the live-oak tree in the center of the town from which, it is said, more robbers and guerillas have

121

been hanged than from any other tree in California. We were delayed at Jackson at least an hour on account of this excitement.

Mokelumne Hill, in Calaveras County, located on Calaveras River, a large rapid mountain stream, was the next mining camp. Soon after leaving Jackson we entered a mountain gorge leading down into the river valley which seemed to me the most dangerous road I ever travelled. Imagine a coach and six horses loaded with twenty-two passengers dashing down a steep, narrow, rocky gorge, around frequent sharp curves, at a speed of ten miles an hour with the coach rocking, swaying, and fairly reeling down the fearful descent, apparently about to be dashed into pieces at any moment, and you have some faint conception of that ride and my fear while taking it. But the driver sat on his seat with a coolness and composure that seemed to me at the time to amount to either indifference or recklessness, handling his six lines and managing his brakes as carelessly as if he were on a level road, whistling or singing some gay air, seemingly totally oblivious to any danger. It was not recklessness, as I soon found out, but rather the result of long experience and familiarity with danger. At the end of the gorge we reached the half way point of our journey and made a half hour's stop for dinner. The next fifty miles to Sonora was through a continuous mountain district, as rough as could be found in California where a six-horse coach could possibly go. With fresh horses and only thirteen passengers, the Chinamen leaving us at Mokelumne Hill, we started down the river, going for two miles over the road by which we came in, then turning off into another gorge similar to the one we had passed through but on the opposite side of the river and up hill instead of down. For three miles we toiled slowly up the grade and then after a rapid drive of five miles came to the Spanish town of San Andreas. Our relay of six fresh horses stood in the street all ready to be hitched on and three minutes after we drove up we were off again at a ten-mile rate for Murphy's Camp. At Mokelumne Hill, with the aid of a five-dollar gold piece, I had obtained permission from the driver to sit on the seat with him during the last fifty miles of our mountain ride, which was considered a great privilege. This driver, who had been on this ten mile section ever since the road was opened two years previous, entertained me with stories of various hold-ups, and showed me scars where he had been struck by bullets in attempting to escape from robbers with his coach and passengers. At the highest point on the road he pointed out to me a high mountain three miles to the right and south of us, where in September, 1852, three of the most dangerous and desperate bandits that ever infested California were captured and executed. Since their capture and execution he said that not a stage coach on that route had been held up. The drive to Murphy's Camp, where we changed horses and drivers again was made in seventy minutes, seven minutes to a mile. Murphy's Camp is noted as the point where stages leave for the Calaveras National Park, the home of the wonderful sequois and redwood trees which grow to a diameter of forty feet. The first grove of these trees is only twenty miles east of Murphy's Camp. There are also celebrated caves in the vicinity and a wonderful natural bridge spanning a river. In the spring of 1855 I visited all these interesting points, and again in 1886 I visited them with friends, finding the spot which had once been nothing but a rough mining camp then a great center for tourists.

An hour's drive from Murphy's Camp brought us to Vallicita, a village settled by Mexicans as early as 1840, where they followed mining for gold in a crude way transporting the ore by mule teams to Mexican cities. The next mining town which we reached was called Angel's Camp. All these little mining villages were located in Calaveras County in the narrow valleys made by small streams, on the upper range of mountains lying between the two large mountain rivers of Calaveras and Stanislaus. The courses of these rivers we could trace with the eye from our route by the heavy growth of pine, spruce and cedar timber that lined their banks. Angel's Camp was strictly a Mexican or "greaser" town. Not a Yankee with his enterprise had yet invaded it or disturbed its lazy, dirty, half-civilized life. Its name could only have orginated from the loveliness of its situation since the appearance and reputation of its inhabitants showed them to be far removed from such a class of beings. The sun was sinking out of sight in the west, throwing its bright rays over the mountains and covering them with a mantle of transient and splendid glory as we left Angel's Camp. Only from the top of a stage coach at such a moment, it seemed to me, could a person have any conception of the almost heavenly beauty of the mountain scenery about the village. We drove down the mountain ridge to reach the ferry across the Stanislaus River, our driver, like the nine others who had preceded him, having perfect command of his teams as they trotted briskly down the steep roadway. The ferry boat was attached to a heavy rope by a system of pulleys, the force of the current supplying the power to propel it across the stream. The grade up from the river was not so steep as to prevent our going at a trot most of the way until we reached the summit of the mountain, four miles further on. From there on we found good roads all the way to Sonora, which we reached about nine o'clock, one hour behind schedule, but having made the distance of one hundred miles in fifteen hours.

It was Saturday evening and the one long, narrow street which ran the length of this, the largest mining town in the State, was packed with people, most of whom were Mexican Greasers, although there were representatives of practically every State of the Union. The principal places of attraction were two large gambling houses, one of them named "Miss Virginne Saloon," owned and managed by a Mexican woman, and the other owned and run by Americans and called "The Long Tom Saloon." All the known gambling games were in operation at these places, and liquor bars were running in each, seven days of the week and twenty-four hours of the day. I had made this trip to Sonora partly that I might find an uncle by the name of Corydon P. Sprague, who had represented Tuolumne County in the State Legislature for the past two years, but I learned that night that he had recently left the town and moved to Oregon. I was therefore at somewhat of a loss just what to do, but that evening I found four brothers, by the name of Gilkey, whom I had formerly known in Lansing, Michigan. One of them, Edwin Gilkey, kept one of the hotels in Sonora and showed me the sights during the evening. I accepted his hospitality and took my first lodgings at his hotel, which was the only temperance house in town. It was a temperance house because Gilkey's wife insisted that he should not sell liquor and because of her position he was finally compelled to close it for want of patronage, for temperance houses were never known to live to any great age in a new mining town.

The next day I visited the father and mother of the Gilkey boys, who were living in Shaw's Flats a mining camp two miles from Sonora. It was Sunday and the Mexicans were to have a Spanish bullfight at three o'clock that afternoon, to which Riley Gilkey asked me to go. Sunday is the great holiday of the Mexicans. This was the second bullfight held in Sonora, and as a grizzly bear was to figure in the show everybody was anxious to see it. Two acres of ground had been inclosed by high pointed posts deeply planted in the ground and fastened at the top, and a grand stand was erected on one side of the circle large enough to accommodate all who would pay one dollar for a reserved seat. There must have been fully five thousand people in the stand that day. A Mexican band entertained the crowd with Spanish tunes, intermixed occasionally with Yankee Doodle and other American tunes, and kept the waiting crowd of many nations and peoples in good humor until the show began. The proceedings opened with the entrance of a small Mexican bull decorated with many colored flags. He stood still a moment, looking in bewilderment at the great crowd of people out of his reach, then circled the ring a few times, and finally tossed with his horns two dummies which were thrown into the ring, much to the delight of the audience. By a side door there now entered a Mexican dressed in a gay colored suit, carrying in one hand a red flag, and in the other a long, sharp lance. The band struck up a gay tune and the death struggle began. The bull dashed and plunged fiercely at his daring antagonist who skillfully evaded the thrust of his horns when it appeared to us that he must certainly be impaled. Then after stepping aside from the bull's mad charge, he would prick him with his lance to enrage him the more, thus torturing the poor brute until it was time to close the first act in the tragedy by thrusting his lance into the heart o the animal. The band then struck up its music again while the audience cheered and waved their hats and applauded, as if a noble deed had been done. The victorious Mexican proudly waved his bloody lance, made many smiling bows to the audience, and backed out of the ring like a great conquerer—over a poor little bull. The slain animal was then dragged out of the ring and act one of the cruel play was ended.

The second act was still more repulsive and inhuman. Two bulls were put into the ring to mangle each other until they became exhausted, whereupon two Spaniards, worthy of their proud blood, exhibited their courage and prowess by entering the ring where they faced the dreadful danger of the two exhausted and mangled bulls. For a full half hour they tortured the poor suffering and bleeding animals with sharp pointed swords to the delight of the crowd of onlookers, and finally when their lust for blood was satisfied, thrust their swords bravely and fearlessly into the hearts of the almost dead animals.

The ring was now cleared for the final act, which had been arranged at the special request of the citizens of Sonora and which was to consist of a fight between a grizzly bear and the fiercest bull which the Mexicans had. The bear had been raised from a cub by one of the citizens, who could play with him as if he were a dog, but who had allowed no other man to lay his hands on him. The bear and its owner first entered the arena together and played with each other to the amusement of the crowd. The man soon left the ring and the bull was let in. The bear took a position near the flag-staff in the arena, while the bull circled around him several times, occasionally stopping to bellow and paw up the ground but approaching nearer and nearer each time. The bear quietly watched the bull as he drew near and suddenly, springing forward, struck him with one forepaw on the side of his head, the blow knocking him down, taking half the skin off his head and tearing out one of his eyes. The bear did not touch the bull again but resumed his upright position, and looked around the arena as much as to say,—"Bring on another." The bull got up and staggered away until he struck the wall, where he laid down. That closed the show. The bear's owner jumped into the ring, and calling him, shook hands with him, hitched the leading chain to his neck and led him away. He had made more by the show than the showmen had, for he had heavy bets on his favorite. This was my first and last bullfight. All my desire to witness such sport was then and there satisfied. I have never wanted to see another such exhibition of brutality. A country that allows such exhibitions has no right to call itself civilized.

Nearly all the neighboring mining camps were represented at Sonora that day and excitement ran high until Monday morning. I had supper at the Gilkey House that evening with the four Gilkey boys, their father, mother and sister, and they entertained me with the story of their experiences in these mining regions, while I told them some of mine in the gold fields of Northern California. They soon learned that my last venture had been unsuccessful and that I was anxious to get at work again. Ed, the hotel keeper, said that he had been estimating for one of the banks in the town on the delivery of five hundred thousand feet of lumber from their saw-mill ten miles up the mountain. At his invitation I went with him to the bank and looked into the proposition. The lumber would have to be brought down a ditch only eight feet wide and three feet deep and delivered on the banks at a point where teams could reach it. It seemed like a difficult job, but I was desperate and after forcing the bankers to come up in their offer as far as possible I took the job for Gilkey and myself promising to have the lumber delivered within a month. The mill men promised on their part to have five hundred rafts of lumber in the stream in six days, ready to run down, to keep three feet of water running in the stream, and to furnish us with enough money to pay our help each Saturday night. I was to superintend the work, for which I was to receive two hundred dollars, provided we made that much. I camped and lived with our hired men along the stream, working a night crew to keep the lumber moving, and by the second week we were sticking lumber at the landing, which proved to be the hardest part of our work. At the end of the fourth week, as we were finishing our job, Gilkey came into camp much excited, saying that a run had been made on the bank that evening which had forced it to close its doors. A mob of depositors had taken possession of the building and had broken open the vaults but had found no gold. All the deposits had disappeared with the bankers the day before. Two other banks, one at Jamestown and the other at Columbia, both of which were owned by the same parties, had then been taken possession of by the depositors, but very little money was found in either of them. The depositors, mostly miners, lost half a million dollars in the three banks. But Gilkey and I did not intend to be defrauded, and the next day we attached the lumber for our pay. The Columbia Company, which had contracted for the lumber through the bank, came forward promptly and paid all claims, and after we had paid the workmen we had eight hundred dollars left to be divided between us. Gilkey received three hundred dollars, although he had done but little, while I got five hundred dollars for the month's hard day and night work.

The day following the winding up of our work for the lumber company I went with Gilkey up into the mountains on the Stanislaus River, about twenty miles from Sonora, to inspect a large ranch. There were five hundred acres of fine prairie land bordering on the river, very level and entirely cleared, but surrounded with mountains which were covered with a fine growth of pine, spruce and cedar. This ranch had been located two years before by a Missouri family who had built a good log house and barn and had occupied it one year. They had been driven out by the deep snows of winter and had abandoned the place for a farm which was away from the mountain snows. Their claim on the land had become outlawed, having been abandoned one year, and Gilkey had paid the man fifty dollars for the buildings and his rights in the ranch. He wanted me to form a partnership with him and to take up the ranch and as I was much pleased with the land and its surroundings I agreed to do so. It was now the early part of May, just the proper time to commence farming in the mountains, so we returned to Sonora, and made preparations for moving the Gilkey family out to the farm. We purchased a team and two cows next day, and on the day following I took a load of supplies and the two cows to the ranch, while Gilkey promised to bring on the family within the next two days.

I had been there but one day when a man named Lyons, who owned a large ranch near Sonora, drove up and asked me what I was doing on his ranch. I explained to him that Gilkey had bought the rights to the ranch, that I had gone into partnership with him and that we were going to develop it. He replied that Gilkey had no claim to the place that would hold because the man whose rights he had bought had nothing to sell, for the ranch was his and he meant to hold it. He carried a revolver in his belt and I noticed a rifle in his buggy so I was afraid that he meant trouble. He came back after an hour or so and told me that I had better send word at once to Gilkey not to come onto the ranch, or otherwise he would get into a great deal of trouble. I knew that Lyons lived near Sonora so I advised him to see Gilkey himself and tell him what he had told me. I explained to him that I was a stranger in the vicinity and not acquainted with the facts in the case and that if he was entitled to the claim I wanted to know so at once so that I could withdraw. I assured him that I didn't care for a ranch that belonged to another as I thought there were plenty of good claims in California without having to buy trouble with one. This seemed to cool him somewhat and he went away saying he would see Gilkey.

The visit from Lyons made me uneasy, and I was very anxious

until Gilkey and his wife and little girl drove in about dark.   At the first opportunity I got him out of his wife's hearing and told him of Lyons' visit and of what he had said.   He replied that this was the first time that he had ever heard of such a claim, and said that although Lyons had met him on the road he had made no mention of the claim.   It didn't make me feel any easier when Gilkey said that Lyons had the reputation of being the most dangerous man in the county, and that he had killed three men since coming to California, but that nevertheless he didn't intend to be scared out of his claim but would hold it until he was either bought out or killed. He thought, however, that there was little likelihood of Lyons molesting us, as he had probably come out to take possession of the ranch and finding me here had tried to scare me off.

But my fears of Lyons had not been groundless.   The next morning we saw a tent located near our house and found Lyons and four other men with two loads of timber starting to build a house. Gilkey and I went over to the spot and asked Lyons on what he based his claim to this ranch.   He replied that he had filed a claim on the ranch to take effect when the first man's claim ran out, that he was on the claim at that time, and finding me there had ordered me off, and that if we didn't want trouble we had better leave at once.   When I asked him why he had not spoken to Mr. Gilkey about the matter the day before as he had promised me, he replied that he had not wished to start trouble in the presence of Gilkey's wife and little girl.   The discussion grew hot and both men became very angry and I feared lest they would use the pistols which they were carrying.   I tried to cool them down by suggesting that we take the matter to court, but Lyons declared with an oath that no court in California would ever decide this case.   I finally took Gilkey by the arm and drew him away from Lyons.   We took counsel at the house and I advised him to go at once to Sonora and consult with the judge and a good lawyer.   Gilkey did not wish to leave his family and urged me to go in his place, and this I agreed to do.   I reached Sonora before noon and laid the matter before the judge, who said that Gilkey would have to contest his case in the United States court, but that he had better leave the ranch at once as Lyons was the worst man in the county to deal with.   I told him the whole story and asked him to write a letter to Gilkey, repeating what he had told me as I feared that if he stayed at

10

the ranch much longer there would be bloodshed. I took the letter which he wrote and called on a friend of Gilkey's who was a lawyer, and who also gave me a letter advising Gilkey if he regarded his life as worth anything, to leave the ranch at once. I returned by way of the home of Gilkey's brother, where I took dinner and he gave me another note to Gilkey advising him to give up the ranch. I reached the ranch soon after dark and found a scene of excitement. Lyons, it seems, had been to the house and ordered Gilkey off the ranch at once. Gilkey had opened fire on him and both men had emptied their revolvers at each other, but they were so excited that neither had been hit, although one ball had passed through the hair of Gilkey's little girl. I handed Gilkey the three letters without a word, and after reading them he said that although the advice was good he was going to stay on the ranch. His wife begged him to leave at once and I, who was tired of the whole affair, told him that I should leave that night as I regarded my life as of more value to me than all the ranches in California. He said that I was a coward to go and leave him, but I didn't bother to answer that. I offered to take the team and carry his wife and child back to Sonora, where they would be out of danger but he would not listen to it. After supper I made Mrs. Gilkey a present of my interest in the team and cows and started on foot for Sonora, carrying my satchel.

My five days' experience at farming in California had proved too exciting for me and I was determined to get so far away from that ranch that I would not be troubled with it again. I kept walking all night and did not halt until I reached a mining claim near Jamestown, which was beyond Sonora, and here I stopped for breakfast. I then walked on until I reached Jacksonville, a mining town on Tuolumne River, seventeen miles from Sonora, where I found a Michigan friend who was mining alone on the south bank of the river. I stopped at his claim and helped him that afternoon. He had built a wing dam to turn the water off from his claim and he said that he had been making good wages for the past four weeks and had all the space he could work until high water came. The claim looked good so I bought an interest in it, and having purchased a long tom, sluice boxes and a large canvas hand pump, went to work in earnest. It proved a fine investment for me. I had been at Jacksonville two weeks when one day the man with whom I boarded showed me an article in the Sonora *Herald*, giving a detailed account of the trouble between Gilkey and Lyons and speaking of me as Gilkey's partner who had left the ranch one night and had not been seen or heard of since. A large number of men had been searching the country for me, as they had concluded from my absence that Lyons had killed me. As soon as I saw the article I got a horse and rode to Sonora where I met Gilkey on the street. He seemed very much surprised as he had believed that I had been killed. He said that his family were still at the ranch, and that he was going to hold it. I went with him to his brother's house and after an hour's persuasion got him to agree to leave the ranch and settle the matter in the United States court. I gave him one hundred dollars and sent one hundred dollars to his wife, on his promise that he would leave the ranch at once.

I returned to Jacksonville that night and worked out the claim, and once more found myself possessing a good sum of money. My partner returned to Michigan while I went to Columbia, where I found Gilkey again keeping hotel. At Columbia I bought another claim. The soil here was a blue clay which had to be dug, then dried in the sun and kept under cover where it would stay dry until the rainy season set in, when there would be water to wash the gold out. Some of these claims were very rich. This gold-bearing clay lay between cliffs of white limestone rocks which pointed up to or near the surface of the ground, and dipped down on some claims for two hundred feet. At the bottom of these clay beds was a bed of fine gravel, which was easily washed without drying, and which was rich in gold. Mining in this clay was an expensive proposition. One set of men dug out the clay in the pit, then hoisted it with ropes and pulleys and man-power to the surface, where others spread it out to dry, pounding and mashing the lumps into smaller pieces to facilitate the drying, while still another set of men wheeled the dried dirt into mounds and covered it with canvas or boards to protect it until the winter rains came. Then with the coming of the rainy season the long toms were put to work and all hands were kept busy reaping the golden harvest. Like other claims some of these made their owners rich, others gave them fair wages and still others were a dead loss.

The Water Company charged so much for the use of their water that the claims could not well pay much. This robbery, as it was called, led to the assembling of a convention of miners who organized a stock company for the purpose of building a ditch to carry water from Stanislaus River, a distance of thirty-five miles. The day following the meeting stock enough was taken to build it and a surveyor was at once put to work. I spent a month assisting the surveyors in this job and later three men and I as partners took one mile of this canal to dig. Our portion of the work was fifteen miles up in the mountains east of Columbia. The canal was to be twelve feet wide and six feet deep and forty rods of our mile ran through solid rock, which had either to be blasted through or built over by a flume. One-half of the contract price was to be paid in company stock and the other half in cash. We built a log shanty to live in, and on the twentieth of May, after about three months' work, our job was finished. The lower fifteen miles of canal was now finished, but the upper ten miles could not be completed until the snow went off. For a time we helped in the construction of a saw-mill which the company was building on the mountain-side near the section of the canal which we had completed, and a ter that was finished returned to our claim and commenced digging out blue clay again and drying it in the sun. On account of our new canal, the stock of the old Tuolumne County Ditch Company that had been selling at an advance of five times its par value went down be!ow par. The new company agreed to furnish water at one-fourth the price of the old company and every claim which the new ditch could reach was taken up and worked, the increase of business giving new life to all the surrounding towns. I again boarded at the Gilkey House. Mrs. Gilkey set a very good table and, as she would not allow the sale of liquor in her house, she had a quiet and orderly lot of boarders.

One Saturday evening, about the first of July, I happened to be at Sonora when a telegram came to the sheriff advising him that a prominent man had been killed by his partner at Columbia and that a mob was determined to hang the murderer. The message called on the sheriff to send the Sonora Grays, a militia company, to protect the man. The wire was cut by the mob after this message was sent and we had no further communication. About thirty of the company and ten citizens armed with revolvers, I among them, started for Columbia on the doub e quick, led by the sheriff and the captain of the Grays. When we reached Columbia we found that the mob had torn the iron door from the calaboose, and had dragged the prisoner, with a rope around his neck, to the trestle work of a high flume. Here, by the light of a bonfire, they were giving him a mob law trial. There was a crowd of probably three thousand men, most of them shouting for his execution before even any kind of trial was had but some of the better and more level-headed citizens risking their own lives in attempts to prevent the outrage. The prisoner who was exhausted by the violence which he had already suffered at the hands o the mob had given up hope, and asked only for time to make his will and for a lawyer to draw it for him. Before the will was finished the crowd heard that the sheriff and the Sonora Grays had arrived. The sheriff ordered us to fire our revolvers over the heads of the mob and to make a dash for the prisoner. We found him with one end of the rope around his neck and the other over the flume. The mob yelled madly to haul him up. The sheriff cut the rope only to have another noose thrown over the man's neck. It was a terrific fight for the prisoner's life. Time and again we cut the rope only to have another one take its place. Once, in the wild excitement, a rope was placed around another man's neck, and he was drawn six feet into the air before the mob saw the mistake. For about ten minutes the struggle went on and for a time we thought we could save the prisoner but he was so injured that he could not help himself, and at last we were overpowered and he was hauled up more dead than alive. But the captain of the Grays had yet another trick to play, for as soon as the prisoner was pulled up above the heads of the mob, he ordered his men to fire at the rope, and the body fell to the ground again. It was a vain effort for the mob drew him up once more, and the leaders, to be sure of their victim, filled his dangling and senseless body with revolver balls. The mob leaders then gave orders to leave his body hanging there until Sunday night, and although thousands of men went to see the dangling corpse that day no one had the courage to take it down and bury it.

I had heard of men being hanged by mobs before, but this was the first lynching I had seen. During the fight two other men had been so badly injured that they died the next day. When I witnessed the bull-fight in Sonora, and saw the brutality of man towards dumb animals, I had concluded that these men had become mere brutes themselves and had struck their lowest level. But when I saw this worse than brutal mob, composed of people professing to be civilized, I made up my mind that human beings sometimes fall far below the brutes, becoming more savage and inhuman than animals, and possessing the full nature and spirit of demons of the lowest pit. During that same month a mob took a horse-thief from the jail at Sonora and hung him from the limb of a tree, in the middle of the street, and left his body dangling all day as a pretended warning to all horse thieves. Some months later two Mexicans were legally tried and convicted of murder before a jury in Sonora and theirs were said to be the first executions ever performed in accordance with the law in a California mining town.

That night when marching with the Sonora Grays to Columbia, I became acquainted with the sheriff and with several men of the military company, who invited me to come and drill with them once a week. This I did for four weeks, thus securing my first lessons in military tactics. I learned easily and the captain said that if I would join the company, they would make me their captain the next year. But I told him that I had been a floater since reaching California and had not stayed long enough in any one place to hold such a position. The Sonora Grays was the only state militia company located in a mining town in California and was composed mainly of young men who were not permanently located, so that it was difficult to keep up the organization. Those four nights of drill in the use of the old bungling flint-lock musket, with that company of daring spirits, fired the military spirit in me and poured a feeling of patriotism through my youthful system which kindled in me a soldierly ardor that has never quite died out.

General William Walker, of filibuster fame, had at this time just conducted an unsuccessful expedition into the State of Sonora, in Northwest Mexico and had been driven out with most of his men, barely escaping with his life. He was now getting up an expedition to Nicaragua, nearly three thousand miles down the coast. I told my partners that if I could sell my mining interest at a fair price I would join the expedition, for I believed Walker would succeed and that Nicaragua would become a prosperous country. But they told me that it would be sure death to join his expedition, and after learning more about the country and its climate, I decided that it was a doubtful proposition and stayed on our claim until it was all worked out.

January, 1856, had come, and I was again out of business with
nothing in sight, unless I searched for another claim. It looked to
me as if mining for gold was an uncertain business. I was still
boarding with Gilkey. Lyons was as yet in possession of our ranch
for the court had not decided the question of ownership. Gilkey
had become discouraged and despondent over the trouble and was
morose and ill-tempered, making it unpleasant for his family and
friends. The father and mother of this family, who once owned a
fine farm on the banks of the Grand River in Michigan and were
fairly prosperous there, died of old age soon after reaching California, and I have learned that afterwards the boys became rough
characters, often getting into trouble, and that three of them died
at different times with their boots on. Similar stories can be told
of too many once happy families who left pleasant and promising
homes to go to the Pacific Coast in the days of "Gold Fever," in
the hope of quickly gaining wealth. I decided to return to Michigan and sold my three thousand dollars worth of stock in the new
canal for two thousand dollars, which I added to the fifteen hundred
I had made working our last claim, packed my clothes in my carpet
bag and started for San Francisco. I travelled by stage to Stockton
where I stopped one day and then took the boat to San Francisco.

CHAPTER VII.

UNDER WALKER IN NICARAGUA.

I found San Francisco bustling with excitement. General Richardson had been murdered by gamblers, and as the authorities seemed unable to do anything to improve conditions a vigilance committee consisting of the best men in the city was organized, proclaimed marshal law, and ordered every gambler and outlaw to leave within three days. The committee also arrested, tried and executed two gamblers named Corey and Casey for the actual murder. At the end of the three days of grace all the gamblers, outlaws and pugilists remaining in the town, numbering over four hundred, were arrested, photographed and measured and then placed upon a sailing vessel bound for Australia with the warning that if they ever returned they would be summarily hanged. The city was intensely excited over this exodus when I arrived and there were also stories in the air regarding Walker's expedition to Nicaragua that increased the excitement. News had come that this expedition was practically sure of success, as the filibustering forces had taken possession of a large part of the country. Several of Walker's officers were in the city actively engaged in collecting funds to aid him, and secretly recruiting men for his force. This had to be carried on under cover as United States officers were watching every move and arresting anyone found to be engaged in filibustering. Two of Walker's lieutenants had been arrested and were in prison awaiting trial at the time of our arrival. But the recruiting was not stopped by these arrests. Even while the trial was going on I, in company with three young miners from Wisconsin, enlisted in the Filibuster's service. Our enlistment was under the following conditions. First, each of us took oath to divulge nothing as to our enlistment, nor to speak of it to anyone outside of our party of four. Secondly, the recruiting officer promised to furnish us with the money for the purchase of tickets to New York via Nicaragua on the regular passenger steamer *Sonora* which was the next boat to leave. Thirdly, we were to serve in Walker's regiment and in case the expedition was a success, were to be given our choice of a large tract of either farming or mineral land, and were also to have positions as officers in Walker's army.

If the *Sonora* arrived on time, she would leave San Francisco twelve days after our enlistment. The time until then was ours to use as we pleased. The first thing that we did was to send home what extra money we had on hand, and after consultation with a banker we did this by means of duplicate drafts, the buyer keeping the original and a duplicate being sent to the one who was to receive the money in case the buyer and the original draft did not appear. Two of the Wisconsin men who were with me sent home thirty thousand dollars and I remarked that if I had half that amount I would never join a filibustering party. They replied that they had left good homes to make a fortune, and did not consider thirty thousand dollars a fortune, that they believed if Nicaragua were conquered it would mean the fortune of every man who had a share in it. We spent most of our time until the *Sonora* arrived in seeing the sights in the city, and in visiting the vessels in the harbor. The only exciting occurrence that happened during this time was a mild earthquake that shook us out of our beds about midnight one night and sent us hurrying into the streets in our night clothes. The quake caused plenty of excitement, but aside from cracking the walls of some new brick buildings it did no damage.

The *Sonora* came in on time and went through the customary process of unloading passengers, cargo, and several boatloads of mail. Again the long lines formed at the postoffice; I suggested to my friends that if we took places in the lines and sold them to the highest bidder we would make more money in a day than Walker would give us for a month's hard service carrying a musket over the mountains and valleys of Nicaragua. They took up with my suggestion and so when the delivery windows were opened we were in line with our dinners and camp stools at window "S", the three Wisconsin men saying that there were probably more men doing business in the city under the name of Smith than under any other and that our chances of selling our positions would be better under the letter S than elsewhere. About one hundred men were in line when we took our places. It was three hours after we got in line before the window opened and men at the head of the line then sold their places for twenty-five dollars each but before we got near the price was down to fifteen dollars. We four had agreed among ourselves to sell out jointly for fifty dollars and just before we reached the window four business men paid us this amount for our places. We went to the rear again in a line now including two hundred men. To buyers who passed along the line we said that the four of us would sell our places for forty dollars, and one buyer offered to pay us that sum if we would hold our places until we got within ten men of the window. We accepted his offer, and he gave us ten dollars to bind the bargain saying that if he was not on hand to take our places at the time mentioned the deposit was ours. He was on hand with three other men at the appointed time, paid us the additional thirty dollars, and again we went to the foot of the line which was now longer than before. We repeated the performance for the third time, again getting forty dollars for our four positions, and then the business men having secured their mail and our ship soon being due to sail, we gave up the profitable business.

The *Sonora* sailed with more than seven hundred passengers on board. The trip took fourteen days, with one stop at All-'chapuleo for coal and water. At this stop the Mexicans came on board by hundreds and amused us by diving from the upper deck after small silver coins which we threw into the water and which they caught before they reached the bottom. The climax of the exhibition came when the captain threw a silver dollar into the air and ten natives dove from the wheel house for the prize. Our trip was a very pleasant one, as we had a well furnished table, good weather and no sickness. We had no means of knowing how many recruits there were for Walker on board as each man had been sworn to speak to no one as to his destination and purpose. On the morning of the fifteenth day we anchored in Salinas Bay, San Juan Del Morte, where we were landed in small boats, the recruits going first. A box of old muskets went with the first boatload of twenty-five men and there was an officer on shore to receive the men, form them into line and give them their arms. My partners and I were in the second boatload and in half an hour after we reached shore one hundred and sixteen young men, all from California, had been landed, armed and equipped for active military duty. The officer who received us read his orders, assigning as our first duty the guarding of the gold that was on board the steamer to Virgin Bay, on Lake Nicaragua, about twenty miles distant.

This California gold, in its native state, was packed in strong boxes and was on the way to the mint in Philadelphia. As General Walker was in control of the district the navigation company had called upon him to protect the treasure over the twenty miles of land transportation. At ten o'clock that morning two six mule teams started with the treasure for Virgin City and our company fell into line, half in front of the teams and half behind, with orders to be ready for an attack at any moment. It was a strangely dressed company of adventurers. Every man was dressed to suit himself. More than half of us were clothed just as we came from the mines of California, with thick boots, heavy wool trousers, a leather belt at the waist to hold up our trousers and to carry a revolver, a heavy woolen shirt worn outside the trousers with from from two to four rows of buttons extending from the shoulders down the front to the waist, and with hats of every style from a close fitting skull cap to a broad brimmed Mexican straw hat. One man, who had evidently been employed in an office, was dressed in a swallow tailed coat and high silk hat. Four Englishmen, seemingly just come over, were dressed in knickerbocker corduroy suits.

The command was given and we started on the first ten miles of the up grade trail, all of us in good spirits after our twenty-five hundred mile voyage. When we reached the top of the watershed, we could look down upon the great fresh water lake of Nicaragua, a splendid body of inland water, forty miles wide and more than one hundred miles long. At this point many of the passengers from our steamer who were mounted on bronchos passed us as they were anxious to reach the harbor on the lake and get aboard the other boat for the night. We made the twenty mile trip in six hours, and went into camp with a few others of Walker's soldiers who were guarding the town which had been captured only a few days previous. There were no wharves and the big steamer was forty rods from shore. As the lake was rough and unsafe for small boats that evening, the disappointed passengers were obliged to spend the night in the small Spanish town which had no hotel nor any kind of decent accommodations. Half of our company were kept on guard during the night, while the other half slept in five tents and were far more comfortable than the six hundred passengers who were stranded in the town. The wind went down towards morning and the people were taken on board. We received orders to go on board the steamer, cross the lake and proceed down the San Juan River to Fort San Carlos, where we were to await further orders from General Walker who was with his main force near Managua, the capital of Nicaragua, eighty miles east of us. Before the steamer was ready to sail, word came by special messenger that Walker and his men had been compelled to surrender and that the General was being tried by court martial at Managua. Our captain did not believe the story, which if true meant the downfall of all our hopes, and said that he would follow his instructions and lead us to Fort San Carlos.

At the foot of the rapids on the San Juan River the passengers and baggage were unloaded from the lake boat and transferred two miles by land around the rapids to a river boat. Here we again did duty as guard for the gold which we were protecting. The San Juan River forms the boundary between Costa Rica and Nicaragua, and runs through a tropical forest so dense that we could not see five rods back from the banks of the river. Alligators lined the banks, monkeys frisked and played in the trees and parrots flew screeching over our heads as we went down the river. We camped at the rapids that night and the next morning boarded two river boats. At noon we landed at Fort San Carlos where we found a company of fifty men, all Californians. I knew the lieutenant in command of this force for he had been a miner at Poor Man's Creek. He had heard of Walker's surrender and had determined to disband his company and to leave the country at once in order to avoid trouble. Our captain after hearing his story became convinced that the game was up and calling us into line explained the situation to us, advising us to get out of the country as soon as we could. He said that although he was a nephew of General Walker he meant to get back to the United States as soon as he possibly could as there was nothing that could be done here. He told us that we might take our guns with us, if we wished, as we would probably receive no other pay for our brief military service. Some of us carried our guns along and started for the river boat which was on its way to Graytown, where we could take a regular passenger steamer for New York. Eighty-five of our company decided to go to their homes in the different states while the balance of our number crossed the Isthmus again and returned to California.

Those of us who were going back to our homes in the States boarded the river boat which carried us to Graytown where we secured transportation on a New York steamer leaving that night. We were only too glad to bid farewell to Nicaragua. The trip required ten days, our only stop being at Havana where we delayed six hours taking on coal. I went ashore for a few hours and thought myself well repaid by the sights of the old Spanish town. The news of Walker's capture had been received by the Spanish with great rejoicing as his first expedition had been made to Cuba, where he had been captured and court martialed and where but for the interference of the United States authorities he would probably have been executed. At Managua the court martial sentenced him to be shot, but again the United States consul saved his life as well as the lives of several of his staff. But his failures and narrow escapes did not deter him. In 1858 he planned an expedition against Honduras, and he and his men, while on board a sailing vessel, were captured by a British man-of-war near the eastern coast and their plans came to naught. Once more and for the last time he left New Orleans in 1860 with over one thousand well armed recruits, landed them on the northern coast of Honduras and having captured several towns, proclaimed himself president. But the forces were too strong for him and he was finally compelled to surrender, and after trial by court-martial at Truxillo, he was shot on the plaza of the capitol grounds in September, 1860.

We encountered rough weather all the way from Havana to New York and most of us had a bad time with sea-sickness. We were seven days in making the usual five days voyage and land never looked so good to me as it did when we reached New York Bay. Some four hundred of the passengers, myself included were dressed in miners clothing and our first act upon reaching shore was to buy new clothes. My three comrades in the Nicaragua campaign left for their homes in Wisconsin and I accompanied them as far as Michigan.   The last stage of my journey was made on horseback, through the woods, to my mother's home where I was warmly welcomed by mother, sisters and brothers after my absence of four years.   And now at the age of seventy-two, as I write from memory the story of my experiences during those four years, it all seems to me like a far distant and pleasant dream.

CHAPTER VIII.

Still a Wanderer.

The first few days after reaching home were spent in visiting relatives and friends and in telling them the story of my experiences and the time passed very pleasantly. But after the novelty of being at home had passed I grew uneasy and restless and once more faced the question of what I should do. The ways of the people at home were so different from what I had grown accustomed to in my four years' life in California that I felt out of place, and determined to return to the Golden West at my earliest opportunity. The opportunity came through the excuse of visiting relatives in New York and placing my favorite sister in school there. We went by way of Niagara Falls where we stopped over for a day to see the sights, and then we visited our relatives in New York State. Having concluded my visit and placed my sister in a good school, I bade my relatives goodbye, and started for New York City intending to take the first steamer for Panama. I reached the city at evening and went at once to the dock, where I found that every berth on the boat had been taken and that if I sailed I would have to sleep on my blankets on the lower floor. In spite of the fact that I had roughed it for years I didn't like this idea and so decided to go to New Orleans with some other miners and sail on a boat which was due to leave there two weeks later. The trip appealed to me as it would give me an opportunity to visit Philadelphia, Washington, Baltimore, Cincinnati, Louisville, Harrisburg and Pittsburg.

The next morning therefore I took the train for Washington arriving at noon, and spent the afternoon in looking over what seemed to me to be a very dirty and dilapidated place for the Capitol of such a great nation. The next two days I spent in Philadelphia and Baltimore, which seemed more interesting to me than Washington. From Baltimore I went by rail to Harrisburg and thence had a delightful daylight ride through the mountains to Pittsburg. I took passage on a river boat that night to Cincinnati where I spent the following day. The journey from Cincinnati to Louisville was made by a small river boat and at Louisville, after a twenty-four hours' wait, we took a large Mississippi packet to New Orleans.

In all the cities near the border of the slave states, and on all the river boats the only public question which we heard agitated was that of slavery. Every man from the north seemed to be closely watched, and if he spoke a single word against the "beautiful southern institution" someone was sure to call him to order, or make dire threats against him. Our party of ten soon saw that it would be our best.policy to keep discreetly quiet on that subject while in a section entertaining views to which our own were hostile. It was during Fremont's campaign for the presidency, four years before the election of Lincoln and the beginning of the War of the Rebellion, yet steamboats had already been stopped on the Ohio River, northern men had been taken from them and landed on the Indiana and Illinois shore and told to return home and stay there and not to meddle with the peculiar institution of the South. Some of the Southerners on the boat inquired what our business was on the lower Mississippi River. Our reply that we were going to New Orleans to take the Panama steamer for California seemed to satisfy them, and to allay their fears of an invasion by us ten young men for the purpose of breaking up their "great and lawful institution." There were slaves on our boat who had been bought in Kentucky by southern slave holders. They were chained and handcuffed together, some of the younger and more powerful ones being chained singly, on the lower deck, to prevent escape. Our boat stopped at many places for passengers or freight and the towns and cities which we saw looked dull and dilapidated, as if dying for want of the enterprise and intelligence which would not enter as long as slavery was alive.

Upon reaching New Orleans we found that the boat from Panama was not yet in, and as it was not due to leave until five days after its arrival we sought boarding places for the length of our stay. After spending three days viewing the sights of the city, we learned that the steamer was quarantined at the mouth of the river one hundred miles below the city, because of cholera on board. The word cholera ended our hopes of reaching California by this route and of any desire we may have had for staying on in New Orleans. The next day we took a boat up the river to St. Louis, twelve hundred miles north, quite undecided as to what we were to do when we reached there. The prospect of an invasion of cholera put a sudden quietus to the slavery question, and on our way to St. Louis we heard very little said about it.

I was the only one of our party who had been in California and the rest expected me to answer the question of what to do next. I told them that there was yet plenty of time to reach California by crossing the plains, provided we could get mustangs to ride. Before reaching St. Louis we had decided to go to Fort Leavenworth on the Missouri River where we thought we could get an outfit for the trip. We stayed but one day in St. Louis, then took a Missouri River boat for Fort Leavenworth, where we found we could get our outfit. The commandant at the Fort told us it would be a hazardous undertaking to cross the plains at this time, however, as the Mormons were in rebellion and had stirred up the neighboring tribes of Indians to assist them. A large force, he said, was then being organized to subjugate the Mormons and to enforce the territorial laws of Utah. This body of troops was expected at the Fort within ten days and he offered us good employment until the expedition should start saying that we could accompany it. I told him that I had crossed the plains a few years before over the same route, and upon hearing this he asked me into his private office, questioned me about the country and said that if I would wait until the expedition was ready to start he felt sure that he could get me a position on the commander's staff as my knowledge of the plains would be of value In the meantime he offered me a job superintending the construction of a long line of temporary barracks and, as this was just the kind of a job I was accustomed to, I accepted it. The next morning all the men who had been with me for the past two weeks went to work for the government. Within a few days troops began to rendezvous at the fort, most of them coming by boat up the Missouri River. Two large trains of supplies composed of six mule teams with a few troops had already been sent forward to Fort Kearney, three hundred miles further west, and by the twenty-fifth of June, the main body of troops numbering three thousand men and composed of cavalry, infantry and three batteries of artillery were ready to move forward. At the last moment orders were received not to undertake the expedition until the next spring because of the lateness of the season.

This order caused me to change my plans once more and I con-

cluded to return home and make a new start. Some of my associates
left for their homes, two enlisted in the Light Artillery and two others
were given steady work at the fort as carpenters. I was offered a
good job but declined it and went back home by way of Chicago.
The last eight miles of my journey was made on foot in the night.
I found all the family asleep, and without awakening anyone went
to the room I had occupied three months before, and on the next
morning (July second) surprised them all by walking out to the
breakfast table just as they were sitting down. The surprise and
shock was too much for my mother, who supposed me to be in
California, and she broke down and sobbed on my shoulder. I told
them of my recent movements and of the incidents which had kept
me from getting back to California, and ended by celebrating the
anniversary of our independence with our family at home. I
decided to stay in Michigan until the next spring and then make
another start for the West. But my mother asked me why I could
not settle down among my friends, as I had a good piece of land and
money with which to improve it. She reminded me that I would soon
be twenty-five years old, and said that it was time for me to cease
being a wanderer and to make a home of my own. She urged me
so hard that I finally promised her that I would do as she wished.
On the sixth of July, therefore, I left my mother's home fully determined to go and clear the piece of new land I had bought of the
government before I left for California, which was located twenty
miles north of Grand Rapids.

There was no stage route to my claim so I was obliged to walk the
distance of seventy miles carrying my satchel and a new ax, the
most important tool in a new and heavily lumbered country. The
second night after leaving I reached the home of an uncle, within
eight miles of my land. I told him of my plans and asked him to
recommend a good chopper who would do his share of clearing forty
acres of land by the first of September. He recommended a man
whom he had hired recently, but said that I would have to pay him
the high wages of twelve dollars per month and board, as he was a
first-class worker. A message was sent to this man and he came to
see me that evening, and as I liked his looks I decided to hire him
for three months. He wanted thirty-six dollars for the three months
wages, and I told him that this was satisfactory and that if we got
forty acres chopped in good shape in three months, I would pay him

forty-five dollars. The next morning my uncle took his ox team and wagon and made the trip to the nearest store, six miles away, where he purchased a load of supplies for me and carried them to my claim. In the afternoon of the following day we began work putting up a log shanty, which we completed by noon of the second day. On the tenth day of September the forty acres of timber along the south side of my claim were chopped into five windrows, each eight rods long. I paid my man his forty-five dollars, left my ax and cooking utensils with a neighbor and started for my uncle's house. The next morning my uncle took his one horse buckboard and drove me to Grand Rapids, and from there I walked to my mother's home.

The following week the Michigan State Agricultural Fair was held in Detroit, and my eldest brother and I attended it. We walked the forty miles to Jackson to reach the Michigan Central Railroad. At Ann Arbor we stopped off for two days and visited relatives at Saline, my birthplace. From Saline we walked the fifteen miles to Ypsilanti and there took the train again for Detroit and the Fair. On our return home we visited the State Prison at Jackson, where the warden, William Hammond, who was a friend of ours, offered me a position as guard, which I accepted. The following day found me walking my beat as an armed guard on top of the high stone wall surrounding the prison grounds, with the promise of a place as overseer in the prison in three months. On January 1, 1857, I received notice of promotion to a position as overseer in one of the shops of the prison with an increase in pay. But the inside work was not what I liked and I soon gave notice of my resignation, to take effect the first of March. In the meantime I had written the officer in command at Fort Leavenworth, asking him if I could have the position which he had promised me the preceding spring in the expedition to Utah, if I returned in the spring. My letter reached him on the Rio Grande River, where he was stationed with his company on guard duty along the Mexican border. He replied that he had written about me to General Sidney Johnson who was in command of the expedition, and advised me to write to him personally. I accordingly wrote General Johnson informing him of my experience on the plains. I received answer that every staff position was filled, but that I could have an appointment as assistant wagon master if I would enlist in the regular service. This I declined to do.

CHAPTER IX.

When the first of March came I left the prison service and went home, but the western fever had its hold upon me and I was restless and dissatisfied. Crowds of settlers were at this time rushing to the new territory of Minnesota and I decided to follow them. Soon after I reached home from Jackson, I started for St. Paul by way of Galena, Dubuque, La Crosse and Winona, getting the first boat that broke throught the ice to St. Paul that spring. At St. Paul I took passage on the *Time and Tide* for the Sioux Agency, five hundred miles up the Minnesota River, beyond the historic Indian town of Mendota on the left bank and Fort Snelling on the right. Fort Snelling was located on a high rocky bluff, near the junction of the Mississippi and Minnesota Rivers, and was for many years the headquarters of the United States forces in the Northwest. Twenty-five miles above Fort Snelling the boat made its first landing at the stirring young town of Shakopee, named in honor of a celebrated Sioux chief. Fifty miles above Shakopee was Shaska, an Indian village, and following it came Belle Plain, a county seat of some importance where many of the passengers left the boat looking for land and many more came on board to go farther up the river in search of better locations. It was said that every piece of good land for two hundred miles above St. Paul had been located and laid out as a village plot or town site, with a hotel or store of some kind erected to start the place, and a saloon and blacksmith shop added as soon as the population made it possible. All these enterprises had been started during the two years time that had elapsed since the land had been purchased from the Sioux Indians. The river formed the line between counties and land speculators had located many "county seats" on the river, so that there was no plot of land which they offered for sale which was not "near a county seat."

We passed many new towns bustling with the constant coming of settlers from the eastern states and from Europe. At Le Sueur, one hundred and fifty miles above St. Paul, two hundred passengers left the boat and about one hundred came on board. We were carry-

151

ing a heavy load of freight for the Indian agencies, and this, with our crowd of passengers, made it very difficult at times for the stern wheeler to make much progress against the swift current.   When we came in sight of Kasota, Colonel Flandran, the Indian agent on board, told some of us that although it was ten miles by river to St. Peter, it was only one mile on foot over a good road and invited us to walk across and lighten the boat.   Nearly all of us took the walk.   The boat did not arrive until late and the captain announced to the crowd that was waiting, that he would not leave until four o'clock the next morning.

Morton L. Wilkinson, a young lawyer whom I had known at home, who was now a member of the Minnesota territorial legislature and also a member of the Constitutional Convention which was soon to be held at St. Paul, had been a passenger on the boat with Agent Flandran and invited me to go to the hotel and stay over night with them.   Colonel Flandran was a young westerner who had lived with the Sioux Indians for several years.   He was dressed in a buckskin suit, wearing his long, straight, light-colored hair hanging down to his shoulders.   He had a kind and pleasant word for everyone and was a favorite among all the passengers.   While at the hotel that night he became interested in my California experiences and kept me telling stories most of the evening.   Wilkinson had left Michigan for Minnesota the same year that I went to California, and he told Flandran that night that the reason he had not gone to California with me was because he could not raise enough money to buy an ox team.   Before and during the Civil War Wilkinson was United States senator from Minnesota and was considered one of the ablest and most loyal men in the Senate.

After a night's rest in a real bed, we boarded the boat early and were soon on our way up the river again, with one hundred less passengers than the previous day.   Our next stop was Mankato, thirty miles by river and ten by land, and it took us six hours to make the distance.   Mankato was then the largest town on the river but our stop was only long enough to let off some passengers, none being taken on.   New Ulm, a town settled by Germans from Cincinnati, seventy-five miles further up the river, was the next stop; here over one hundred Germans left the boat, while fifty others came on board for the trip up to the Indian agencies.   Three miles above New Ulm we came to the lands owned by the Sioux

Indians, which lay on both sides of the river and extended north to Big Stone Lake at the river's head and to the Dakota line. Soon after dark we reached Fort Ridgely where a large quantity of government supplies were unloaded, delaying us so that we did not leave again until daylight. At noon we arrived at the lower Redwood Agency, located on a beautiful prairie, skirted with timber and about two hundred feet above the river.

Colonel Flandran and Mr. Wilkinson invited the passengers to visit the agency to get an idea of the inside management of a United States government Indian Agency, during the distribution of the government supplies. Several thousand Indians were gathered from different parts of the reservation, all awaiting the distribution of the government supplies which were brought for them. Many of the Indians were at the landing place and cordially welcomed their agent, Colonel Flandran. Flandran invited Wilkinson and myself to a good supper and lodging at the agency that night.

The next day Wilkinson and I took the boat for Yellow Medicine or Upper Indian Agency, one hundred and fifty miles by water, where Flandran met us, having driven across the forty miles of prairie with his team of Indian ponies. The Upper Agency was two miles from the landing place, and since it was late in the day and the boat was to stay there two nights before starting on the return trip most of the passengers remained on board until the next morning. Wilkinson and I, however, got off and walked up the pleasant valley of Yellow Medicine River to the agency, which was located in a fine oak grove, one hundred feet or more above the river valley. The Agency buildings were of brick, which had been made by hand by the Indians. Here again we met Colonel Flandran and also Major Gelbraith, another agent, who had been sent as one of three men to investigate the condition and needs of those Indians who had sold their lands to the government for a small sum and had received their payment in goods for which they had paid exorbitant prices. Here I found another friend from Michigan, who had filled the contract for erecting the buildings of the agency. He was living at the agency with his family and I stayed at his house for two days.

At the end of our stay three other men and I hired Indian ponies, and, accompanied by an Indian guide, made the journey across country to the Lower Agency. It was a ride of forty miles, over a beauti-

ful prairie dotted with fine growths of timber bordering the streams
and lakes. We passed a number of small brick houses, built by
the government for Indian families who had chosen to adopt a
civilized mode of life, and to follow the business of farming. To
each of these families had been allotted eighty acres of land, a brick
house, sixteen by twenty-four feet in size and one and one-half
stories high, and the necessary agricultural implements. A white
man had been appointed for each group of several families to act as
instructor.in teaching them the white man's way of farming. On
this ride we frequently passed Indians dressed like white men, working with plows and harrows in the fields or making bricks, and we
saw two well built Indian churches. All these changes were the
result of two years of white men's control of these once wild savages.
Reaching Redwood Agency, I obtained lodgings with one of the Boss
Indian farmers who lived in good style in a new brick house.

The following day was the semi-annual payment day when the
Great White Father gave out supplies to his red children. The
payments were made partly in gold, but mainly in provisions,
blankets and other goods. A company of troops had come in from
Fort Ridgely to keep order during the payment. The Sioux braves
with their families, from as far north as the Canadian border and
for two hundred miles west, were on hand to receive their government pay at the two agencies. Children and the aged and feeble
who were unable to walk came on conveyances made of two long
poles fastened at one end to each side of a pony, the other end dragging on the ground and the poles covered with skins. Several
hundred such conveyances which had been drawn for hundreds of
miles, were in sight that day. Payment was made by number, each
family having been given a registered number. When the number
was called the head of the family presented himself for his allowance
for the next six months, less the amount which he had traded out in
advance with such traders as were licensed by the government to
sell to the Indians. Very many of these Indians found but little
coming to them and were left poor for the next six months, while
the traders who had made enormous profits on their goods, as the
Indians had no real idea of the value of money, reaped a golden
harvest. This ignorance on the part of the Indian and greed on the
part of the trader caused a great part of the dissatisfaction and
trouble, violence and war which this country has suffered in Indian

history. This Indian pay day was the only one I ever saw and it was very interesting to me.

The following day four of us hired a double team and driver to take us twelve miles across the prairie to Fort Ridgely. We crossed the river by ferry and were soon riding over a beautiful, unpopulated prairie. We reached Fort Ridgely at nine o'clock in the morning, where we found five companies of United States troops and two batteries of light artillery. We remained four hours, visiting the Fort and taking dinner with the soldiers. The fort was situated on a government reservation of several sections of land which had been selected when the treaty was made with the Indians and they were placed upon the reservation. A celebrated war chief named Ink-pa-du-ta and his band had never consented to the sale of the Sioux lands, had declared themselves independent, and early in March of this year had made an attack on the scattered settlers around Spirit Lake, near the northern line of Iowa, one hundred miles northwest of Fort Ridgely. They had killed all the settlers near the lake, and several families on the Des Moines River in Minnesota, carrying with them as prisoners four women whom they held for ransom. The names of these women were Mrs. Noble, Mrs. Thatcher, Mrs. Marble and Miss Gardner. Mrs. Noble and Mrs. Thatcher were unable to keep up with the band and, were killed soon after their capture. Mrs. Marble was ransomed by two friendly Indians who had been sent out for the purpose by the missionaries Riggs and Williamson and who gave for her freedom all the horses and guns they had, being later reimbursed by the governor of the territory. It was learned that Miss Gardner had been sold to a Yankton warrior and many friendly Indians offered their services to undertake her rescue or ransom. Three prominent members of the Indian church were selected for the work, one of whom, by the name of Otherday, later proved of great friendship and service to the whites at the time of the terrible Sioux massacre in 1862. These three men were furnished with four horses valued at six hundred dollars, a double wagon and harness valued at one hundred dollars, blankets and squaw cloth worth one hundred dollars and other articles amounting in all to one thousand dollars, with which to ransom the captive. They left on their mission on the twentieth of May and on the thirtieth reached the Indian camp of one hundred and ninety lodges of Yankton warriors and three of Ink-pa-du-ta's

band. They succeeded in ransoming Miss Gardner for two horses,
seven blankets, two kegs of powder, one box of tobacco and several
small fancy articles, but to secure themselves against Ink-pa-du-ta
and his fierce warriors, they had to obtain the escort of two sons of
the Yankton chief back to the agency. While this rescue party was
carrying out its work the governor and the commander at Fort
Ridgely were planning a movement against Ink-pa-du-ta and his
band to be begun just as soon as Miss Gardner was safe. On the
day that the commander at the fort learned of her safety he received
orders to join General Johnson with his force in the expedition against
the Mormons; this put an end to all hope of punishing the Indians
that Spring. Only a few of these events had transpired at the time
of our visit at Fort Ridgely but the entire story is told here as it
had a considerable effect on my movements. The news of the Spirit
Lake massacre was brought to the fort by the liveryman with whom
we were to go on to New Ulm and caused great excitement at the
post.

The ride across the plains was a lovely one. It was the most
beautiful country we had seen. We reached our destination at sunset and put up at a German hotel which furnished good accommodations. There was but one American born citizen in this town of
fifteen hundred people and he was a veteran of the Mexican War.
He owned the largest general store in town, which was housed in
the only brick building yet erected, from the top of which the Stars
and Stripes floated every day of the year. He kept both Indian and
German clerks in order to accommodate all his customers. The first
inhabitants of this town had come from Cincinnati two years previous, and since then more than five thousand other Germans had settled in the town and on farms in the vicinity. There were two beer
gardens in the town; one of them had an opera house connected with
it, which we attended that night, where we witnessed a German play.
The Ink-pa-du-ta massacre at Spirit Lake had greatly alarmed the
farmers in the vicinity and many of them left their homes and brought
their families into New Ulm for safety that night. The leading
men advised the building of a fort for their protection in case of an
Indian attack and a militia company was organized. Settlers out
on the Big Cottonwood River towards Spirit Lake, twenty miles
from New Ulm, came into town in large numbers and added greatly

to the excitement and fear.   In consequence of this alarm our night was a sleepless one.

The next morning we secured conveyance by lumber wagon to Garden City in the Blue Earth Valley, twenty-five miles southeast of New Ulm, where the men who were with me had friends and relatives living.   Our journey lay through a fine prairie country, across the Big and the Little Cottonwood Rivers and past several small lakes bordered with timber.   On each of the streams and lakes we found settlers living in log houses whose first inquiry was for news concerning the Spirit Lake massacre.   Each one was ready to move his family to some place of safety at a moment's warning. We reached Garden City a little after noon and found the people at work building a log fort around a large boarding house which was owned by the company erecting the grist and saw mill on the river.   My friends found their relatives all at work on the Fort, for many families had left their farms and had come into town for protection.   Most of the people in this section had come from Boston, Massachusetts, and knew very little about western life, or of the handling of an ax, the principal tool of the pioneer.   After dinner I saw how they were situated, bought a good ax, and went to work with them on the fort.   Before night I had gained such a reputation at that kind of work that I was chosen to boss the job.   In two days we had a half acre surrounded by a wall of logs ten feet high.   After it was finished and the women and children were placed inside, all felt more secure.   Reports continued coming in that made the situation look worse every hour.   Some families had already left the territory until the Indian question was settled.   I tried to quiet their fears by telling them that the New Ulm people had organized a militia company and had sent a committee to the governor for arms and ammunition.   Reliable news soon came direct to us from Fort Ridgely and the Indian agencies that Ink-pa-du-ta and his warriors had gone westward into Dakota.   The messenger bringing this news had letters with him from Flandran, Riggs and Williamson, and also from the Commander of the Fort, advising all the settlers to return to their homes as the danger had passed.   By the end of the week most of the settlers had returned home and were at work again on their farms.   I was given a good job in one of the mills which were being built.

I had been working at the mill for two weeks when a Norwegian settler living on the south branch of the Wattonwan River, twenty miles southwest of us, came riding into the village with the news that the Indians were burning and robbing the homes of the settlers on the river and that they were fleeing from the country. In less than two hours families that had left the log fort two weeks before were returning to it again, and that night it sheltered more people than formerly. Each report that came in was to the effect that the Indians were advancing down the river, plundering the vacant homes and stealing the stock which the settlers had failed to drive off with them. No one had been reported killed but every settler was on the run to save himself and family. Two days previous to this raid word had been received that Colonel Alexander's Regiment had left Fort Ridgely by boat and gone to Fort Leavenworth to join the Mormon expedition, so that there were no troops on the frontier for the protection of settlers, with the exception of the handful left to protect the Fort. This fact caused the settlers to lose courage for they felt that without the regulars there was no hope or safety for them except the entire abandonment of the country. Nothing gives a settler on the Indian border such confidence as the knowledge that he is protected by his government through the presence of an adequate force of regular soldiers. The regulars are the only force that the outlawed savages fear and that can keep them from plundering and killing scattered settlers. In the absence of regular troops the best thing for settlers to do is to organize militia companies. That evening, in our log fort, sixty men volunteered to sign the roll of a territorial militia company and I was elected captain, with a young man by the name of Pease for lieutenant. Pease was a picturesque figure; he had been brought up on the frontier and always wore buckskin.

We raised one hundred dollars that night and this sum was turned over to me with instructions to go at once to St. Paul, get arms and ammunition for the company and return as soon as possible. A team took us twelve miles to Mankato that night, and early in the morning we boarded a steamer down the river that landed us at St. Paul the next morning, in time to visit Governor Medary at his house before he was out of bed. He invited us to breakfast with him and at once ordered a team to be in readiness to take us to Fort Snelling. We first drove to the residence of Senator H. M. Rice, and the four of us were at Fort Snelling at nine o'clock where we secured sixty

Springfield rifles with cartridge boxes and plenty of ammunition. After dinner at the Fort, Senator Rice gave me his personal check for two hundred dollars, with instructions to use it in the best way possible to make our new territorial militia company comfortable. At two o'clock p. m. we had our equipment on board the steamer *Favorite*, the best and fastest boat on the river, and the next morning at ten o'clock we reached Mankato.   Teams and wagons from Garden City were waiting for us and we reached our blockhouse in time to give "The Garden City Sharp-Shooters," as we named ourselves, a drill that afternoon.   The experience and knowledge I had gained with the Sonora Grays in California, less than two years previous was of value to me now.   The boys thought from the way in which I formed them into platoons and drilled them in primary tactics that I must have been in the regular service.   For two weeks we kept up this drill daily, and stayed close to our guns waiting for orders. Letters from the governor and Indian agents which reached us at the end of the two weeks informed us that no one had been killed during this last raid, that only one house had been burned, a few cattle and horses stolen and several abandoned houses entered and goods carried off.   Less than forty Indians had been engaged in the raid, and these apparently only for the purpose of theft and of frightening the settlers into leaving the country.   We also received the welcome news that two companies of regular infantry had been ordered to Fort Ridgely to protect the settlers from further depredations, and that Ink-pa-du-ta and his followers had had nothing to do with the raid, but were in Dakota.   The settlers now went back to their farms and for years suffered no disturbance.

The citizens of Garden City and vicinity took a lively interest in our home company and raised four hundred dollars to build an armory on the public square for use as a drill room.   Our organization was kept up until the Civil War broke out and its presence gave the settlers in the vicinity a feeling of security from 1857 to 1861. With the beginning of the war the government ordered our guns and outfits sent back to Fort Snelling where they were used in arming the First Regiment of Minnesota Volunteer Infantry, said to have been the first volunteer regiment offered to the government in the war of the Rebellion.   This regiment had the credit of losing the largest percentage of men of any regiment during the four years' struggle for national life and liberty.   The guns which our home Militia

Company had used received their baptism of fire in the First Battle of Bull Run.

The financial crisis of 1857 struck Minnesota like a blight. The territory had experienced a great boom, in common with other new frontier territories. Villages and cities had sprung up like mushrooms in nearly every county in the eastern half of the territory, most of them built on borrowed capital on which interest was paid at from one to three per cent a month. When the panic came most of the new improvements became a dead loss to both borrower and lender. What little money I carried into the territory soon disappeared and in 1858 I could figure out without the aid of higher mathematics that my six years of hard labor in the west had been a financial failure.

I now decided not to try life any longer single-handed, and returned to Michigan where I married Miss Diantha O. DeGraff, to whom I had been engaged a short time, and whom I had known when a boy in Michigan. In November, 1858, we returned to Garden City and commenced keeping house in part of the log Fort which I had helped build during the previous year. My wife was an experienced school teacher and started a private school in our rooms which gave her pleasant occupation during her first winter in the new Northwest country. This was the first private school opened in that part of the country. I ran the only grist mill in operation that winter. About the first of January, 1859, it became so cold that the river froze nearly solid and the water wheels in the mill became a mass of solid ice. We could not start the wheels again until the following March, and most of the settlers had to grind their corn and wheat for food in hand coffee-mills or pound it in a mortar. As I lived in part of the house owned by the miller and worked for him, we managed to save out enough flour, meal and buckwheat to last until the mill ran again.

CHAPTER X.

THE SIOUX WAR.

During the years 1859 and 1860, Minnesota filled up rapidly with settlers. The government had a strong force of troops along the borders of the settlements and the Indians were kept on their reservations. But in 1861, soon after the Civil War began, the Sioux became bold and defiant and left their reservations without permission; scattered settlers on the frontier lost horses and cattle, and in two instances children disappeared, all of which occurrences were charged up to the renegade Sioux. In the spring and summer of 1862, Minnesota was called upon to furnish seven regiments of volunteers for the war. Two companies were enlisted from the Sioux reservations in the State. The Indian agents were nearly all opposed to the war and openly showed their joy at any reverse to our arms. The Indians, learning that the north was divided, became more bold, passing at will through the border settlements and causing an unusual feeling of uneasiness and alarm. Many families fled for safety from their homes to the larger and older settlements. An instance in our own family will serve to illustrate the annoyance we suffered. One day when my wife was alone with our little two-year-old daughter, two powerful, six-foot Sioux warriors came into the house without warning. One of them picked up the child as if to carry her off while the other offered my wife a large new brass kettle. My wife as decidedly as possible rejected their offer and they finally left, only to return later bringing two more Indians with them. They had the same brass kettle and carried in it a hog's head which they had stolen. They set the kettle heavily down on the floor, and offered it and the hog's head for the child, and, when they were again refused, went away deeply disgusted and displeased. These Indians were thirty miles from their reservation. When we told the incident to our neighbors we were warned to keep close watch over the child, lest she be stolen away by them.

Six months afterwards these same Indians were massacring hundreds of settlers all the way south from the Canadian border to the boundary of Iowa. In 1863, after the Sioux had been driven from Minnesota, it was learned that these prowling bands of Indians, one of which had visited us, had been sent out by Little Crow, the most warlike chief of the Sioux, for the purpose of locating the settlements, spying out their situation and strength and learning where to strike most safely and successfully when they commenced war the following August. The Sioux planned to involve the Winnebago tribe, and obtain from them over five hundred additional warriors to assist them in the attack on the Minnesota settlements. The situation looked so gloomy that in the early summer of 1862 I sent my wife and two small children to Michigan, where they would be out of danger. I did not see them again until the hostile Indians had been driven westward out of Minnesota. This hostile feeling on the part of the Indians located a few miles west of us, and of those on the Winnebago reservation, only two miles east of Garden City, taken together with the recruiting of the best of our young men for service in the war of the Rebellion, contributed to make the situation very unsafe for the people of the border settlements. The United States troops had all been ordered south from Forts Ridgely, Ripley and Abercrombie, only a sergeant with a handful of men being left to hold each fort and to protect its property. Every night for weeks, the hostile Indians held councils up to the time that Little Crow took the war-path.

On the morning of the nineteenth of August, 1862, two citizens from New Ulm came riding into Garden City with the news that the Sioux were massacring the settlers near Redwood Agency and Fort Ridgely. The advancing bands of savages were within a short distance of New Ulm at the time these messengers had left and couriers had been sent to all the valley towns, warning the settlers of the danger and appealing to them to hasten to the aid of New Ulm, the largest town in the Indian country west of Mankato. Within four hours from the time we received the news sixty men were enlisted, armed with such guns as could be found and mounted on farmers' horses. The men elected me their captain. During the excitement of preparation the ladies of the village prepared a good dinner and rations for our journey. At noon we formed into line and started for New Ulm, twenty-five miles to the northwest, the men and women who stayed behind cheering us bravely on and bidding us Godspeed as we rode away. All the men wanted to go with us but there were not enough horses to go around so some had to content themselves with wishing us good luck and warning us not to lose our scalps.

We followed the Mankato road three miles until we struck a fresh Indian trail leading from the Winnebago Agency towards the Sioux Agency and became convinced that a party of Winnebagos had joined the Sioux. We followed this trail a short distance, then turned to the right and struck out for the Mankato and New Ulm wagon road which ran on the south bank of the Minnesota river. We reached this road at the point where it crossed the Butternut Creek, about ten miles from New Ulm, where we passed through the first timber since leaving Garden City. At Butternut Creek we met four families who were greatly excited and were fleeing to safety with their teams and stock. They told us that it was sure death for us to go on as the Indians were out in large numbers, massacring all they could find and begged us to escort them to Mankato. They admitted, however, that they themselves had not seen an Indian for a week. This incident had the effect of alarming some of our boys for the safety of the families they had left at Garden City, and four of them decided to return home. They agreed to go with the four families and protect them as far as the fork where the main road to Garden City branched off.

Our little band was now decreased to fifty-six men. Soon after crossing the Creek we reached a large log cabin occupied by a Mr. Shaw who was the oldest settler in the country. He was over seventy years of age and for ten years his house had been a stopping place for all who travelled the road. We found him and three of his neighbors busy preparing the house for a siege. He regarded this work as merely precautionary, for he thought the Indians would not harm him and his wife, as he was well-known to the chieftains and had always treated them kindly. While we were talking with Shaw a double team drove up with a party of four land seekers, who intended staying over-night with "Uncle Shaw." They said that they had met and talked with a mounted party of Winnebagos about one hundred in number and that all in the party were young braves, well armed and decorated for war. These men were young fellows from Wisconsin and well armed. They had heard nothing of the uprising until we told them, when they at once decided to go with us. This addition made our original number good.

From Shaw's house on Butternut Creek we had five miles of open prairie before reaching Little Cottonwood River, and from the Little Cottonwood it was three miles to the Big Cottonwood. We made fast time, for it was getting late in the day and we were anxious to reach New Ulm before dark. While making the three miles between the Big and Little Cottonwood rivers we saw, about two miles to our left, a party moving towards New Ulm. At first we thought that this was a band of Indians, but our Wisconsin friends took a look at them through a field glass and said that it was a group of settlers with ox teams. As we galloped along the high bluff of the Big Cottonwood, we could look over the intervening timber and see the buildings of New Ulm nearly three miles distant. There was a beautiful clear sky and we could see the town plainly. Several buildings in the western part of the city were in flames and we concluded that the Indians had arrived. We had to go through a half mile of timber and willow brush to reach the open ground on the opposite side of the river, and many of us thought of the death that might be lurking behind those very willows if the Indians were in ambush. There was hesitation among my men as we neared the ravine, but I reminded them that we had already passed through two places fully as bad as this for an ambush and that if we turned back now we would have to pass through them again. I also told them that it would be far safer to go on into New Ulm from the eastern side than to go back, for if the Indians knew we were making for home over the road they would undoubtedly ambush us on our way. The situation was a critical one and there was no time to lose. My men still hesitated. Once more I urged them, telling them that I had been elected their captain but eight hours before, that we had fully agreed to go to the relief of New Ulm, and that if we retreated now after we were in full sight of those who so badly needed our help we would be disgraced forever. This was sufficient. There was a cheer from the company and a shout to lead them forward. I ordered them to follow in single file and putting our horses on the run we broke through the ravine and onto the prairie on the other side of the river. In less time than it takes to tell the story we were formed into columns of four and with our horses on the gallop entered the eastern part of the city.

As we reached the road running down the Minnesota River Valley, we met two companies of militia, one from St. Peter under command of Captain Dodd, the other from Le Sueur, commanded by Captain Saunders, one of the leading ministers of the Minnesota Valley. Both of the companies were mounted and they aggregated about one hundred men. We had just joined forces when down the road over which we had come there galloped a company from Mankato, under Captain Bearbour. This company consisted of about fifty men and raised our strength to a full two hundred. With Captain Saunders at our head, we swept four abreast through the main business street of the city as fast as our horses could carry us. We were within a half mile of the Indians before they knew of our presence, and we took them completely by surprise. They dropped their torches and scalping knives, mounted their ponies in the utmost haste and scattered each one for himself in the direction of the reservation. There appeared to be about one hundred of them. They had burned two of the breweries and twenty-one houses, and had it not been for our arrival they no doubt would have burned the entire town and massacred all the people that night, as there was no other armed force to check them.

We could not follow the Indians in the dusk, and so after they had scattered we returned to the city and took care of our horses as well as we could. Coffee was furnished us by the ladies, and with the rations which we had brought from home we had a good campaign supper that first night out. Colonel Charles E. Flandran, the Indian agent whom I had met at the Redwood Agency six years previous, had arrived from St. Peter during the afternoon and taken command of the city. He had placed the town under martial law and stationed guards on all roads leading out of the city with orders to allow every person to come in, but no one to pass out except such as held a permit from him. Nineteen dead bodies, mostly those of women and children killed inside the city limits, were brought in that evening. All had been scalped and terribly mutilated. They were laid out in a row on the floor of a blacksmith shop for identification and it made a scene such as none of us had ever witnessed before. Most of those who had left their families that morning to rescue others now felt anxious to return at once to the protection of their own homes. In eight hours after leaving our homes twenty-five miles away we had met the Indians in our first skirmish and driven them away; had seen the destruction of homes by fire, and gazed upon a score of mutilated bodies of women and children who had been tomahawked and scalped by the savages. Many of my men that night asked for passes to go home, but Colonel Flandran refused them, saying that if we all stayed we could whip the Indians here and prevent them from penetrating the more settled country to the east of us, while if we abandoned New Ulm we might lose the entire State. Most of my men were determined to go for they feared that their own families might now be in danger; four of them left their horses that night, escaped through the guard on foot and started for home. Two of these men went in the wrong direction and nearly lost their lives before reaching home. The next morning all but fifteen of my company signed a petition asking for passes to return home that they might protect their own families, and the percentage in the other companies was fully as large. Colonel Flandran called the captains together for consultation and the officers all agreed to stand by him. We admitted, however, that if our men were determined to leave that they would be of little use in case of an attack. My men had said to me that morning,—"If our families were in the east like yours, we would gladly stay and fight it out here. But place yourself in our positions and then answer the question as to what you would do if your own family was within twenty-five miles of you and exposed to slaughter?" I admitted that my first duty would be to protect my family.

The meeting of the officers that morning resulted in the decision to give passes to all the men who had families. Some of the men on leaving exchanged their rifles with those who stayed and who had only shot-guns, which were of little use in Indian warfare; others left their extra firearms and ammunition, for they all felt that we would have a hard fight on our hands. When those receiving passes had left I had fifteen out of my original sixty men remaining and this was about the proportion with the other companies. Some of the officers were in favor of evacuating the town but Colonel Flandran and most of us would not listen to this, as there were over two thousand recruits stationed at Fort Snelling who could be armed and sent to our relief within forty-eight hours. We decided to hold the town as long as we possibly could.

It was Wednesday, August twentieth, when most of our men

left us. The previous day the Indians had murdered people all along
the western line of Minnesota, and by Thursday night five or six
hundred refugees, many of them wounded, had straggled into
New Ulm seeking safety. Rude hospitals were made up for the sick
and wounded, while the few physicians in the town worked night and
day and the women volunteered as nurses. We were greatly encour-
aged by the arrival of four companies, one from Blue Earth City,
one from Shelbyville, one from Waseca and one from Henderson,
in all about two hundred men. On Wednesday night news was
brought in by two men, one of whom had an arm broken from a
rifle bullet, that fifteen miles away in a swamp near Leavenworth
on the Big Cottonwood River a party of one hundred settlers had
been surrounded by Indians. A force of one hundred men was at
once organized to go to their relief, leaving one hundred and fifty
to protect the city. During the day we had heard the cannon
booming at Fort Ridgely at the Sioux Agency, eighteen miles up
the Minnesota River, and we took this to mean that the main body
of the Sioux had attacked the fort. Before starting on this relief expedition which would lead us within ten miles of Fort
Ridgely, Colonel Flandran, who remained in command at New
Ulm, gave us orders to return at once if the firing at Fort Ridgely
ceased. We started out well mounted, taking several wagons
to bring in the sick and wounded. Before we got out of sight of
the city we began finding dead bodies, and before reaching the besieged settlers we had discovered sixty-five bodies of those slain
by the Indians. The firing at the Fort still continued. Though we
saw many scattered bodies of Indians, they all kept out of range
of our rifles. The settlers whom we relieved were all foreigners,
very few of whom could speak a word of English. After much difficulty we found out that they had been attacked by the Indians
on Tuesday, the nineteenth, and had been surrounded in the swamp
for three days, during which time six of their number had died and
still lay unburied. The wounded and the women and children
were put in the wagons and we started to return at once, not even
taking time to bury the dead, for an hour's delay might mean the
death of us all. We had only fairly started, when a man came gal-
loping up to tell us that three families with their teams were surrounded by the Indians only two miles away. We halted at once
while half the force went to the rescue. We found the wagons

within a half hour from our departure but even then we were too late to save the occupants, for all had been murdered and scalped.

We had just resumed our march when the sounds of the cannon at Fort Ridgely died out and we saw smoke and flames from that direction. This could mean but one thing and that was that the Fort had been captured by the Indians, who would now doubtless attack New Ulm with fresh forces. It was nearly dark and we were still fifteen miles by the shortest route from New Ulm. If we took this short route we must cross the Cottonwood River three times, each time passing through a ravine where the Indians might easily ambush us. Small groups of Indians were in sight watching us, and we knew that the main body was being kept informed of our movements. We decided to outwit them if possible, so, late that afternoon, made camp. As soon as night came we left our camp fires burning and moved away over the river road, reaching New Ulm before daylight on Saturday, August twenty-third.

The four Wisconsin men who had joined us at Butternut Creek while on our way to the relief of New Ulm proved to be made of the right kind of stuff for Indian fighting and acquitted themselves well. One of them was taken violently sick on Friday while on the Cottonwood trip, and on Saturday morning desired to start for his home. His companions promised him that he should go and early that morning these four men started for St. Peter, thirty miles down the river, where they were to cross by ferry. Soon after reaching the river they were attacked by a band of Indians, who had been sent out from Fort Ridgely after its capture to destroy the ferry, and three of them were killed.

After destroying the two ferries at New Ulm and the one on the road to Fort Ridgely in order to prevent escape from the town by those routes, the entire force of Indians who had been besieging Fort Ridgely for three days appeared at New Ulm and at nine o'clock Saturday morning made a desperate attack on the west side of the town. It was their plan to burn the city, murder all who were in it, and then to strike Mankato and reach the Winnebago Agency, where they felt sure they could persuade several hundred Winnebago warriors to join them in massacring the whites. They had been greatly disappointed in not cutting off our party that night on the Cottonwood River as they had planned to do; but our night march deceived them, and no doubt saved our lives.

This march was also one of the causes which saved the city and its people from destruction for if our force had been cut off the city could soon have fallen.

During the opening of the attack on Saturday two white men were seen, almost in front and a little to the right of the Indians, running towards the city from a narrow skirt of timber on the west side of the river bluff. They turned out to be W. W. Dooley and Henry W. Smith from Lake Shetook, sixty-five miles west of New Ulm, where there was a settlement of about one hundred persons, the farthest west of any settlement in the State. On Monday, the eighteenth, the Indians had attacked them and after defending themselves as long as possible, these two men, with their wives, who were sisters, and their six children started for New Ulm. Early on Wednesday the Indians had overtaken them and they were compelled to abandon their wagon and conceal themselves in the tall grass. During the day the Indians killed the six children and captured the two women, who were held prisoners for eleven months, until the Government ransomed them. The two men made their escape, and, supposing their wives as well as children to be dead, worked their way through the tall grass to the river and thence down to New Ulm. Their story is told here because they were later members of the cavalry company I commanded, though, before we were mustered into service, Dooley was made chief of scouts over seventy-five loyal Indians, with the rank of captain, which position he held until the close of the Indian war. H. W. Smith was a first-class soldier and served in my company until the regiment was mustered out. Both of them were out on the Dakota plains doing good service at the time their wives were ransomed and brought in and presented to them on the Missouri River. Who can imagine the feelings of those men at that happy surprise? Both men have since passed away, but the two wives and sisters, when last heard from, were still living together in Blue Earth County, Minnesota.

But let us return to the battle of New Ulm. This second attack was made on the west side of the city where many of the buildings had already been burned. The savages came on with their ponies on the run, yelling and whooping and singing their war songs, their naked bodies painted in all colors, and their feather head-dresses flying in the wind. They made a bold dash to cut off Dooley and Smith and this attempt cost them the lives of several of their warriors. For three days we had been busy throwing up breastworks at different points around the borders of the city, and between two and three hundred men were behind these breast-works, besides fifty or more men who were on horse-back. The Indians spread out before us like a great fan, riding back and forth, coming closer and closer, leaning on the opposite side of their ponies, and firing at us from under their horses' necks, their yells and war-whoops becoming more hideous as they came nearer. Suddenly a panic seized our men in the trenches and they made a wild rush for the center of the city, followed by the Indians, who yelled and whooped louder and more hideously than ever. When they reached the houses the savages stopped to plunder and set them on fire, and this looting alone saved us for it gave us a chance to check the panic of our men. Captain Saunders, the minister commanding the Le Sueur Company, was seriously wounded and fell from his horse. My horse was shot and killed from under me, either by the Indians or by my own panic-stricken men who fired as they retreated. Several men were injured while trying to check and rally the fugitives, some of whom never stopped, however, until they reached their homes from ten to forty miles away. Most of these runaways were killed by Indian scouts who had been sent out to guard the roads leading east from the city and to prevent our escape.

During the previous night Colonel Flandran had ordered a barricade built through the main street to serve as a protection for the refugees and their families who had come into the city, and also for a central rallying point if our men were driven in. This blockade consisted of wagons formed in two lines, one on each side of the street, each wagon stationed a few feet from the next one and a plank run in between them. This barricade was about forty rods long, with a space of eight feet between the two rows of wagons. It was almost completed when the panic occurred and most of our men stopped when they reached it. This, together with the fact that the Indians had stopped to plunder and burn houses, gave them time to recover their confidence and courage. That delay of an hour on the part of the Indians was our salvation. We rallied our men and determined to give the Indians the best fight they ever had. By noon they were burning houses in nearly all directions on the outskirts of the town. Up to this time no help had come. We had learned that one thousand men under General Sibley were at St. Peter, well-armed, but without ammunition. A large body of men appeared on the opposite side of the river near the lower ferry, which had been destroyed, but they left, being unable to cross. We found out later that they were two companies of militia from Henderson and Shakopee, who, seeing the city on fire and the ferry destroyed, concluded to return to St. Peter.

About two o'clock the wind began to blow strongly from the east and the Indians decided to set fire on that side, and burn us out completely. For that purpose about five hundred of their braves approached from the east. This was the direction from which we were expecting aid, and the report started that the advancing body of men, under Sibley, was coming to our relief. Captain Dodd was so certain of this that in spite of our protests he started out on his fine black horse to meet them. In vain we tried to stop him; he went on at full speed, until the Indians fired a volley at him, then turned back and fell dead before he reached us, pierced by many bullets. As the Indians would surely burn us out if they succeeded in setting fire to the eastern side of the city, Colonel Flandran saw that something must be done at once, and called for volunteers to drive them out of a thick piece of oak brush which ran alongside the Mankato road of which they had taken possession. As the call for volunteers was made I was struck in my left cheek with two buck-shot and momentarily stunned. I fell, and those with me, seeing that I was hit in the face, thought I was dead, and took my Sharp's rifle, Colt's revolver, and ammunition and were about to leave me, when I sat up. I walked to a nearby temporary hospital, where the doctor took the shot from my face and gave me a stimulant. All this occurred in such a short time that I was able to get my arms and join the volunteers in driving the Indians from their shelter in the brush. We had about one hundred of our best men, well armed and led by Colonel Flandran; we dashed into that brush with a rush and a war-whoop that made the Indians conclude we could fight and beat them at their own game. It was a bloody, close range, desperate battle. Many on each side were killed. Colonel Flandran's clothes were pierced with bullets in many places and his gunstock was shattered. A fine young man at my side was shot in the mouth, his tongue cut off, and he died the next day. In fifteen minutes we had driven them out of their ambush and they made no further attempt to burn us out again that day from that direction.

From movements of the Indians during the afternoon, we felt sure that they expected reinforcements and that then another attack would be made. When night came they built fires to the south and west of us, out of range of our guns, and held war dances all night long, preparing for the next day's battle. Colonel Flandran called a council of the officers, and we discussed the situation in all its phases. Some were for vacating the place that night, but others who knew the Indians better were certain that such a move would result in death to us all. We finally decided to burn all the buildings that were in the way of our rifle fire or that might afford shelter to the Indians in an attack upon our barricade. We burned about forty such buildings that night, barricaded the remainder as much as possible and lined their sides with loop-holes. Our best marksmen were placed in these houses, with instructions not to fire until the Indians came within close range. Ammunition was scarce and every shot must count. The women were engaged throughout the night in casting bullets, preparing bandages, or making coffee and carrying it around to the men, while the men kept busy strengthening the fortifications in every possible way. Some few who felt sure we would all be massacred the next day stole away and left for their homes; some of these reached home but more did not.

When Sunday morning came, our courage was high and we all felt confident that the Indians could not conquer us. During the night some of the men had made dummy cannon out of stove-pipe mounted on wheels and had placed one at each end of our barricade, where the Indians could see them. Indians are superstitiously afraid of cannon. Near the "cannon" we placed blacksmith's anvils to do the firing with, in case an attack was made in force. Soon after daylight we could see the Indians forming in large bodies to the east and south of the city. About fifty of them soon appeared to the westward for the purpose of drawing our men out of the barricade in that direction. They put on a bold front, came within rifle range and dared us to come out for a fair fight. But our men kept under cover and held their fire. In the meantime the main parties from the south and east advanced in battle array, their leaders mounted on ponies. They made a great display, beating Indian drums and other instruments, the noise of which, mingled with their war-whoops, seemed to encourage them to their work of slaughter. As they came nearer, it was clear that heavy reinforcements had been received during the night. Occasionally a gun was fired by them, but not a gun had as yet been fired by us. They were led by a chieftain dressed in white man's clothes, wearing a tall silk hat and mounted on a fine American horse, all of which he had stolen. They halted within twenty rods of the east end of our barricade, and then orders were given our men to fire. Such a volley as Indians rarely experience poured into them from the houses and the east part of the barricade. As soon as the smoke cleared away we saw the fatal effect of our fire, for the enemy were in disorder. At the instant of firing the volley, the anvils were also let loose several times for the moral effect, and we afterwards learned that the Indians believed we had secured cannon during the night.

They did not make a second attack, but withdrew about two miles to the westward where they held a short council on the high bluffs in plain sight from our blockade, and then disappeared from our view. As soon as they had disappeared we decided to evacuate the town. There were about two thousand people in the city, eighty of whom were wounded and dying for want of proper care, and there were less than thirty houses left standing for shelter, and provisions for only twenty-four hours. There seemed no prospect of relief from the towns below, so orders were given to have all the teams made ready to carry the sick and wounded to Mankato. By noon we were ready to start on our retreat. No sadder sight could well be imagined than that which attended our going. For five days the bodies of men, women and children had laid unburied in the little city and we could not stop now to bury them. Most of the buildings were smouldering ruins. Every inhabitant was a fugitive from his home, and scores of them were badly wounded. We knew that our hope of escape was a slim one, for if the Indians learned of our retreat they might ambush our column and massacre us all before we reached Mankato. It was a sad procession that started out from the ruins that noon. When about ready to start we found that a number of wagons were loaded with household stuff and this we unceremoniously dumped out in order to give space for the wounded and the women and children.

When nearing the Cottonwood River we met a relief train consisting of Captain Cox with two hundred men. But they had no provisions and so we did not turn back. Captain Cox countermarched his men and returned with us. Reaching the bluff of the Big Cottonwood, Senator Swift, who afterwards became governor of Minnesota, and who was at this time in command of the rearguard, noticed that the stars and stripes had been left flying from the Fuller Block, the only brick building in the city. He halted his men and called for volunteers to go back for the flag. His men hesitated and told him they thought it unnecessary to spend the time and run the risk simply for the flag. The sentiment attached to that flag of battle seized me and I offered to go back alone for it if he would loan me his own horse which was much better than mine. My offer was accepted and the rear-guard was halted to wait for me. The horse was a good one and I made the trip quickly and safely, and upon my return received the cheers of the men who thought the deed a dangerous one. We soon overtook the rest of our column and early on Monday morning reached Mankato, having kept on the march all night. Nine of the wounded died on the way. One of the women in the wagons was a Swede whose husband and three children had been killed in the rush to New Ulm, while she herself had been wounded. On that retreat from New Ulm to Mankato she gave birth to a baby boy, and I have recently learned that at the present time this boy, who was in truth born on the battlefield, is now living in Montana and is one of the millionaires of that State.

Upon reaching Mankato we found that most of the settlers in Minnesota were leaving the State for Wisconsin, being determined to place the Mississippi River between them and the hostile Indians before stopping. The stampede was caused largely by the burning of New Ulm on the previous Saturday and the report which had been circulated that all its inhabitants and those who had gone to their relief had been murdered by the Indians. Colonel Flandran decided that something must be done at once to stop the stampede, and called for three volunteers to take good horses and follow the three main roads through the State telling the people that the Indians had been whipped and were returning to their reservations.

I was one of the volunteers. I secured a good horse from Daniel Tyner, the sheriff of Blue Earth County, who had been in the siege of New Ulm and whose horse I had ridden after my own was killed. While the horse was being fed, I took breakfast with a Mr. Piper and his wife from Garden City. My shirt and left side were covered with blood from the wound in my face and Mrs. Piper wanted me to put on some clean clothes before I left. This I decided not to do, as I felt that my bloody clothing would be better evidence than any words of mine to the fleeing settlers that I had been in the fight at New Ulm, and would lead them to believe my message. Upon starting, Colonel Flandran handed me the following order:— "I have ordered Captain Potter, who has been with me for five days in the siege of New Ulm, to inform all settlers who are leaving the State on account of the Sioux War that the Indians have been whipped at New Ulm and driven back onto their reservations; and he is authorized to say to you that it will now be safe for you to return to your homes. I have empowered him to place guards on all roads and bridges to give this information, and also empower him to press any horse he needs into his service for these purposes. Charles E. Flandran, Commander in Chief of State Militia."

As I mounted my horse to start on my mission, a stranger stepped up to me and handed over a new Colt's revolver, belt and ammunition, with the words, "You may need this, keep it until I call for it." I strapped this belt over my own pistol belt and bidding the boys good-bye rode rapidly away. The first twelve miles was through a timbered country and I made the distance in an hour and a quarter. My first stop was at the Winnebago Indian Agency where I gave the agent the first news he had received of the result of the fight at New Ulm. Many of the Winnebagos were present and greatly excited. The agent told them the news by means of an interpreter and then called on one of the Boss Farmers to take six of his most reliable Indians and escort me through the reservation to Wilton, in Waseca County, just outside the reservation lines. We passed many settlers on the way, with their families, in wagons, and I told them of the defeat of the Indians and advised them to return to their homes. At Wilton we crossed Le Sueur River on a long wooden bridge where I stationed a guard with orders to let no teams pass going east, and to post copies of my orders on the bridge for all to read for themselves. Some of

the settlers became very angry and were disposed to force their
way across. As an illustration of the panic, I will mention the case
of one man who lived six miles south of Garden City, and who
owned six hundred and forty acres of land. He had left his home
in the night, with his family and two wagon-loads of household
goods and was determined to cross the river. He insisted that he
had seen Garden City on fire at the time he left, and althoug he
knew I had been in the fight at New Ulm believed that I was only
one of a few to escape, and that within a week the entire State would
be in the hands of the Sioux. He offered to give me a deed to all
his land, if I would give him enough for it so that he and his family
could get across the Mississippi River. I laughingly declined his
offer and prophesied that he would be back in his home within ten
days, which prophecy proved true.

From Wilton, accompanied by two other mounted men, I hurried
on to Waseca fifteen miles further east. On our way we met a
company of sixty mounted men from Dodge County to whom I
showed my orders, whereupon they returned with us to Waseca.
I had ridden my horse forty miles in less than six hours and he now
began to show signs of giving out. I told the captain of this
company that it was necessary for me to go on to Owatona that
night, and that I must have the best horse in Waseca. I also asked
him to have Colonel Flandran's orders printed and posted on each
road in the vicinity. While a horse was being secured the print-
ing was done, and, before I left, copies of the orders were carried
in every direction by the captain's men. By this time the buck-
shot wounds in my face had become very painful. I had a physician in Waseca examine them, who advised me to have them
attended to at once, as there was danger of blood-poisoning.
I told him that I would attend to the wounds as soon as I
reached Owatona but that there was no time for it now, as it was
nearly four o'clock and I had twenty-five miles yet to ride. Two
men of the militia company lived in Owatona and their captain
ordered them to accompany me. We passed many settlers hurrying
east across the Mississippi River, all of whom we advised to turn
back to their homes. Among them were several men who knew
me. The wounds in my face, my blood-stained shirt, and the
revolvers in my belt, convinced them that I had really been in the
fight and was telling them the truth. We reached Owatona at

seven o'clock, and gave the inhabitants their first information of the defeat of the Indians.

After having my horse cared for, I asked the landlord for a good surgeon to attend to my wound, and in less than five minutes two physicians were at work. In probing and cleaning the wound, they found a sliver which had been driven into my face. The shot had evidently first passed through the board of a fence which had afforded us a slight protection at the time I was wounded. I told the doctors that I had not removed my clothes for six days, and that I did not remember having had any sleep during that time. They brought me a clean shirt and pair of trousers in exchange for my bloody ones, but I told them that I believed my bloody clothes and wounded face, taken with Colonel Flandran's order had done more than anything else that day to keep hundreds of people from leaving the State and that I had better wear them to the end of my journey. I scrubbed up, however, and after ordering a fresh horse or team to be ready to start at twelve o'clock that night for Albert Lee, forty miles south of Owatona, and arranging with the doctors to have Colonel Flandran's orders printed during the night and distributed the next day I borrowed a night-shirt and went to bed. I got four hours of good sleep, my first in six days, and at twelve o'clock was called to take the night ride to Albert Lee, which I made with a good team and driver. During our six-hours' ride we were halted four times by camp guards put out to watch against Indians. We were well supplied with copies of the paper containing Colonel Flandran's order and the news from New Ulm, and these we distributed in all the camps of settlers along the road. At seven o'clock Tuesday morning we were at Albert Lee, bringing in the first good news they had received from New Ulm. We found here a great crowd of settlers rushing out of the State, as nearly all those located south and west of Mankato had taken a southern route to avoid crossing the Winnebago reservation. At this point there were two roads leading east to the Mississippi River, one crossing at La Crosse, the other going into the northern part of Iowa and crossing at Prairie Du Chien. Mounted messengers were sent out at once to notify those who had passed through town during the preceding day of the needlessness of their going farther. I concluded to stay over until noon and then ride to Wells in Faribault County, forty miles west. By this delay I got another

13

short sleep, which I greatly needed, and also a fresh poultice for my face. My bloody clothes attracted much attention, and many wild and foolish questions were asked me by men who were still so frightened that they insisted on getting the great river between them and the Indians.

After a good dinner I mounted a fresh horse and in less than six hours was in Wells. Here the news of the defeat of the Indians had already been received, and most of the refugees had gone into camp awaiting its confirmation before starting back to their homes. I found one camp where they were burying a woman who had died from fright; and another where a woman had died from exposure during the flight, showing me that there had been suffering other than that caused by the bullet or the tomahawk. I stayed over night at Wells where I found several men I knew, four of whom had gone with me to New Ulm and taken part in the first day's fight, and had then returned to care for their families. Next morning, the excitement at Wells having subsided and most of the families now preparing to return to their homes, I made arrangements for a fresh horse to take me back to Mankato via Minnesota Lake, Mapleton and Garden City, a distance of fifty miles. I met but few teams or camps on the way and the persons whom I did see were on their way home. At Mapleton I found most of our Garden City people in camp awaiting my coming, as they had heard that I was to return to Garden City that way. As I rode into their camp they gave me three cheers. The man in command of the camp was the one who gave me his horse to ride when I left for New Ulm in command of our militia company and the first question he asked me was what had become of his horse. I told him that in our fight the Indians had taken his horse with them to their happy hunting grounds beyond the clouds where he probably would be well cared for, as they knew he was a "brave" horse, because he was killed in the line of battle along with a number of them. He muttered that it was a good horse and someone would have to pay for it, whereupon I assured him that he should be paid if I had to pay him myself. I took dinner with the campers and tried to get them to go back to Garden City with me, but they declined to go until they were absolutely sure that all was safe.

I reached Garden City at sunset, without meeting a person on the lonely fifteen-mile ride. Of the population of four hundred in

this village the week before, not one was now left. I put my horse
in the stable and then went to some of the stores, two of which I
found open, and helped myself to coffee, crackers, cheese and
sardines. I took these provisions to my own home, made a fire
and got a good, hot supper. After supper I washed my week-
old, blood-stiff clothes and exchanged them for clean ones, and
having cared for my horse, went to the Williams store and camped
out for the night. My bed was a bolt of cotton cloth laid on the
floor and I had a roll of cotton-batten for a pillow, but no sleep
could have been sweeter or sounder than mine. After breakfast
I rode around town to most of the houses, finding the doors locked
and everything undisturbed and then started for Mankato supposing that I had been the only person in the town that night. I afterwards learned, however, that a Polish doctor with his wife and six
children, for whom there had been no conveyance when the rest of
the people left, had stayed over night in the log school-house. They
barricaded the doors and windows, making it practically a block-
house, and stayed there for four days until the people came back to
their homes. On the way to Mankato I met the Williams brothers,
merchants of Garden City, with two other men going back home, and
assured them that the village was all right and that their store was
undisturbed except that I had forgotten to make up my bed there.
They said that the people in Mankato believed the Indian War
was over, and were awaiting my report as to the condition of the
country I had been through. I rode on and soon reached Mankato
reporting at the headquarters of Colonel Flandran, where I was
highly complimented upon the execution of my mission.

Colonel Flandran informed me that he had been ordered to
establish his headquarters at South Bend, three miles west of Mankato, and asked me to act as one of his aides with the rank of first
lieutenant, my work to include the carrying of dispatches through
the Indian country and the command of special details of troops
sent out from headquarters. He also told me that I had been
elected the day before as first lieutenant of a company to be stationed at South Bend and that I would have all the work I was
looking for during the next thirty days. That night we took up
quarters in a large hotel at South Bend where our company of sixty
men, mounted on the best of horses, awaited special duty. My
first outside duty was the carrying of a dispatch to General Sibley

at Fort Ridgely where he was stationed with two thousand men, preparing to follow up and punish the Indians for the recent depredations and murders. I had a detail of twenty men on the trip and spent the night at the fort. While here I visited the hospital and saw ten wounded men, the only ones of Captain Marsh's company to escape death at the Indian ambush at the ferry crossing of the Redwood Agency. I also met others who had been wounded in the ambush at Birch Cooley near the Redwood Agency. These two massacres, with the later ambush of General Custer on the Little Big Horn in 1876, were the deadliest assaults made by the Indians in the nineteenth century.

My next dispatch duty of any importance occurred soon afterwards when I carried the news of General Sibley's victory over the Indians in the battle of Wood Lake, near the Yellow Medicine Agency, to Fort Snelling seventy-five miles away. I took only one man with me on this trip, as there was little or no danger. We made the ride in one day. After stopping a day at the fort and at St. Paul, I was ordered to take a picked body of sixty mounted men and report to Captain Cox who had been sent to Madelia with a company of soldiers to build a block-house for the protection of the settlers on this exposed point of the frontier. We started about dark, taking the shortest route straight across the unbroken prairie passing Loon and Crystal Lakes. We were aided by the bright moonlight until about midnight when clouds obscured the heavens and a driving rain commenced. We kept on through the rain and darkness, only being able to keep the trail by having a dismounted scout, carrying a tallow candle lantern, lead the way.

It was nearly two o'clock in the morning when we reached our destination and were halted by the guard at the block-house. The garrison had finished their fort with the exception of the roof. Our coming was a great relief to them, for four persons had been killed by the Indians in sight of the village during the preceding day and their dead bodies had been brought in. At ten o'clock that night a wounded Norwegian settler had come in from his home eight miles southwest of Madelia, on the south fork of the Wattonwan River, and reported that four members of his family had been killed, he alone having escaped. He said that the Indians were making their way up the river towards a settlement consisting of about twenty five families of foreigners who had just returned to their farms, thinking their troubles ended. I heard this story as soon as I reached the block-house and told Captain Cox that it meant sure death to these exposed families unless we went to their protection. He replied that he could not leave his post without orders. I told him that I had not been assigned to the post but had been placed under his orders and asked him if he would be willing to let me take my men to the rescue. He finally consented, but warned me that we might fall into an ambush and be annihilated as the St. Paul company had been at Birch Cooley only two weeks before. I knew that some of Captain Cox's men wanted to go with me and asked him if he was willing to let them go, but he would not consent as he said his company was under orders to protect the block-house. My company had rations with them, the cooks of Cox's company made us coffee and after a hurried breakfast we took the trail to the threatened valley. It was four o'clock in the morning when we started, only two hours after our arrival, and so dark that I could not tell how many men I had. As soon as it was sufficiently light to see, after we had gone several miles from the camp I rode down the double line and found that I had one hundred mounted men and three wagons loaded with infantrymen, instead of the sixty men of my own command. Occasionally a man volunteered that he belonged to Cox's company but intended to go with us.

About daybreak a dense fog settled down and we could not see a rod in front of us. I was riding at the head of the column with two pioneer guides, who were showing us the road, when a man suddenly appeared before us. He could not speak a word of English, but a number of my men were Norwegians and we soon learned his name. He proved to be one of those whom we were hastening to relieve. He had been shot in the breast just at nightfall and was holding his straw hat, which had been pierced with two balls, against the wound to stop the bleeding. He was sure that his wife and two boys had been killed at the time he was wounded. We learned that we were near his home, which was at a ford of the river, and that by crossing the river here we could save eight miles in reaching the settlement. Some of the men thought it dangerous to go down into the brush at the river bottom which would afford a fine ambush for the savages, but I knew that if we expected to reach the threatened families ahead of the Indians we must take every chance and gave orders to cross at once. When we struck the river bottom the fog was still so dense that we could hardly see twenty feet ahead of us, but as soon as we reached the high bank on the other side, we were above the thick fog and could see quite clearly. Here we found the badly wounded wife of the wounded Norwegian, hidden in a thick grove of plum trees near their log house, and told her that her husband was still alive and that they would at once be sent back to Medalia for medical treatment.

Leaving ten men to take care of the wounded couple, we hurried on to the larger settlement, travelling rapidly over the open prairie. About eight o'clock we reached the first house in the valley and found it deserted, but a kettle of potatoes was boiling on the fire and there was no evidence that the place had been disturbed. It seemed that the settlers had seen us coming and, believing us to be Indians, had spread the alarm and fled. It was three hours before we found them, the entire settlement having gathered in one house three miles further up the river where they had planned to defend themselves. It was one o'clock before we could get the people together with their teams and more valuable possessions and start back for Medalia. There were twenty-seven wagons in line and with the crowd of women and children we decided to take no chances but to return by the long trail over the open country. It was a distance of twenty-eight miles and proved a tedious trip for the people who had only just got back to their homes from the first stampede of over two hundred miles, as well as for us who had been in the saddle all night long. Late in the afternoon we saw four mounted Indian scouts on the opposite side of the river riding in the same direction as we were. They fired at us and then rode out of sight in the timber. This incident gave me some anxiety and I decided to send a dispatch to Captain Cox asking for immediate assistance. The two men with this dispatch returned at nine o'clock that night, saying that Captain Cox could not reinforce us, as most of his men were already with us and as he himself was in danger of being attacked in the morning. We continued our march without a stop and reached Medalia safely about two o'clock the next morning. At the trial of the Indian chieftains which took place the next December at Mankato, it was shown that only twenty-five Indians took part in the raids and massacres around

Medalia, but that this small number had killed seventeen settlers and wounded as many more, and had captured two white women whom they carried for fifty miles and then murdered upon hearing of the failure of their cause. The chief of this party was one of the thirty-eight hanged at Mankato on December 26, 1862. We remained at Medalia until these Indians were driven away, and then returned to South Bend.

Our thirty days' enlistment had now about expired. Colonel Flandran had received notice that Colonel Montgomery with the 25th Wisconsin Volunteers was to be stationed at South Bend, that the militia was to be mustered out and the Indians were to be pursued by United States troops under General Pope, whose headquarters were to be at Fort Snelling. The National government, however, was short on cavalry and called for a regiment to be raised in Minnesota for the Indian War. I received a commission to recruit one of the companies in this regiment and the day after the expiration of my thirty days' commission I led seventy-five men to St. Peter where we were to unite with twenty-five others whom Horace Austin had recruited. I was entitled to the command as captain from the fact that I had recruited most of the men. Austin who was well-educated and a brilliant lawyer wanted the command, and in order not to cause any delay in getting our muster rolls to headquarters first so as to become entitled to the coveted position as Company "A" in the regiment, I waived the point in his favor and was sworn in as first lieutenant. Austin had already served as captain in the militia and remained captain of our company until the regiment was mustered out. After the war he was elected circuit judge for a term of six years, leaving the bench to become governor of the State for two terms. He is now living in California, where I had the pleasure of meeting him again at the National G. A. R. encampment in San Francisco in 1903. Thomas F. West was elected second lieutenant. As I write this he is eighty years of age and living at Medford, Oregon.

As soon as the company officers were elected, Captain Austin and I took the stage for St. Paul, which we reached the same day, and handed in our company muster roll. We were told that ours was the first company to be put on record. By some kind of wire-pulling a Minneapolis Company was given letter "A," however,

and we had to put up with second place and be called Company
"B." The horses for the regiment soon arrived and were held
at Fort Snelling. Company "A" had the first choice of horses
and selected bays, while we selected all grays for Company "B."
The captain returned to St. Peter to look after his men, while I
remained to look after the horses until arrangements could be made
to get them and our equipment to St. Peter. In less than a week
we were mustered into the United States service, were uniformed,
armed and mounted, and ready for orders.

Most of the hostile Indians had now been driven out of the
State into Dakota, and the season was too late to follow them that
fall. Many had been captured and were under trial by court-
martial at Camp Release, one hundred miles up the river from St.
Peter. The court was in session nearly three weeks, and condemned
to death three hundred and twenty-one of the Indians who had been
implicated in the murders of defenseless settlers in the State.
The prisoners were brought to Mankato chained in pairs, where
they were confined in the barracks and guarded by our soldiers
until the president could review the proceedings and pass upon
the verdict. President Lincoln was not hasty in coming to a decision, and a great many in the State began to think that the condemned Indians would be set free, as many petitions had been sent
to him from people in the Eastern States asking for their release.
Fear lest these guilty wretches should escape justice led to several
attempts by the enraged settlers, who had suffered so terribly,
to surprise and kill all of the condemned prisoners. One attempt
came near execution. One hundred and fifty men, who had lost
members of their families in the attacks, banded together under
oath to kill these prisoners and were armed with revolvers and
officered by some of the best and bravest men in Minnesota. The
day and hour was fixed for the deed, but at the last moment one
of their own number betrayed the secret to the colonel commanding the regiment which guarded the prisoners, and their attempt
was frustrated. About the fifteenth of December President Lincoln's message was received ordering the execution of thirty-nine
of the chieftains included in the list of three hundred and twenty-
one who had been condemned. The order read as follows:

"Executive Mansion, Washington, D. C., December 6, 1862.

"Brigadier Gen. Sibley, St. Paul, Minnesota.

"Ordered, That of the Indians and half-breeds sentenced to be hanged by the Military Commission composed of Col. Crooks, Lt. Col. Marshall, Capt. Grant, Capt. Bailey, & Lieut. Olin, and lately sitting in Minnesota, you cause to be executed on Friday, the 26th day of December, instant, the following named, to-wit:— (list of names of thirty-nine.) The other condemned prisoners you hold subject to further orders, taking care that they neither escape nor be subjected to any unlawful violence.

"Abraham Lincoln, President of the United States."

On the morning of December twenty-sixth our company was ordered to march to Mankato and act as guard at the execution. We were in our saddles and on the way before daylight. The distance was only twelve miles, but the thermometer registered thirty-five degrees below zero, and before we reached Mankato many of the men had frozen ears and feet, and all suffered severely from the intense cold. At Mankato we met several other companies of our regiment who had been ordered here for the same purpose as we. Hundreds of angry men who had suffered at the hands of these savages were camped within sight of town. They were well armed and officered and were determined that the two hundred and eighty-two Indians who were not to be executed that day by the law, should suffer execution at their hands. Colonel Miller, who was in command of the troops had a force of fully two thousand men, including one battery of artillery, with which to protect his prisoners. The execution took place in the early afternoon. The thirty-nine Indians were ranged on one long platform and executed at the same moment, in sight of a vast multitude of people besides the two thousand troops. At the appointed moment W. W. Dooley, a former member of my militia company and a chief of scouts, whose family had been killed by the Indians at Lake Shetook, stepped forward and cut with an axe the two-inch rope that held the scaffold suspended and the entire number were plunged to death. The prisoners met their end like true soldiers of the plains. Missionaries who had been with them for years were permitted with them during their last days. When the time came for them to go to the gallows the braves asked to have the chains taken from their legs so that they could go in Indian style, single file. This was allowed, and they marched to the scaffold singing their Indian war-song, which was joined in by all the other prisoners. Each Indian placed the rope around his own neck and sang while the death cap was drawn down over his eyes. For five minutes after the scaffold fell everything was as hushed and silent as death itself. Then the crowd began to quietly disperse. The settlers who had formed in companies prepared to make an attack on the barracks, but Colonel Miller had his force well disposed to repel any attack, and the people saw that it would be foolhardy to make an attempt to storm the jail protected as it was by the force of disciplined soldiers. Nearly all the soldiers present were Minnesota men and many of them had had friends killed by the Indians, so that their sympathies were with the settlers and it was well understood among them that if an attack was made on the barracks, and they were ordered to fire on their own friends, they would do so indeed, but would see that none of the attacking party should get hurt. Fortunately the attack was not made and the settlers dispersed.

The executed Indians were ordered buried on an island in the river near the spot of their execution. All were to lie in one grave and a strong guard was stationed to protect their remains. That night our company returned to St. Peter. On the way several sleighs passed us at different times with only two men in each sleigh. The surgeon of our regiment, a Dr. Weiser, who was riding at my side, remarked that it looked as if those sleighs might have dead Indians in them in spite of the guard at the grave. I jokingly assured him that even if there were dead Indians in those sleighs, there was no danger of his losing his scalp to them. That night after reaching St. Peter and supper at the Nicolet Hotel, the doctor invited me upstairs to the third floor, saying that he had some valuable Indian relics he would like to show me. There on the floor lay three of the Indians that had been buried that afternoon and placed under a guard consisting of a full company of *live* Minnesota soldiers. The great mystery was how those Indians were smuggled out of the grave, in spite of the watchfulness of those guards. It was soon known to all that their bodies had escaped the grave and were distributed among museums and hospitals in this country and abroad.

CHAPTER XI.

The Dakota Campaign.

About March 1, 1863, four companies of our regiment were ordered to Fort Ridgely where we were thoroughly drilled for a month in preparation for the expedition planned by General Pope to enter Dakota in the early spring and punish the hostile Indians who had escaped the previous fall. The winter had been severe and many Indians had died from cold and hunger. Yet in spite of the severity of the winter several war parties returned to Minnesota in April and commenced their work of destruction. Our battalion had plenty to do to protect the settlements. One party of fifteen passed within three miles of Fort Ridgely and killed several people near New Ulm. Our entire battalion was ordered out by companies in different directions to capture this party. As Captain Austin was on court martial duty I was ordered to take the Company and strike the Cottonwood River near Sleepy Lake. Soon after starting we saw Indians on the opposite side of the river hurriedly making their way west, leading horses which they had evidently stolen from the settlers. They saw us as soon as we saw them and hurried off, but we gained on them so rapidly that they abandoned their stolen horses and scattered in different directions, each by himself. We had with us four half-breed scouts besides W. W. Dooley and his brother-in-law Smith, both noted scouts who had been in the siege of New Ulm. These men agreed that the Indians after separating would make for a certain point where they would meet, and that if we could make this point before they did we would stand some chance of capturing them. We started at once for this spot deciding to make Walnut Grove, twenty miles away, that night where we knew we would find hay for our horses, and log houses for shelter. We reached Walnut Grove about midnight and, after feeding our horses and making coffee, rolled up in our blankets for a few hours' rest with orders to start at day-light for Lake Shetook, fifteen miles away. Six miles brought us to the spot where Dooley's and Smith's families were overtaken and murdered the previous August. The men had not been there since

187

the occurrence and were greatly disappointed to find the swampy
ground covered with water, making it useless to search for the
bodies of their families. At nine o'clock we came to Dooley's and
Smith's homes at the south end of the lake and found that their
hay and grain had all been used by troops that had stopped there in
the fall. Here I divided our force sending twenty men under W. W.
Dooley seven miles up the east side of the lake to the Ireland Farm
at the north end where they were to secrete themselves and watch
for the Indians, while the rest of us returned to the south end of the
lake, crossing the Des Moines River, which was then high and full
of floating ice. The floating ice came near causing us the loss of
three men and horses in crossing. Beyond the river we found stacks
of hay and two log houses whose occupants had been killed by the
Indians, and here we made fires, dried our clothes and fed our
horses. We then divided the company again, leaving ten men with
the poorest horses to remain until five o'clock in the afternoon when
they were to go up the west side of the lake, while I took thirty men
and went to the Great Oasis, ten miles west, near the Pipe Stone, a
place of great resort for the Indians of the Northwest because of
the quantity of soft red stone out of which they made their pipes.
We met that night at Ireland's Farm without having seen an Indian.

We were now sixty miles from Fort Ridgely but concluded
to return by way of the Redwood River Agency which would make
the distance eighty miles. This route would enable us to obtain
forage and replenish our meagre rations at the agency, and would
also give us a chance to get game, so the half-breeds told us, in the
timber along the Redwood River. We started early, our route
taking us over an open prairie. A few men were sent out as scouts
on each flank, with the double object of locating the trail of the
hostile Indians, and of finding game which would be very
welcome to sixty men who had been living two days on dry bread
and coffee. The scouting parties and the main column were to
meet at Linn's Crossing on the Redwood River twenty miles from
our starting point. When nearing the Redwood the scouts on the
east flank saw five mounted Indians making north at a rapid pace,
and at once gave chase. The Indians crossed the river at Linn's
Ford and our main force came up just in time to see them pass out
of sight on the opposite side of the river. Twenty of us, mounted
on the best horses, crossed the river and followed them rapidly until

we again came in sight of them, when they separated and scattered in different directions making pursuit useless. We returned to the ford where the rest of the company had arrived and found that our hunting parties had secured quite a variety of game during the forenoon, including prairie wolves, foxes, badgers, and wild geese, which was already in the process of cooking when we arrived. The fresh meat afforded us a fine change from our bread and coffee.

By riding twenty miles that afternoon we would shorten our distance so as to be able to reach Fort Ridgely the next day. We made this ride and went into camp on the south bank of the river under very unpleasant conditions. It was a cold, dark April night. We had but one full ration of bread and took our supper on a half ration with our coffee. The horses had only dry dead grass with a little corn. It was so cold that we could not sleep, and sleepy and hungry as we were, we were not in very good humor. Our situation was so bad that we decided to push on twenty miles to Redwood Agency. We started at midnight. We were in a section of the country that had not been settled by white men and there was nothing to guide us but the narrow and almost indistinguishable Indian trails. Often our half-breed guides had to dismount in the darkness and feel for the way on their hands and knees and we made slow progress. Not even the glimmer of a single star broke the gloom of the night. We rode four abreast, and many of the men fell asleep on their horses. It took us eight hours to make the distance of twenty miles over the trackless plains. The Agency was deserted, but we found shelter, plenty of hay and about five bushels of corn in the ear. We used the logs of some of the Indian camps for wood to warm ourselves and cook by, and having divided the corn with our horses, roasted our share by the log fires and enjoyed it very much. We stayed here until noon and then proceeded on our way, reaching Fort Ridgely that evening, without the capture of an Indian or the loss of a man.

The companies which had been sent out in other directions returned either that night or the next day with the exception of the company ordered up the Minnesota River to Big Stone Lake, which returned on the sixth day bringing a single Indian who claimed to be a friend of the whites and who had voluntarily surrendered. Two days later I was detailed to take this Indian to Fort Snelling and deliver him to General Pope. David Quinn, a half-breed government interpreter who accompanied me was positive that this Indian was one of the outlaws who had participated in the last raid. We took our shackled prisoner in a two-horse wagon to St. Peter, placed him in the county jail that night, and after a day's stage ride delivered him to General Pope. The interpreter, Quinn, made an investigation of this prisoner and finally obtained positive evidence of his participation in the massacre. He was thereupon tried, found guilty and hanged at Fort Snelling in the fall of 1863.

I went on from Fort Snelling to St. Paul as I was expecting my wife and two small children from Michigan as soon as navigation opened on the river. Boats had already come up as far as St. Paul and the first one after my arrival brought my family, on their return to our home in Garden City. I went to General Sibley and obtained a furlough for one week so that I might go home with them and see them comfortably settled. The day after their arrival at St. Paul we took passage to Mankato on one of the first boats up the Minnesota River that spring, and thence obtained conveyance by wagon to Garden City. We found that most of the people had returned to their homes. Two companies of troops had been stationed in the village early in the winter and had built good log barracks, which gave the citizens a feeling of confidence and safety. In four days I had everything comfortably arranged for my family and then returned to Mankato, taking the first boat up the river to Fort Ridgely.

We had a busy time preparing for the summer campaign in Dakota. A large amount of supplies was sent up the river by boat to Camp Pope, which was the rendezvous of the expedition. Our entire force was composed of Minnesota troops consisting of three regiments of infantry, one of cavalry, two batteries of light artillery, two companies of half-breed scouts and one company of pioneers— in all over four thousand men. On account of the wild and unsettled nature of the country the expedition had to depend on its own supplies and we were accompanied by two hundred and twenty-five six-mule wagons of provisions and a pontoon train of forty six-mule teams for use in crossing the Missouri or other large rivers if necessary. Our expedition moved from Camp Pope on June 16, 1863. Our course was northwest, keeping to the valley of the Minnesota River, crossing many small tributaries and making from fifteen to twenty miles a day. The scouts were kept busy in advance and on both flanks, with orders to report at once if any hostile Indians were seen within ten miles of us. The pioneers located our camps and constructed earthworks every night. Ten days of this progress brought us to Big Stone Lake, near the eastern line of Dakota, where we camped one day in Brown's Valley, noted on account of its being the source of the headwaters of the Minnesota River flowing southeast into the Mississippi, and of the Red River of the North, flowing north into the Hudson Bay. From here our march continued northwest towards the big bend of the Cheyenne River, over one hundred miles away. After about fifty miles of this journey the scouts reported that the grasshoppers had destroyed all the grass in front of us and we halted while the extent of the devastated area was ascertained. It was discovered that it extended only about twenty miles, so the next day we crossed the barren prairie where not a spear of green grass was to be seen.

We reached the big bend of the Cheyenne River on July third, crossed the river and made our camp in a beautiful valley, where we remained while a detachment was sent to Fort Abercrombie, sixty miles northeast on the Red River, for news from General Pope and for the mail for our command. General Sibley assigned to me the duty of making the trip to Fort Abercrombie and offered me a force of five hundred men if I desired them, as he said he considered it a dangerous mission. I replied that if he would furnish me with sixty men from my own company, forty from any other companies he might select and fifty half-breed scouts under the command of Captain Dooley, I would undertake the service and would be back in three days. As the weather was hot I told the general that I thought it best to start at midnight. I returned from the general's quarters to my company, called the men into line and asked them if there were sixty who would volunteer for the service. Every man offered to go. At midnight we were in our saddles ready for the start. The scouts told us we would find water half way to the Fort, but nevertheless I halted the column as we crossed the river and ordered every man to fill his canteen as we were to pass through an enemy's country and might be delayed before getting half way. The night was warm and clear, a full moon was shining and we made good progress, so that by daylight we were twenty miles from our camp. Before leaving General Sibley's orders were read to us. These required us to keep scouts out in front and rear and on both flanks and to kill no game going or returning. Two sutlers' wagons, each drawn by ten mules, accompanied us to be loaded with supplies at the Fort. At daylight a dense fog settled down that detained us over two hours and when it lifted we saw within close gunshot six fine elk standing and looking directly at us. It was a severe test to the self restraint and military discipline of our men and to the power of the orders given by our commanding general. Some of the men looked at me as if to ask if I did not want elk for dinner. I shook my head and not a shot was fired, but how the spirit and appetite did rebel against the orders!

The sun soon came out bright again and we were on our way. It became very hot, but we kept moving, our scouts always on the watch for fresh signs of Indians. When in sight of a valley covered with scattering timber where the scouts had told us we would find water, a herd of buffalo that had been started up by the scouts came rushing down a ravine near the sutlers' wagons. The sutlers, who had probably not heard the orders read, or else did not think themselves under strict military discipline like the soldiers, fired into the herd killing one and breaking the leg of another, and before I fairly knew what was up, or could interfere, many of my men had joined the chase. Corporal Dudley of my company was charged by a large wounded bull and was so excited that in using his revolver he shot his own horse in the top of its head so that it fell as if dead. Seeing the danger of the fallen corporal from the enraged animal, I shot the buffalo in the head with my Sharps Carbine. The supposed dead horse recovered, and proved to have received only a scalp wound and Dudley rode him until mustered out.

This incident and the dressing of the game detained us another hour. When we reached the stream where we expected water, there was none to be found. The next watering place was at Wolfe Creek, twenty-five miles further on, and men and horses were already very thirsty. The scouts now came in with reports of a fresh Indian trail where a band had camped the day before, and Captain Dooley, their commander, was very uneasy. About noon we crossed another Indian trail which led like the other in the direction of the Canadian line. Later we learned that the Indians who left these trails had started out for Minnesota to renew their depredations on the settlers but that upon reaching Lake Traverse, a few miles north of Big Stone Lake and learning of the approach of General Sibley's expedition, had returned to a position near the Canadian line, where all the hostile Indians of Minnesota were then assembled. They had chosen this spot so that if attacked by our forces and overpowered, they could take refuge in Canadian territory, where our forces could not follow them. They also expected to receive reinforcements from the tribes located in Canada. After striking this last trail we moved cautiously. We reached Goose Creek Valley about four o'clock and within another hour found abundance of water to relieve the sufferings of the men and of the animals, whose tongues were parched and swollen from thirst. Major Camp, in command of Fort Abercrombie, had been notified of our coming and when he caught sight of us started out at once with fifty cavalrymen to escort us to the Fort. We were well provided for at the Fort after our continuous sixty-mile ride during the extreme heat of that fourth of July.

We had brought with us a six-mule wagon for the purpose of taking back the mail for the men of our expedition, which the major showed us, all ready to be loaded. I informed him that my orders were to stay at the Fort one day and to return the next, and so on the fifth we rested. The veterinarian of the Post informed me that five of our horses were unfit to return, and the post surgeon told me that three of our men would not be able to be back with us. On the morning of the sixth everything was ready for us to start on our return and we set out at two o'clock in the morning. Major Camp with one hundred men accompanied us part of the way. We reached our camp the next evening just at dark, without any incident of note having occurred and I delivered the mail at headquarters, made a verbal report—not including the story of our buffalo hunt—and received the thanks of the general for the success of my service.

Next morning the expedition was on the march again up the valley of the Cheyenne River. On the seventeenth of the month the general learned of a movement of the Indians Southwest from the border of Canada towards the Missouri River, news which was confirmed on the twentieth by three hundred half-breed Chippewas who were on their summer hunt for buffalo meat and skins and who visited our camp. This information necessitated a change of plan in order to prevent the Indians from escaping. About fifty miles south of Devil's Lake General Sibley established a fortified camp,

14

leaving there under a strong guard, the major part of his wagon train, together with the sick and injured men and animals. Travelling in light marching order and carrying twenty-five days' rations the balance of the command, eighteen hundred infantry, six hundred cavalry, one hundred pioneers, one hundred scouts, and two batteries of artillery started on a rapid march to intercept the Indians before they reached the Missouri River. On the twenty-second we crossed the James River, fifty miles west of the camp and on the twenty-fourth the scouts reported hostile Indians in large numbers under the command of Red Plume and Standing Buffalo near Big Mound, about sixty miles north of the Missouri River.

Positive orders had been issued against the killing of game, but these orders were not always obeyed. Lieutenant Freeman of my regiment and a few of his friends found the temptation too great for them, and while outside the lines hunting buffalo were ambushed and four of the party killed. A sergeant with two arrows in his body escaped to bring the news to the general. The scouts soon came in reporting that the main body of the Indians were within five miles of us. We moved forward a short distance and went into camp near the east bank of a large lake just west of the Big Mound. The pioneers started throwing up earthworks and the cavalry and infantry were drawn up in line of battle while Riggs and Williamson, the Indians' former missionaries were sent to treat with them. Large bodies of Indians appeared in plain sight near the top of Big Mound, and Dr. Weiser, surgeon of our regiment, who had lived with the Indians several years, mounted his horse and rode up to the painted warriors, several of whom he greeted as old friends. As he rode back and passed our lines, Colonel McPhail said to him, "Doctor, I expected to see you killed." The doctor replied, "They will not kill a medicine man. They are my best friends." He stated that there would be no fight that day, as the Indians said they intended to surrender. Nine companies of our cavalry had been sitting their horses for three hours, drawn up in line of battle under a blistering sun, awaiting orders. Riggs and Williamson finally returned, bringing with them two white boys whom the Indians had taken in Minnesota the year before and whom they now returned as an earnest of their good faith. The savages asked that General Sibley meet them in council.

At this news Dr. Weiser became so confident of their peaceful intentions, that he again mounted his horse to visit them. He disobeyed orders in doing this and paid no attention to our attempt to dissuade him. Off he went up the hill, dressed in full uniform and his horse on a gallop, but before he reached their lines a number of shots rang out and he fell dead, pierced with many bullets. His orderly who was with him returned unharmed. The battle was soon raging. The Indians spread out and advanced rapidly upon us, some on horseback, others on foot, all shouting their terrible war cries. Colonel McPhail ordered our nine companies of cavalry forward at a gallop, while Colonel Brooks with the 6th Minnesota Infantry on the double quick made for the left flank of the Indians to cut them off from their camp. Both batteries followed close after the infantry and cavalry. The Indians were soon on the run and we hot after them. As we reached the top of the hill a heavy thunder storm broke over us. As we charged down the opposite side of Big Mound, Indians firing at us from front and right flank, private Murphy and his horse fell dead at my left. At the same instant Colonel McPhail, who with drawn sword was directing our men to cut off the Indians directly in front of us from their main body on our right, had the sword struck from his hand, while my horse fell to the ground. My horse was soon on his feet again and after a few staggers went forward in the charge as if nothing had occurred. I thought that he had been shot, but after the fight when we went back to get Murphy's body we found that a bolt of lightning had struck him, killing him and his horse, disarming the colonel and knocking my horse to the ground.

On we went in the charge as fast as our horses would carry us, driving the savages through their camp, which they abandoned, leaving behind tons of buffalo meat and other heavy articles which they could not carry in their hasty flight. Colonel Crooks' Infantry and the batteries soon came up and we set fire to the camp and abandoned articles, and took up the trail of the fugitives directly towards the Missouri River. We soon overhauled them and then began a desperate running fight. One of Sibley's aides reached us with orders to return to headquarters, but Colonel McPhail did not understand the orders to mean to return at once, so we did not slacken our pace. The fugitives finally turned upon us in their desperation, but we quickly put them to flight again and in the last five miles of the running fight before darkness overtook us forced them to abandon nearly everything they had stolen the previous summer from the Minnesota settlers, as well as valuable furs and buffalo robes which they had taken since leaving their reservations. Many of our soldiers found bundles of mink, otter, and beaver skins, and it was said that one of the sutlers had a wagon load of valuable furs when the regiment returned to St. Paul. As the darkness came on another aide galloped up with emphatic orders to return to headquarters at once. We were now eighteen miles away from headquarters and after the severe service and excitement of the day had a long and trying march back, arriving at headquarters just at daylight, thoroughly worn out. We were all disgusted, feeling that Sibley ought to have brought his headquarters to us on the field, as then we would have been able to capture the Indians before they crossed the Missouri. The next day we laid over to bury our dead consisting of two officers and seven men. There were more than one hundred dead braves stretched out on the route of our pursuit.

I had in my company of cavalry a fine young man by the name of Andrew Moore who came from the Blue Earth Valley, south of my home in Garden City and who stood six feet two inches in his bare feet. In this fight at Big Mound three Indians hid in a buffalo wallow on a hill at our right from which they kept up a persistent fire upon us. Colonel McPhail gave orders to Captain Austin to deploy to the right, under protection of the hill, cut off these marksmen if possible and drive them from their position. Within two minutes we were in their rear. They fired at us and then tried to escape. Two of them were killed and the other one threw down his gun and offered to surrender, but some of the men fired and wounded him. He instantly turned, ran for his gun and fired before any one could shoot him, the ball striking Andrew Moore in the abdomen. He, as well as we, knew from the nature of the wound that he could not recover. We carried him in an ambulance with us to the Missouri River, but being on the move and having no proper treatment, he died on the twenty-fifth, and we buried him with military honors on the bank of a beautiful lake. We marked his grave with a large mound of stones and named the lake after him. The most pathetic feature of the case was that while he knew he could not live he hoped and longed to be able to reach home and look once more upon the faces of his wife and children before he died. Ten years after his death the valley in which he was buried was well settled, and a railroad ran along the bank of this lake, which was still known as Moore's Lake.

When we overtook the savages again they were within twenty miles of the Missouri River. They had received reinforcements and gave us battle at Stony Lake. The whole country in our front seemed covered with mounted Indians. Our columns were halted while our batteries threw a few shells into their midst which put them to flight. Indians cannot stand the fire of artillery and the bursting of shells when the range is too great for them to use their rifles. This fight, which occurred in the morning, did not last over thirty minutes and by nine o'clock we had driven them back until we reached a point several miles from the river's bank, yet overlooking the broad valley. It was a beautiful day, the sun shining bright and clear. Across the river on the highland opposite, some fifteen miles away, we saw bright flashes of light reflected to us. At first we thought these to be the glitter of the sabers of General Sully's command, which had been ordered up the south side of the Missouri, to act in concert with us in the capture of these Indians. But our scouts soon disillusioned us by saying that the flashes of light were from small oval looking-glasses which the Indian warriors were proud of wearing, and which they used both for ornament and for signalling. These flashes, they said, were made by Indians who had crossed the river and were signalling to those who were still on this side. General Sibley had relied on capturing the families of the Indians before they could cross the river, believing that if he had the women and children in his hands the warriors would quickly surrender. The half-breed scouts told him that the Indians could quickly make rafts out of willows overlaid with buffalo skins to take their women and children over and that unless we hurried they would escape capture. Seeing a large body of Indians making for the timber that skirted the river, we galloped rapidly forward to reach them. As we were entering the river bottom the scouts brought in several Teton Sioux whom they had just captured. This tribe belonged on the other side of the river, and said that a large body of their tribe had come to assist their brothers in crossing the river, and that they had seen nothing of General Sully's white soldiers. The timber was too thick to get our horses and artillery through and we delayed while the pioneers chopped a road through it for us. When we reached the bank the Indians and their families could be seen on the opposite side. A few shells from the cannon quickly drove them from sight again.

Convinced now that the Indians had escaped him, General Sibley sent his favorite aide, Lieutenant Beaver, to order the artillery to return, but before reaching his destination the lieutenant was shot down by Indians, still secreted in the lumber. A second aide reached the destination, the artillery was recalled and we went into camp about dark on a level mound with Apple Creek bordered with a thick growth of willow brush on one side and a heavy body of timber on another side. The mound was from ten to twenty feet higher than the bottom on which the creek willows grew and its banks were steep, so that it was an excellent camping place. Strong earthworks were thrown up and a heavy guard placed that night. Just at daybreak several shots were fired from the timber, four of them passing through our company officers' tent, though too high to do damage, and one of them wounding my horse and disabling him for several weeks. A small party of Indians also made their appearance from the brush along Apple Creek and tried to stampede our horses, but we stopped their little game with a few shells from our batteries and all was quiet again. The rest of the Indians evidently escaped across the river that morning. Alarmed and mystified at the failure of Sully's command to co-operate with him, Sibley sent his scouts down the river to learn what had become of them. They returned on the second day with the news that Sully's supply boats had grounded on a sand bar one hundred and fifty miles below, and that he had been unable to push on. While the scouts were out on this duty, we buried Lieutenant Beaver and his orderly with military honors. Beaver was a young man of English birth who had hunted large game in Africa and had come to St. Paul with two other young Englishmen to spend a season hunting large game on the plains and in the mountains of the west. Finding that it was inadvisable and dangerous to carry out their plans while the Indians were at war, they offered their services to General Sibley for his expedition, were given lieutenants' commissions, and served on his staff as volunteer aides without pay. They were well educated and we understood that they belonged to noble families. Lieutenant Beaver was the oldest of the three and always claimed the honor of carrying dispatches where the bullets flew thickest, and now after three months' faithful and courageous service, he laid down his life on the banks of the upper Missouri River, five hundred miles west of the border of civilization. His two comrades felt his loss keenly and resolved to avenge his death. They continued to fight the Indians and both of them lost their lives on the frontier before the war closed.

On the third day after the Indians had crossed the Missouri, co-operation with General Sully having proved a failure, Sibley ordered a return to Fort Snelling. It took us four days to reach Camp Atchison, the fortified camp where we had left our supplies and a part of our force. On reaching this camp we learned that the scouts who had been left here during our absence had captured the son of Little Crow who was the chief disturber in bringing on the Indian War. Little Crow's influence had been so great that he had actually persuaded the Indians that they would drive all the settlers out of the country west of the Mississippi River if they would follow him. They followed him but instead of the glory which he had prophesied they had found themselves driven away from their reservations and homes out onto the bleak plains of Dakota where they suffered and starved the next winter as the result of their war with the whites. Then Little Crow's followers had turned against him, saying that he had deceived them and could lead them no longer, nor live among them, and that it would be safer for him to go and live in the white men's country than to stay with them. So he left them and taking his son returned to Minnesota, where he was recognized by a settler who shot him on the spot. His son escaped and fled into Dakota again, and there while searching for his mother's family had been captured by our scouts near Devil's Lake. He was taken to General Pope's headquarters at Fort Snelling where valuable information was obtained from him. He was then imprisoned at Rock Island with the Indians who had been condemned to death by court martial but had been saved by the reprieve of the president. Later these murderers were taken up the Missouri River and liberated in Montana, where, in June, 1876, most of them took part in the battle of Little Big Horn River, aiding in the massacre of the gallant Custer and his five companies of cavalry. It was believed at that time, and is still thought by the old settlers, that if those Indians condemned to death by court martial had all been executed at Mankato, the battle and massacre on the Little Big Horn would never have occurred. The bitter enmity of these savage chieftains and their burning spirit of revenge, was in my opinion the direct cause of the Montana uprising.

The day before we reached Camp Atchison, a body of one hundred men under command of a Captain Fisk, all well mounted and well armed and carrying two pieces of artillery stopped at the camp on their way to the newly discovered gold fields in Montana. Major Atchison, who was in command, tried to persuade them not to go on as they were almost sure to be attacked by the Indians. But they felt confident that they would have no trouble, since they were well mounted and armed, and were sure that they could protect themselves until they reached Fort Benton, at the great North Bend of the Missouri River, where there was a small garrison of United States troops, so Major Atchison's words had little effect and they moved on. When they were about fifty miles from Camp Atchison the Indians attacked them one morning before they had broken camp, and killed four of them at their first fire. They held the Indians off with their artillery the first day and that night two of their best men crawled through the Indian lines and hastened to Fort Atchison for assistance. These couriers reached Camp Atchison just at daybreak. Our force had come in the day before and General Sibley soon had four hundred cavalrymen and one battery on the way to their relief. We reached them at twelve o'clock that night. The next morning about two hundred Indians came in sight to reconnoitre, and perhaps to make an attack. Before they fairly knew what was up the charge was sounded and four hundred mounted men were on their heels and a battery pouring shells among them. This reception was too much for them and they quickly scattered over the plains as fast as their ponies could carry them. We soon returned from the chase, reporting five Indians killed. Thus delivered, Fisk and his men were glad to return with us and acknowledged that but for the prompt relief they must all have been slaughtered. We were soon on our way back to camp and within forty hours after setting out on the relief expedition we were safe in the fort again without the loss of a man.

The morning after our return Camp Atchison was broken up, General Sibley with the infantry and one battery, marching by way of the Cheyenne River and Fort Abercrombie, while Colonel McPhail with six companies of cavalry and the other battery, took an easterly route running south of Big Stone Lake to Fort Ridgely. I was in

McPhail's division and we saw no signs of Indians on our way. Colonel McPhail was a Minnesota farmer and knew but little of military tactics or discipline. He knew that there was little possibility of meeting hostile Indians and so gave us an easy time on our home march. Buffaloes were plenty and we had hunting parties out each day, bringing in an abundance of fresh meat for the command. We arrived at Fort Ridgely about the tenth of September. During our absence General Pope had constructed two lines of stockades, reaching from the northern line of Iowa to the border of Canada. These stockades were from ten to twenty miles apart, depending upon convenience to wood and water, were made of prairie sod and included accommodations for men and stables for their horses. The first lines of stockades ran on a line parallel with New Ulm, and the other was from ten to twenty miles west and parallel with it. A small force of cavalry was stationed at each of these stockades to assist in capturing any bands of Indians that might come within these lines which practically covered the entire settled portion of the state. These stockades proved of great benefit, as the Indians soon learned that it meant capture or death for them to venture within them.

As our regiment, by the terms of its enlistment, could not be sent into service in the Civil War and as the Indian war was now practically over, after two months at Fort Ridgely we were ordered to Fort Snelling to be mustered out. The Sioux War on our northwest border occurred during the intense anxiety of the Civil War. Although it was of considerable magnitude itself, and was fairly successful as a campaign, it was hardly noticed by the country at large for the attention of all was absorbed in the changing fortunes of the far greater and more important conflict in the South.

CAPTAIN THEODORE EDGAR POTTER

From a photograph taken at St. Paul, Minnesota, in 1864, in the uniform of the 11th
Minnesota Infantry

CHAPTER XII.

UNDER THOMAS IN TENNESSEE.

After our regiment was mustered out, many of the young unmarried men re-enlisted and went south to take part in the War of the Rebellion. I went home to Garden City and spent the winter with my family. In the spring Indian war parties again entered the State and began their depredations and murders. One evening a band of fifteen attacked a small settlement at Willow Creek, only twelve miles southwest of Garden City, killing several families and stealing a number of horses. I learned the news at ten o'clock the same night and saddling the old war horse that had borne me through the Dakota campaign started for the nearest stockade, which was twenty miles west of us, to notify the garrison. I passed through Madelia where I gave warning to the settlers, then hastened on to the stockade. The commander immediately dispatched a courier to the next stockade in the line, twenty miles west. He furnished me with a fresh horse and I rode twelve miles north to the next stockade, where my sudden arrival in the night stampeded some of the cavalry horses. Twenty-five mounted men were immediately sent southwest to try to pick up the trail of the murderers. After breakfast at the stockade I returned to the post where I had changed horses, intending to return home by way of Willow Creek. Here, however, I found that the entire force had been sent out to the northwest and that no warning had been sent to the stockade ten miles southwest of them. I therefore mounted my own horse which was now rested, and carried the news to this stockade and finding that there were others that had not been warned rode on south to still another one. At this last stockade the news had just been received and the cavalry were in their saddles ready to start when I rode in. I gave them what information I had, especially as to the direction taken by the troopers from the other stockades. It was now ten o'clock in the morning and as I had ridden fully sixty-five miles in twelve hours, I felt the need of a little rest. I remained at this post for dinner, then started home for Garden City, forty miles away. I passed through Willow Creek, the scene of the massacre on my return, and found that five persons had been killed and ten horses stolen. I reached home at nine o'clock that night, having been gone twenty-three hours, during which time I had ridden over one hundred miles and had not had a wink of sleep.

As the result of my journey the party from the second stockade which I notified struck the trail of the Indians about ten o'clock that morning and soon overtook them. The Indians hid in the thick brush near a bluff and finally escaped in the night leaving the stolen horses behind them. The next morning another party of troopers struck their trail and followed it until they had killed or captured the entire band. That ended the Indian raids in that part of the state for the spring and summer of 1864. Such was the animosity against the Indians after this massacre that one of them could not have passed through the state safely even if he had had the stars and stripes wound around him.

Major Brackett, who had taken an acitve part in the pursuit of the Indians, obtained a commission to raise a battalion of cavalry to be mounted on Canadian ponies for frontier service. He asked me to raise one of the companies, but my wife objected so seriously that I declined. I sold my old war horse, that had seen service in the Sibley campaign, to M. T. Fall of Garden City, who was commissioned as first lieutenant in Brackett's battalion, and so it saw two years more of service in Indian fighting.

Soon after this raid the federal government called upon Minnesota to furnish another regiment of infantry for service in the south and Governor Miller sent me a commission to raise one company of this regiment in Blue Earth Valley. The command of this company was promised to me if I desired it. I soon had the company made up, consisting largely of men who had already seen service in the Indian war. My wife believed that I had fully done my part and that I ought now to stay at home with my family. I told her that the war would soon be over and that I thought it was my duty to go. The company gathered at Mankato to choose their officers before starting for Fort Snelling and I told them that, although I had recruited the company and was by right entitled to the command, yet on account of the fact that my wife was confined in bed, our youngest child being only five days old, I would relinquish my right to the command. But the men would have none of this, telling me that I had recruited them and was their choice for captain and that they would not be satisfied to go to the front under another officer. In spite of my objections they unanimously elected me captain, and left the choice of the other company officers until we reached Fort Snelling. There was nothing for me to do but to go if my men were to go at all and I proceeded with them to Fort Snelling, making this distance of seventy miles in two days by wagon train, where we were mustered in as "Company C" of the Eleventh Regiment of Minnesota Infantry. As soon as we had been mustered in I called on the governor and told him how things were at home. When he had heard my story he granted me a furlough so that I could stay with my family until the regiment was ready to leave for the south and said that if my wife was not well enough for me to leave by the time of the departure of the regiment he would have the furlough extended for me. I returned home where I found my wife much better and reconciled to my going south. I remained at home a week and so arranged affairs that my family would be comfortably provided for during my absence, and then returned to Fort Snelling just in time to go South with the regiment.

We marched from Fort Snelling to St. Paul, where we were taken aboard a river steamer which had two large barges lashed one to each side, the whole furnishing comfortable quarters for the one thousand men. Our regimental band played "The Girl I Left Behind Me" as we left the city. We debarked at LaCrosse, Wisconsin, which was the nearest point to a railroad, and the next day proceeded in freight cars to Chicago where we camped for two days in one of the city parks before we could obtain transportation for Louisville, Kentucky. At Indianapolis we were transferred from the cars which we had occupied from Chicago to the airy upper decks of two freight trains which were filled with fighting humanity below. This change detained us another day. At Jeffersonville, just opposite Louisville, we camped for one night and the next day crossed the Ohio River to Louisville by ferry. Here we were detained three days, for our officers were determined to have something better in the line of transportation than the tops of old freight cars for the balance of our trip to the south.

In Louisville we were soon made aware of the fact that we were in an enemy's country. All the way from St. Paul to Jeffersonville we had been greeted with hearty cheers and demonstrations of loyalty. But no sooner had we crossed the Ohio River than the cheering stopped and we met with the frowns, scowls and sneers of people who did not dare express their insults openly but who showed us as plainly as they dared how they hated the soldiers wearing the Yankee blue. Upon reaching Louisville we marched up one of the finest residential streets of the city where the homes of the wealthy rebels were situated. We were halted in this street while our regimental officers arranged for transportation to Nashville, Tennessee, and during this halt it commenced to rain heavily. We had become thoroughly drenched when Lieutenant-Colonel Ball, who had seen hard service in the First Minnesota Infantry and who was temporarily in command, sent orders for us to take shelter from the rain on the porches of the residences which lined the street. This gave much offense to the disloyal and we were ordered off the porches by the owners but we paid no attention to such orders, maintaining our protected positions. We remained on these porches for five hours when the order came to fall in and we marched back, as we supposed, to entrain for Nashville. Instead of this we marched to a large tobacco warehouse which was nearly empty and which the owners had been requested to throw open to us for shelter until transportation was provided. The owners, being rebels, had refused and had guards at the locked doors to keep us out but these were thrust aside, the doors broken open, and we secured good quarters for the balance of our stay.

Up to this time our regiment had been in command of Lieutenant-Colonel Ball, as Colonel James B. Gilfillan, who had been promoted to the leadership of the regiment from a captaincy in one of the Minnesota regiments then in New Orleans, had not yet arrived. Lieutenant-Colonel Ball had received a telegram from him that he was on the way by boat and would join us at Louisville. He was one of the early pioneer settlers of Minnesota and so we officers decided to give him a real western pioneer reception on his arrival. We met him at the boat and escorted him to the United States Hotel where Lieutenant-Colonel Ball had secured the largest parlor for the occasion. Nearly all the officers had served in the Indian war and we conducted the reception in approved Indian style. All except Lieutenant-Colonel Ball sat in a circle on the floor with our feet curled under us, while he brought the colonel into our circle and introduced him as our Great War Chief, whereupon we uttered ugh! ugh! in recognition and welcome. The colonel then made a war speech to us, his braves, saying that if his warriors would follow him the great war would be closed before many moons. When he had finished his harangue the colonel was handed a large Sioux chief's pipe made from the famous red pipe stone of Minnesota that one of our men had brought with him and he smoked with us the pipe of peace. At the close of these ceremonies refreshments consisting of some of the best of coffee and some of the hardest of hardtack were served. After refreshments an officer started a Sioux War Chant, which brought us all to our feet and we took part in an Indian war dance which closed the exercises of the evening. I wonder whether any other military officer during the Civil War was ever given just such a reception by his comrades?

The day after our colonel's arrival the regiment was called into line and marched through the main street of the city to a large open field where we had our first regimental drill. Reports showed that every company was full and that there was not a man on the sick list. Most of our men had seen service before, so the officers found their task as drill masters an easy and pleasant one. The regiment made a fine appearance with its full complement of men. In 1864 it was a rare sight to see an infantry regiment with its full quota of one thousand men. Old soldiers who had served three years inquired what brigade was going to the front as we marched by, newly uniformed. Many questions were asked, and remarks made about this Minnesota Brigade for we were not taken for raw troops. The day following our first regimental drill we left at noon for Nashville via the Louisville & Nashville Railroad, our travelling accommodations being the best we had had since leaving St. Paul. We reached Bowling Green at dark where we were detained until next morning, as guerillas had burned a freight train on the track. That night our men received ammunition and the next morning our two trains moved out cautiously, passing the wrecked freight train where an immense amount of army stores had been destroyed. At several places on the line we saw spots where trains had been destroyed. At the railroad tunnel thirty miles north of Nashville, the guerilla General Morgan had earlier captured a passenger train, robbed its passengers and then run the train into the tunnel and set it on fire, thus putting the tunnel out of commission for several months, during which time passengers and freight had to be transferred over the hills by six horse mule teams. The tunnel, however, had been entirely repaired when we passed over the road.

We reached Nashville about dark and were marched a distance of about three miles to a camping place near Fort Nigley and the Chattanooga Railroad. For the next ten days we were stationed at this place, details being made from our regiment each day to guard freight trains to Chattanooga, the guards riding on top of the loaded cars. This was a dangerous duty in a country infested with bands of guerillas, who were worse to fight than even the wily and treacherous Indians. After ten days of this duty orders were received to fall in and march to the Louisville and Nashville Depot. We were delighted at the orders expecting that we were to be sent to Sherman's Army, but to our great disappointment we were detailed by companies for guard duty to keep the railroad communication open from Nashville to the Kentucky line. Our regimental headquarters was established at Gallatin, a town of about four thousand population, twenty-five miles north of Nashville. A negro regiment had preceded us in this guard duty and had built stockades of poles and split logs set upright which afforded rather poor shelter. My company was stationed at Richmond Station, five miles north of the Kentucky border, and the first work that we did was to build ten small log houses, each accommodating ten men, which made comfortable quarters for all of us. We sent out patrols of six men each twice a day and these met similar patrols from the stations to the north and south of us, each company making daily reports to headquarters.

The country near our station was well settled. There were several large plantations in the vicinity most of which had been abandoned by their owners who had enlisted in the rebel army, while the youngest and ablest of the slave men had joined the Union forces. The non-slave holding population was mostly loyal and many of the men of this class had entered the Union ranks. The section was therefore almost equally divided in sentiment and there was now deadly animosity between former neighbors and friends. We were told that during the six weeks of their stay, the colored regiment that had been on guard before us had lost nearly one third of their number by guerillas who had picked them off, that the government had found it almost sure death to use them as railroad guards, and so had sent them to the front where they made good soldiers.

In sight of our camp lived a family, consisting of a man and his wife, three sons and one daughter. They had a small plantation and ten slaves. The father was a pronounced Union man, and had offered himself for service in the Union armies but had been refused on account of his age. His three boys enlisted in the Confederate army and his daughter entered the Confederate hospital service while the mother claimed to be neutral. The two youngest boys were killed in battle and the girl came home. The oldest boy had become captain of a band of guerillas which operated in the rear of Sherman's army, destroying railroads and murdering Union soldiers and even non-combatants. This band was known as Harper's Guerillas and operated in unison with another band of outlaws known as McKay's Guerillas, both bands doing most of their work along the line of the road we were guarding. McKay shortly previous to our arrival had been surrounded with a few of his men in a log house near Gallatin and upon their refusal to surrender, the house was set on fire and all had perished. The survivors of McKay's band joined Harper, thus giving him a party of one hundred and fifty men with which he committed an outrage nearly every day. As Harper's old father, mother and sister lived near our camp he was careful not to let his band kill our patrols, because he feared that if he did so his people would be molested. The camps on either side of us did not fare so well. One Sunday two men from the station five miles south of ours left their camp without leave, taking their guns with them, and went to a church two miles away from the railroad. During the service some guerillas of Harper's band rode up to the church and called on them to come out and surrender. After they had surrendered and given up their arms, they were shot down in cold blood and their bodies more savagely mutilated than any which I had ever found mutilated by the Sioux Indians. Word was left with one of the church members to tell the officers of these men to come and take care of their bodies. I later talked with men who were present at the church at the time and who told me that the occurrence caused very little excitement, the preacher going on with his services and closing them at the usual time as though nothing unusual had happened.

Government engineers came to our camp soon after our arrival and located a place for us to build a strong block house of hewn timbers twelve inches square. This block house was of octagonal shape

15

and large enough to accommodate one hundred men. The building of this block house, with our patrol duties, kept us very busy up to the Battle of Nashville. As soon as it was known that General Hood with his army was marching towards Nashville the guerillas became more active than ever in our vicinity, attempting to destroy all railroad connection between Nashville and the north in order to hinder the bringing of reinforcements and supplies to General Thomas. For four weeks before the battle of Nashville not a day passed during which the railroad or telegraph lines between Bowling Green and Nashville were not cut. At the time of the battle of Franklin Harper's Guerillas cut the railroad ten miles north of our station at a point where there was a steep grade, derailed two engines pulling a train of thirty cars loaded with army stores, uncoupled the cars near the engines, and let the train run down the steep grade and crash into another train which was coming up, finally setting fire to the wreckage of the two trains. Three soldiers in charge of some officers' horses were on one of these trains. As soon as the news of the wreck reached Nashville, I was ordered to take fifty men and proceed at once to the scene of disaster. We reached the spot about two o'clock in the morning and found a condition of appalling confusion. Among the wreckage were the remains of these three soldiers. They had been shot and their bodies cut up into small pieces by sabres to gratify the brutal lust of these worse than savages. Fully one thousand soldiers were soon on the spot as witnesses of this ghastly atrocity. With the entire force we cleared the road of wreckage and enabled trains to pass to Nashville that evening. Within the next week we caught and executed five of the savage brutes who perpetrated this outrage but this only rendered the others still more desperate, causing them either to drive every Union family out of that part of the country or to kill them in cold blood. Many of the refugees sought shelter in our camps, appealing for protection. An old man of eighty years with his wife, who had been a neighbor and friend of the Harpers, was ordered to leave his home but did not go. Thereupon the brutal guerillas, many of whom were from well-bred families, took all animals which the old folks owned, killed them in their dooryard in front of the house and threatened to shoot the old man if he attempted to move the carcasses. Friends in Louisville heard of the plight of this family and took care of them. A man by the name of Pardue, over sixty-five years of age, was driven from his home. He sent his wife and daughters to the north while he himself came to our camp, where he was of great service as a guide and scout. He was well acquainted with the country and people and was absolutely without fear. He led our men to the guerillas' haunts where we destroyed many of them.

Three days before Hood arrived in front of Nashville a large force of Union troops under command of General Green made a forced march over the Louisville and Nashville Pike, and one night camped only six miles west of our station. Foraging parties were sent out in different directions. One of these parties, which was composed of sixteen men, was cut off from the main force by Harper's Guerillas, and compelled to surrender. After giving up their arms they were all shot in cold blood, except one, a teamster, who was sent back to headquarters to notify the commander of what had happened to his party. That night Harper visited his old father and mother to carry to them the story of his complete destruction of this party.

Soon after this incident we heard the booming of cannon at Nashville and on the river below where batteries had been planted by the rebels to block the river against our gunboats. We hoped and prayed for orders to proceed to the front. Instead of being called into battle, however, we received reinforcements of two more regiments which were sent up to help us guard the railroad. This road was the only railroad running north over which supplies and reinforcements could be brought into Nashville and it was of such importance to General Thomas that he had given orders to keep it open even if it took twenty regiments to perform the task. The rebels made several attempts to cross the Cumberland River both above and below Nashville and to get possession of this road, cutting off communication with the north, but they were defeated each time. During the battle of Nashville, guerilla bands, anticipating the defeat of Thomas by Hood, made desperate efforts to destroy the road and telegraph lines and cut off any retreat north. Scarcely an hour passed during these few days that the road or the telegraph lines were not broken in some place. The fate of the battle turned the tide. Instead of Thomas having to retreat, Hood lost his army and whole regiments of Kentucky and Tennessee troops, now sick of fighting, surrendered to our forces and were sent north as prisoners of war over the road we were guarding.

They were ragged, bedraggled and half starved and orders were given to all the guards along the railroad to give these men on the way north to prison all the hardtack and coffee that could be spared. For three days, after the battle, our principal work was in feeding these poor, ragged, starving foes from boxes of hardtack which we had piled up near the track and from pails of hot coffee which we dealt out to them. The conductor of one train of five hundred prisoners ordered his train stopped at our camp for ten minutes for refreshments. Our men were transformed into waiters for the occasion and served the rebels as they sat in their box cars as temporary prisons, with two Union guards at each door. Never could a lot of men receive a happier service than was given by us, their enemies, during those ten minutes. When the train started on, three as hearty cheers as ever men could give went up to their foes from those five hundred refreshed prisoners. Such was the treatment which was accorded them all along the way until they reached the army prisons.

After the victory of Nashville and the destruction of Hood's army, our regiment was assigned to the Sixteenth Corps under General A. J. Smith and received the credit of having been in the battle of Nashville, which was true as far as our desires were concerned but not true in respect of our position, unless guarding the important railroad and fighting off guerilla attacks can be said to have been in some sense participating in the battle of Nashville. After this victory all the guerilla bands except Harper's ceased their operations in our vicinity. Harper's band, however, continued to make it lively for us until after Lee's surrender, often tearing up the track and cutting telegraph wires causing more annoyance than real damage.

Everybody felt that the war would soon be over and our men talked constantly of the probability of early orders to return home. In February, 1865, nearly all of us suffered severely from jaundice and several of my men died. We would much rather have borne the brunt of battle than have endured such a siege of the poisonous yellow enemy, the results of which never entirely left some of us. In the midst of our scourge came the stunning and paralyzing news of Lincoln's assassination. What effect it would have upon the war, whether or not it would stimulate the South to renewed effort, was to us a much debated subject. For awhile after the assassination the guerillas became more bold and active, but this was not for long and there was quiet as soon as it became known that Johnston had followed Lee's example and surrendered.

Upon the arrival of mail at our camp from headquarters one spring morning I received a letter from my wife at Garden City, on the back of the envelope of which was written, in the handwriting of the postmaster at Garden City, the following note:—"A. J. Jewett, his wife, four-year-old boy, his father, mother and wife's sister, were all murdered and scalped by Indians this morning. If possible, return home at once." Under this was written the following memorandum signed by Colonel Gilfillan, "If you wish to return home, come to headquarters on the first train, and I will see that you have a furlough and transportation." I took the first train to Gallatin but after talking with the colonel concluded not to start for home until I received further news, as the murder had taken place at a time when hostile Indians were not known to have been within three hundred miles of the section. The Jewett family and mine were intimate friends and I felt a deep interest in the case. A few days later I learned the facts. An Indian half-breed by the name of Campbell, who had been an interpreter for the whites through the war with the Sioux, had accompanied Brackett's Battalion to Fort Rice on the Missouri River for the winter of 1864–1865. Lieutenant Fall of the battalion, who came from Garden City and to whom I had sold my Indian war horse, was a relative of Mr. Jewett's, and was in the habit of sending his surplus money to Jewett for safe-keeping. Campbell knew of this and left the battalion secretly, engaging six desperadoes from the renegade Sioux to go with him. They made the winter's journey of four hundred miles across the plains on foot, with three ponies to carry their supplies. They reached Jewett's farm, two miles east of Garden City, before the snow was gone, attacked the family just at daylight, murdered them all, ransacked everything in search of the money, even cutting open the feather beds, cooked themselves a breakfast, then divided the spoils and separated. The six renegade Indians took the ponies, while Campbell dressed himself in Jewett's best suit of clothes and started on foot for Mankato intending to visit his father's family at Henderson, twenty miles down the river. A neighbor of Jewett's, who was returning home from Mankato with a horse and buggy, met Campbell and spoke with him and noticed that the half-

breed appeared to be in a great hurry. He drove on thinking there
was something wrong about the man and when he got to Jewett's
place he met two neighbors who told him of the crime. He
immediately turned his horse around and, asking one of the
men to accompany him, started on the road to Mankato to try
and catch Campbell whom he now felt was at least a suspicious
person.

They had reached the hill overlooking the town when they
saw the fugitive hurrying along the road. As they came nearer
they both noticed that he wore a suit of Jewett's clothes, and drawing their pistols halted him and ordered him to throw up his hands.
They took away his two revolvers, made him get into the buggy
with them at the point of their pistols and in less than ten minutes
had him in the prison in Mankato before anyone in that city had
heard of the murder. The courthouse bell and the church bells
were rung as an alarm, and in a few minutes nearly all the citizens
had gathered around the courthouse and jail. Campbell realized
that his shrift of life was a short one, and asking for a Catholic priest
confessed the whole crime and turned over four hundred dollars
which was his share of the plunder. He also gave information as
to where the other six murderers could be found. After his confes-
sion he was given an hour to prepare for death and at two o'clock
that afternoon, less than ten hours after the murder, the guilty
wretch was hanged at the end of a rope thrown over the limb of a
tree in the courthouse yard in the presence of practically the entire
population of the city. Thus closed in ignominy the career of one
who had been of much service to the whites during nearly three
years of Indian warfare.

The leader of the band having been so promptly disposed of, the
whole country turned out armed to kill or capture the other six
Indians before they reached their homes in the wilds of Dakota.
The soldiers in all the stockades were notified and parties were sent
out into the large timber south of Mankato, where Campbell had
said that the renegades would be found. The day following his
death their hiding place was discovered and they fired on the small
squad of soldiers that surrounded them, killing one and wounding
another, escaping for the time. They were not heard of again
for ten days, but the search and pursuit was kept up so persistently
that they all were killed before reaching Dakota.

When the bodies of Jewett's family were examined it was found that the four-year-old boy, who had been struck on the head by an Indian war club and had been left for dead, was still alive and the doctors finally succeeded in restoring him. Jewett's relatives came on from Boston, settled up his estate and took the boy home with them. They gave him a good education and the last I knew of him he was a prominent lawyer in Boston carrying a distinguishing mark which no other carried—the imprint of an Indian war club on the top of his head.

The people of Minnesota were very much wrought up over this murder and the county commissioners of Blue Earth County voted the sum of one thousand dollars for the purchase of bloodhounds with which to run down the bands of Indian outlaws who still infested the country. The county clerk wrote to me inquiring if bloodhounds could be purchased in the section of Tennessee where we were situated and I replied that there was a man in the vicinity who had them for sale. A later letter informed me that the commissioners had appointed a Garden City man named E. P. Evans to come to Tennessee and make the purchase. Evans soon reached camp and in a few days we had secured six fine blooded hounds to be taken back to Minnesota. It was a considerable undertaking to transport these dogs to Minnesota. Evans had with him a letter from the governor of Minnesota to Colonel Gilfillan, asking him for a detail of two men from the regiment to accompany him and the dogs on the journey. The main southern armies had surrendered and the war was practically over so the colonel told Evans that as he felt sure the regiment would soon be on the way to Fort Snelling to be mustered out it would be better to wait and take the dogs with them, thus saving transportation charges. He promised that in case orders for the return home were not received by the first of July, he would make the detail as requested. Our orders arrived before that time and the dogs went with us. Upon trial, it was found that, although these hounds had been trained to follow the scent of a negro to his death, as soon as they were placed on the trail of an Indian they stuck their tails between their legs and made a cowardly sneak in the opposite direction. So Blue Earth County lost its one thousand dollars, so far as the specific object of the expenditure was concerned.

Returning now to the remainder of our story in the South:

Following the Battle of Nashville we still kept our stations guarding the railroad although the guerillas were very quiet. A Methodist camp meeting was held in the church about two miles from our camp, in the same church where the two men of our regiment had been so brutally murdered by guerillas one Sunday. I received orders from headquarters one day, during the continuance of this camp meeting, to take my company with two other companies of the regiment, surround the camp grounds and search the crowd for some of Harper's Guerillas who were understood to be present. We executed the orders to the letter but failed to get our men, as they had learned our purpose by some underground means.

The week before orders reached us to return north Harper sent word to Colonel Gilfillan that he and his company of guerillas would surrender. The surrender took place a short distance from Gallatin and seventy-five men laid down their arms, took the same oath as Lee's army had taken and were permitted to return to their homes. The officers were allowed to retain their side arms and horses. Such was the feeling against Harper and his two lieutenants that they thought it best to leave the state until their Union neighbors had forgotten their depredations. A guard was given these officers for their protection while they visited Harper's home, near my headquarters, to say farewell before leaving the state. This guard consisted of fifty men from my company, my first lieutenant and I accompanying them to see that protection was really afforded. Our guard lasted from 10 A. M. until 2 P. M. and during our stay the family prepared dinner for us all. The three ex-officers were constantly on the watch for danger, two of them watching the roads while the other ate his dinner. While my men were having their dinner inside Harper asked me and Lieutenant Neal to stay outside with him, as he had something to say to us. This we did and he told us that he and his lieutenants were planning to go to Mexico as they could not with safety stay in the state, hundreds of men having sworn to shoot them on sight. He asked me if Pardue, a former neighbor, was still at my camp saying that he was his worst enemy and that his life would not be worth a shilling if Pardue knew that he was at home. I freed his mind of most of his fears by telling him that Pardue was in Nashville on duty and had not even heard of his surrender.

During this conversation he was free to tell us of several narrow escapes from capture or death when my company was on his trail.

At one time he was staying over night at a plantation when he was informed of our approach by the slave of a neighboring planter and escaped by a back path as we marched up in front.   Again he told us how one night he had visited our encampment with ten men when he had come so close to our guard line that he could see us distinctly through the lighted windows of the house and might have killed some of us by firing.   His company had had several opportunities to kill members of my company, he said, but he had given strict orders not to kill any of them unless attacked, as he feared that by so doing he would draw down our vengeance upon the families of himself and his friends.   This story we discounted as we felt sure that none of his men would let pass any chance of shedding human blood.   He also told us of an attempt to capture Lieutenant Neal and myself at our boarding place, about a hundred rods from our quarters, which had been unsuccessful because we had just changed boarding places.   Orders had been given to kill us if we resisted, he said, and Neal replied by saying that we would never have been taken alive as we understood only too well that surrender to a guerilla meant a death of the cruelest kind.

Neal asked Harper how he and his lieutenants happened to have U. S. A. saddles on their horses and he answered jovially that they had taken them from the freight trains they had wrecked ten miles from Richmond Station.   I asked him if he and his men were responsible for the killing and mutilating of the three soldiers whose bodies we had found there and he responded, without any show of feeling, that they were.   Neal then spoke up and told him that we had been through the worst of Indian wars, had seen the results of Indian massacres and witnessed many horrible butcheries, but that in all our experience we had never looked upon bodies so horribly mutilated and mangled as those of the three soldiers whom his men had killed.   He replied that it was war, and that his actions were justified.   But we told him that such inhuman brutality as this on the part of an intelligent man was enough in our minds to justify us, his victors, in taking his life even though he had surrendered and was under our protection.   But we were soldiers under orders to give him protection and in spite of our convictions those orders had to be carried out.   If our men had known the story then, as well as their officers, I doubt if we could have prevented them from shooting down those three gentlemanly brutes.

Our conversation ended with the call to dinner with the family. It was an excellent farmer's meal and we partook heartily. After the meal there was an affecting farewell scene between Harper and his family; although they were divided in political opinion and loyalty they were an affectionate family. Harper asked for a guard to the pike five miles west of Richmond, but I had no authority to furnish this and refused; when we came to a by-path that led into the woods on the way to our camp, he thanked us for our kindness and bade us good-bye. I was immensely relieved to be rid of the loathsome duty of protecting one who had no moral right to protection, and congratulated myself upon seeing the last of this wretch. If he went to Mexico he made a quick trip of it, for I later learned that he was back home within two months, and at work again killing his enemies. Pardue, our well loved scout, was one of those whose life was taken by him that next fall. This enmity between the Union men and guerillas in that country was so bitter that assassinations continued until both parties were practically destroyed, doubtless Harper among the number.

Our regiment was relieved from duty the latter part of June and we started for home. All along the way, after leaving Kentucky, we received the same welcome and hospitality as that received by others who had served longer and had been in scores of battles. One Sunday the train carrying us was sidetracked near a small town in Indiana and the engine detached, the intention being to leave us there until Monday. But we were too eager to get home to be sidetracked that way and pushed the train a mile into town and cheered until an engine was attached to it. We reached Chicago that evening, having stopped at Indianapolis long enough for a sumptuous dinner. On this trip our six bloodhounds attracted more attention than the nine hundred soldiers and officers. We had decorated them with the stars and stripes and had printed the following words on a cloth blanket which each wore: "Purchased by Blue Earth County, Minnesota. No more slaves to run down. Enlisted with the U. S. A. for the Sioux War. Deserted our Rebel Master and bound for Minnesota, or bust." That night in Chicago the entire regiment, except for a few of the officers, rolled themselves in their blankets and slept on the soft side of the pavement on Michigan Avenue with the cool breezes from Lake Michigan to dispel the intense heat. Hundreds of people came to our spacious bedroom for a look at the "war worn veterans," and more often the "Tennessee recruits." Early the next morning we marched to the station and took the train for LaCrosse, Wisconsin, where we were to embark on steamboats for the journey up the Mississippi River. At every station in Wisconsin flags were flying from the house tops in our honor and ladies were at the train with flowers to pin on our coats and baskets of fruit and food to distribute among us. The nearer we got to home the greater became the enthusiasm. At LaCrosse, which we reached just at dark, the mayor and citizens prepared us fine quarters for the night in the courthouse and the city hall.

In the morning two large boats were at the wharf ready to take us on board for the fine daylight ride up the "Father of Waters," and through historic Lake Pepin. It was the morning of July fourth and it looked as if nearly all the people of the city wished passage with us on those boats, so great was the crowd at the dock.

Half the regiment went on each boat and after the soldiers had boarded, others were let on board to the full extent of the boat's capacity. It was stated that the War Eagle, the floating palace of the Mississippi at that time, had fully two thousand passengers on board that day. There was a fine brass band on each boat which afforded a pleasant attraction, but many said that our dogs, the like of which they had never seen, provided a greater attraction than the band. Winona, Red Wing, Wabashaw and Lake City where we stopped were wild with enthusiasm over the return of the 11th Regiment. None of the men were allowed ashore, but baskets of flowers and refreshments were sent on board and distributed among them, for which we returned our thanks to the kind people by exhibiting our dogs to the crowd from the hurricane deck. Just before dark we passed Hastings where we were saluted by the firing of cannon and at eight o'clock reached St. Paul where the city had provided every comfort for us. Such recognition of our services on the part of people everywhere, such a hearty welcome back, such overflowing kindness and hospitality as we received can never be forgotten and was in itself almost enough to repay us for the hardships and exposures we had passed through.

The next day we marched to Fort Snelling with nine hundred men, one hundred less than when we left and on the eleventh of July were mustered out of service and discharged. We had served less than a year, and had been in no important battles; but many lives had been sacrificed by exposure, hardship, and strenuous service against the guerilla bands of northern Tennessee. The grass-covered mounds where our comrades lie buried at every station along the Louisville and Nashville Railroad from the Kentucky line to Nashville bear mute witness to the fact that the Eleventh Minnesota, though late in the field, contributed its portion to the Union of States and the salvation of the Nation. And of those who returned, nearly all carried with them the seeds of disease that had been sown in their systems by such exposure and hardships as were unavoidably incidental to army life. After being mustered out the members of my company were furnished conveyance by government wagons to Mankato and thence went to their homes in the Blue Earth Valley where nearly all of them had enlisted, as we were mostly farmers and farmers' sons. After our separation at Mankato I returned to my home in Garden City, to enjoy once more the blessings of peace in the undisturbed society of my family and friends.

CHAPTER XIII.

The Capture of the Younger Brothers.

Soon after reaching home from the South I purchased the beautiful farm of Colonel J. H. Baker, on the Wattonwan River one mile from Garden City. Here we lived in happiness for the next ten years. Minnesota during this period became a great and prosperous state. Railroads were built to reach nearly every county in the southern part of the state and the two former Indian reservations were opened and transformed into a populous and prosperous farming district. The three years of Indian warfare, in which the lives of one thousand five hundred settlers were sacrificed, were now almost forgotten except by those of the oldest residents who had had a hand in driving the savages out of the state. The Indian War, notwithstanding its cruelties and sufferings, proved a final benefit since it resulted in ridding the very best agricultural part of the state of its dangerous occupants much sooner than could have otherwise been done.

In the summers of 1873–4–5 the grasshoppers from the plains west of us came into the state in such vast numbers as to destroy nearly all the crops during those three years. Such was the devastation that most of the farmers who remained on their farms were obliged to accept aid from the state or to borrow from friends outside the state. Every possible plan was tried to drive off the locusts or to kill them off but we found that though we could drive off and kill off the Indians the locusts were too much for our skill and power. Our county commissioners voted a bounty of ten cents a quart for them and the schools were closed to allow the children, as well as adults, to catch and destroy them. The principal of the Garden City School and his pupils spent one day on my farm with their canvas nets. My nearest neighbor attached a canvas net to his hayrake and hauled in the pests by horse power. Other improved methods of getting grasshoppers so increased the catch that the bounty was put down to five cents a quart on the second day and after the third day's harvest the crop was so great that it was taken off entirely for fear of bankrupting the county.

One farmer in the vicinity attached a funnel-shaped net to two hay-rakes which he fastened twenty feet apart and drew up and down his fields. His one day's catch filled as many grain sacks as could be loaded on a hayrack and required four horses to draw them to the place where the bounty was paid. The locusts were killed in the sacks with kerosene oil and the supervisor of each township had to attend to measuring them and burying them in long deep trenches. But all efforts availed nothing. Thousands of farmers were compelled to leave the state, taking their stock with them and moving into other western states.

I had now lived west of the Mississippi River nearly twenty-five years and had had my share of a pioneer's troubles, so after the three barren years I concluded to go back to my native state until the scourge had passed away, when I would return again to my farm and to making a living by hard labor without having the results of my labor destroyed by insects. With this end in view I rented my farm to a man who had no means with which to leave the country and who depended on the state to furnish him seed for the next season's planting, sold my live stock to parties living outside the scourged district and in the fall of 1875 started with my family for Michigan. The following winter I travelled as a book agent, but, my health being poor, I abandoned that employment and decided to go once more to farming.

During the summer of 1876 I went back to Minnesota to see how my farm, which I had rented, was doing and by chance became involved in another of the most stirring incidents in Minnesota's history. One day a couple of well-dressed men drove up to my farm and asked me what I would take for it. They said that they had capital and intended buying up a group of the farms which had been practically abandoned because of the scourge of grasshoppers. My price seemed to be too high for them however and they rode on towards Mankato. The next day I met these same men with six others on the streets of Mankato. They were negotiating with several farmers for the purchase of their farms and seeing me inquired whether I had not now decided to take a lower price. Our conversation was disturbed by the passing of a procession, led by a brass band, and the land buyers soon mounted their horses and rode off to St. Peter. At St. Peter, these men, as I later learned, put up at the best hotel in town and during the early afternoon called on some of the principal business men and went to the banks to get some bills changed. After these business errands were ended they returned to the hotel and sat on the hotel porch during the balance of the afternoon, amusing themselves by throwing coins into the street for the small boys to scramble for. That evening they had many offers of cheap farms which they promised to go and see.

The next morning they left St. Peter and rode east through Le-Seuer County and on the second day took dinner at a restaurant in Northfield, Rice County. After dinner six of the men mounted their horses while the other two went to the only bank in the town, leveled their revolvers at the cashier and ordered him to hand over all the money there was in the bank. The cashier did not obey but closed the doors of the money vault, and was instantly shot dead. The robbers also shot down the janitor of the bank and wounded a customer who was in the building. At the sound of the first shot in the bank the six men stationed outside rode up and down the street firing their revolvers and ordering all persons to keep indoors. But the citizens were quickly aroused and in a moment a deadly fire poured out on the mounted robbers from windows and doorways and two of them fell dead and two others were badly wounded. The two bandits who were in the bank took what little money was in sight, joined the others outside, mounted hurriedly and fled to the woods a few miles from the village. Here they remained in hiding for several days until they thought the excitement was over and the search for them ended, and then leaving their horses behind started on foot to get out of Minnesota.

A search of the two dead robbers brought to light maps and documents which were positive proof that this was the gang of the James and Younger brothers, outlaws and robbers from Missouri, composed of the refuse from the Civil War who had found it impossible to settle down at the end of that struggle and had organized to prey on society. The survivors in their attempts to get safely out of the state entered a farm house by night, four miles east of Mankato, ordered the family to prepare them a good supper, the first real meal they had been able to get in eight days, paid for it and then left for the woods again. News that the robbers had been seen again caused the utmost excitement. Special trains were made up on all the railroads and word was sent out that all who would volunteer to run down this robber band would be given free transportation. Immediately the whole southwestern part of the state was under arms and hastening to the conflict. Old Indian fighters and Civil War veterans rendezvoused at every available point with the arms they had used in their former campaigns and, before another night, guards and patrols were stationed at all bridges over Blue Earth River which was now swollen by recent rains and which the robbers would have to cross in order to get out of the state towards Missouri. At the covered wagon bridge, one mile west of Mankato, some one threw stones into the east end to ascertain if there was a guard inside about ten o'clock one night, but did not attempt to cross. About thirty rods south of this wagon bridge was a long high railroad bridge which was guarded by railroad section men. The robbers fired at these men that same night, causing them to flee for safety, whereupon they crawled over the bridge on their hands and knees, stole two horses on which they mounted their wounded comrades and took the road to Lake Crystal. On reaching the Garden City road the band was fired on by guards who were stationed there and separated. The James brothers stole two farm horses belonging to the Reverend Mr. Rockwood, a minister living in Garden City, and at daybreak next morning were seen riding them bareback one mile north of Madelia.

That morning Captain Ara Barton, sheriff of Rice County, who had served with me in the cavalry regiment through the Indian War came to Garden City seeking information about the horses stolen from the minister and asked me to go with him on the robbers' trail. I told him that I had been in Michigan with my family for the last eight months and that I was now only a visitor here, that my health was far from good and that I thought I could not stand the hard riding that it meant. He urged me so persistently that I finally yielded and taking the carbine and revolvers I had used through the Indian War, rode with him to Lake Crystal where we boarded the first train for St. James, thirty miles west. At St. James we hired a team to take us north with the idea of heading off the robbers, but before we started a man came in on horseback to inform us that they had passed five miles north of us only an hour before. We unhitched our horses, got some section men to take eight of us on two hand-cars to Windom, thirty miles farther west, where we arrived at two o'clock P. M. Here we got our dinner and secured a good team to take the eight of us twenty miles north-west to a ford on the Des Moines River for which we felt the robbers were aiming. We reached the ford about dark and immediately stationed guards to let no one pass. The next morning we learned that the James brothers had spent the night with a settler ten miles northeast of us, and this news was encouraging as it meant that we were now ahead of them. No further news being received we rode forty miles into Pipestone County close to the west state line but got no further track of the fugitives. The fol-lowing day we rode south to the railroad where we boarded the first train east towards home. On reaching Madelia we learned that the hiding place of the other four robbers had been discovered five miles north of that town. Two hundred armed men surrounded their camp that afternoon and before night one of the four robbers lay dead and the three Younger brothers, all wounded, were in Sheriff Barton's hands.

As soon as the news reached St. Paul a large delegation came by special train to take the prisoners to the capital, but Sheriff Barton insisted that as the crime had been committed in Rice County and in his jurisdiction he should take the prisoners there for trial and refused to give them up. The St. Paul delegation thought that if the prisoners were taken to Rice County by the way of Owatona, they would be captured and hanged by a mob before we reached the jail, as we would have to change cars twice during the journey. The sheriff had legal possession of the prisoners and a strong guard to protect them, however, and refused to take them to St. Paul, so the dispute was finally settled by allowing them to take the body of the dead robber to St. Paul while the sheriff took the live ones on to the Rice County jail. The three robbers, whose wounds had not yet been dressed, were taken into a passenger car and a doctor called in who, after an examination, said that two of them would probably die before reaching their destination. Cole Younger, the oldest of the three, was able to sit up and willing to tell his story of all they had passed through since coming into the state. I was one of his guard and sat in the seat with him. He asked me many questions about our pursuit and said that he remembered looking at my farm. One of the leading Mankato bankers was on the train and Younger said that he would like to speak with him. I went to Mr. S. and told him the prisoner was anxious to see him.

16

Younger said, "I was in your bank fifteen days ago to get a $20 bill changed, and talked with you about some farms you had for sale." "Yes," said Mr. S., "and you agreed to return or let me hear from you." Younger replied, "I did not lie, I have done both. I have returned and you now hear from me. Our plans were laid to rob your bank and make our escape through the unsettled country near Mankato, but that band came along the street just as we were ready to begin the game, all the people came out into the street to hear the music and we lost our nerve and our chance. We left Mankato and rode on into the thickest settled part of the state to our death. I hear that the two James brothers have been killed and that we three brothers are all that are left of the eight who visited your city fifteen days ago." Mr. S. then started in to lecture him on the bad business he was in, whereupon Younger asked him if he would like to know the difference between the business he was following and that of the banker. Mr. S. said that he would and Younger said, "In your business you are robbing the poor and in mine I am robbing the rich." Another man from Mankato who stood by said, "Less than fourteen years ago we hanged thirty-eight men on one scaffold in our city, and every one of them was as good if not better than you are." Younger replied, "I expect to hang before I leave your city, but these two boys are my brothers, both mortally wounded and one of them under twenty years of age, this being his first raid. I blame myself for their being here. All I ask of you people is not to hang those boys but to let them die as they are."

The train soon reached the city where a crowd of several thousand people was waiting to see the robbers. Here we had to change to another railroad a quarter of a mile away and we feared trouble. But when the crowd saw how badly wounded the men were their feeling of murder gave way to one of pity. At Owatona another transfer was made and here again it seemed that the entire population of the city and country round about was out to get a glimpse of the captured outlaws but no demonstration was made. At Owatona the sheriff received a telegram that a mob of thousands of angry people had gathered at Fairibault and had determined to hang the robbers. Barton telegraphed back that he would be at Fairibault with his prisoners on the regular train at three o'clock, that he had a strong guard and that any one who tried to take possession of his prisoners would be shot to death. Instead of taking the regular train, however, we boarded a freight that started earlier than the passenger train and stopped a mile south of the Fairibault depot. Two teams were ready for us here and prisoners and guards were driven direct to the jail. By this unexpected move we had the prisoners inside the prison walls and under the doctor's care before the passenger train pulled into the depot. There was talk for a time of storming the jail but when the news was received that the men were so badly wounded as to be practically dying the mob decided to let the law take its course with them.

At the request of Sheriff Barton I stayed on at the jail for five days helping him. At the end of this time, the excitement having quieted down, I returned home to Garden City, leaving my army carbine to be used by a guard who the next night killed a man with it who approached the jail without halting at his order. Twenty years after the event I wrote Captain Barton asking him to send me the carbine by express, as I desired to have it go to my posterity as a relic and souvenir of the Indian wars in Minnesota. He informed me, much to my sorrow, that it had been destroyed by fire. All three of the Younger brothers recovered from their wounds and were brought to trial. They pleaded guilty and were sentenced to life imprisonment at hard labor. The state law was such that the penalty for a murderer who pleaded guilty, was life imprisonment instead of hanging. The five days which I spent in the attempt to capture the two James brothers and in the capture of the three Younger brothers were fully as exciting, though not as dangerous, as my experiences in the Indian War. It showed me that the people of Minnesota had not forgotten how to defend themselves and that they would never allow robbery and murder without instantly rallying and making a brave fight for lives and property.

After the exciting occurrences connected with the capture of the Younger brothers I returned to my family in Michigan. They were anxious to remain in Michigan and as I had a good opportunity at this time to exchange my Minnesota farm for one at Vermontville, Michigan, I decided to settle definitely there. Here we lived until our family of five children were all of age. During this time in addition to my farming I also engaged with two of my brothers in the hard wood lumber business at Potterville, Michigan, about

fifteen miles from my farm. In 1890 I sold my Vermontville farm
and bought another in the same county, located on the new line of
railroad being built by the Pere Marquette Railroad where I laid out
the present village of Mulliken, Michigan, and continued a few
years longer as a farmer with an incidental lumber business. My
Mulliken farm I soon sold to my eldest son and purchased a quarter
interest in the Potter Furniture Manufacturing Company at Lansing,
Michigan, which city has been my home during the past thirteen
years.

My life has not been filled with such important and thrilling events
as have the lives of some other pioneers. But such incidents as
have occurred in my life in their relation to the growth of a nation
I have considered worthy of record, if for no other purpose than to
teach my posterity of the labor and toil on the part of all who helped
to carve a great country out of a wilderness. Though I did not
suffer any great hardships in my experience still there have been
many exposures, trials and dangers. As I now look back upon
those earlier experiences of pioneer and army life, they seem through
the distance more like pleasures than hardships or perils. And
now, at seventy-two years of age, man's usual life limit, as I find
myself still enjoying the companionship of the wife of my youth
and that of all my five children and thirteen grandchildren, not a
death having yet occurred among us, enjoying the unbroken love
as well as the companionship of all these, I ask what more can
I have to comfort me in this life except to know that after this
mortal body is cared for there will be an immortal body and a still
happier home.